READINGS ON EQUAL EDUCATION
(Formerly *Educating the Disadvantaged*)

READINGS
ON EQUAL
EDUCATION

Volume 15

RACE, THE COURTS, AND
EQUAL EDUCATION: THE
LIMITS OF THE LAW

Volume Editor
Richard Fossey

Co-Managing Editors
Robin Garrett Jarvis
Elizabeth A. Kemper

AMS PRESS
NEW YORK

Library of Congress Catalogue Number 77-83137
International Standard Book Number: Set 0-404-10100-3
International Standard Book Number: Vol.15: 0-404-10115-1
International Standard Series Number: 0270-1448

All AMS Books are printed on acid-free paper that meets the guidelines for performance and durability of the Committee on Production
Guidelines for Book Longevity of the Council On Library Resources.

Manufactured in the United States of America

AMS Press, Inc.
56 East 13th Street
New York, N.Y. 10003

This book is dedicated to the blessings of Feliciana:
Kim, Elizabeth, Austin, Charlie, and Polly

CONTENTS

VOLUME 15

MONIQUE WESTON CLAGUE is a resident faculty scholar at the University of Maryland's Center for Education Policy and Leadership (CEPAL). She received her Ph.D. from Harvard University in the area of Political Science and served as an expert witness for the U.S. Justice Department on faculty issues in *U.S. & Ayers v. Fordice*. Her recent publications include "Affirmative Action Employment Discrimination: The Higher Education Fragment," in J. Smart (Ed.) *Higher Education: Handbook of Theory & Research* (1996) and "The Affirmative Action Showdown of 1986: Implications for Higher Education," in *The Journal of College and University Law,* (fall, 1987).

RICHARD FOSSEY is associate professor of education law and policy at Louisiana State University. He received his doctorate in education policy from Harvard University and received his law degree from the University of Texas School of Law. Prior to beginning an academic career, he practiced education law in Alaska, where he represented school boards in Inuit, Athabaskan, and other Alaska Native communities. His research interests include education law, school choice, child abuse and neglect, and school reform. Fossey is co-author, with Michael Clay Smith, of *Crime on Campus: Liability Issues and Campus Administration,* published by Oryx Press and the American Council on Education. He is also co-author, with Todd A. DeMitchell, of *The Limits of Law-Based School Reform: Vain Hopes and Fair Promises*, published by Technomic Publishing Company.

LINO A. GRAGLIA is the A. Dalton Cross professor of Law at the University of Texas School of Law. A native of Brooklyn, New York, he received his B.A. from City College of New York in 1952 ad his LL.B. from Columbia University Law School in 1954, where he was editor of the law review. He was an attorney with the U.S. Department of Justice and practiced law in Washington, D.C. and New York City before joining the Texas law faculty in 1966. He has also taught at the Universities of Virginia, Utah, and Puget Sound. Professor Graglia teaches courses in constitutional law and Antitrust. He is the author of *Disaster by Decree: the Supreme Court Decisions on Race and the Schools* (Cornell University Press, 1976), a critical analysis of the school busing decisions. He has written widely in both scholarly and popular journals on currents issues of constitutional law and the role of the Supreme Court in the American system of government, and is a frequent speaker at scholarly symposia and on radio and television. His most recent publications include, "Church of the Lukumi Babalu Aye: Of Animal Sacrifice and Religious Prejudice," *Georgetown Law Journal* (1996), and *"United States v. Lopez*: Judicial Review Under the Commerce Clause," *Texas Law Review* 719 (1996).

DON HOSSLER is a professor of Educational Leadership and Policy Studies and executive associate dean for the School of Education at Indiana University. He earned his Ph.D. from the Claremont Graduate University in 1979. His research interests include student college choice, higher education finance, enrollment management, and more recently, higher education desegregation. He has been a consulting reviewer and served on editorial boards for several journals. Don is currently completing a book that summarizes the results from an eight-year longitudinal study of the college decision-making process.

ROBIN GARRETT JARVIS is a doctoral student in Educational Leadership and Research at Louisiana State University. She presently serves as a research assistant in the Department of Administrative and Foundational Services. With 11 years of teaching experience in the elementary grades, her research interests include school effectiveness and school improvement, middle level education, and equal education. She also served as co-managing editor for this volume.

ELIZABETH A. KEMPER is a doctoral student and research assistant in Educational Leadership and Research at Louisiana State University. A former high school teacher, her research interests include educational policy implementation, school restructuring, and equal education. She also served as co-managing editor for this volume.

RALPH MAWSDLEY is professor and chair, Department of Counseling, Administration, Supervision, and Adult Learning, Cleveland State University. He received his J.D. from the

Cleveland State University. He received his J.D. from the University of Illinois and his Ph.D. from the University of Minnesota. Among his 200 publications on a wide range of legal topics are 12 books, including *Legal Problems of Religious and Private Schools, Academic Misconduct: Cheating and Plagiarism,* and *Pupil Transportation and the Law.* He is a member of the Editorial Advisory Committee of *West's Education Law Reporter.*

GARY S. MATHEWS is completing his second year as superintendent of the East Baton Rouge Parish School System in Baton Rouge, Louisiana. Having served as teacher, principal, and central office administrator, he was named one of the top 100 school executives in North America by the magazine *The Executive Educator* in 1988. Dr. Mathews' school improvement work in Jackson, Mississippi, Spring Branch ISD (Houston), Texas, and St. Johns County, Florida, have earned him recognition in *Making School Reform Happen* (Allyn & Bacon, 1993), *Keepers of the Dream* (Excelsior, 1994), and *The Revolution Revisited: Effective Schools* (Phi Delta Kappan, 1995).

VIRGINIA DAVIS NORDIN teaches in a graduate program of Higher Education Policy Studies at the University of Kentucky. She is a graduate of Harvard Law School, and has taught at the Universities of Michigan and Wisconsin. She was the affirmative action officer at Dartmouth, and practiced law on Wall Street, and in the Poverty Law Program in Detroit. Her publications include, *Higher Education and the Law,* with Harry Edwards, "Affirmative Action" in M. Chamberlain (Ed.) *Women in Academe*, and "Legal Protection of Academic Freedom" in the NSSE Yearbook, *The Courts and Education.*

CHRISTINE H. ROSSELL is professor of Political Science at Boston University. Her research interests include school desegregation, bilingual education, and educational policy. She has written four books on school desegregation and bilingual education and about 50 articles on school desegregation for the *Connecticut Law Review, Urban Affairs Quarterly* (now *Urban Affairs Review*), *William and Mary Law Review,* the *American Journal of Political Science, Political Science Quarterly, Urban Education, American Politics Quarterly,* the *Journal of Legal Studies, Law and Contemporary Problems, Educational Evaluation and Policy*

Analysis, and on bilingual education in *Research in the Teaching of English*, the *Journal of Law and Education, Educational Policy*, and *Bilingual Research Journal*, among others. She has written numerous reports to the court and other government agencies and testified for parties in more than 20 school desegregation cases and one bilingual education case.

EDWARD P. ST. JOHN is professor of Educational Administration at the University of Dayton. His research focuses on student choice, finance, and policy in higher education, and he has published extensively on these topics. He recently co-edited (with Don Hossler) *Rethinking College Desegregation*, a special issue of the *Journal for a Just and Caring Education* (1997). His other recent books include *Prices, Productivity, and Investment: Assessing Financial Strategies in Higher Education* (1994, an ASHE/ERIC Higher Education Study), and *Rethinking Tuition and Student Aid Strategies* (an edited volume in the *New Directions for Higher Education Series*). Dr. St. John has conducted numerous state and federal policy studies, serves on several editorial boards, and has received awards for his research from national associations. He received his Ed.D. from Harvard University and his M.Ed. and B.S. from the University of California, Davis.

JOHN L. STROPE, JR. is a former secondary school teacher, counselor, and principal in Nebraska. He spent twelve years as a professor at the University of South Alabama. Since 1991, he has been a professor and chair in the Department of Administration and Higher Education at the University of Louisville. His articles have appeared in numerous publications including *West Education Law Reporter, The Journal of Student Financial Aid*, and *Academic Medicine*. Over the years he has made presentations for the National Association of School Boards, the National Association of Secondary Schools, and the Education Law Association.

CHARLES TEDDLIE is professor of educational research methodology in the College of Education at Louisiana State University. He also taught at the University of New Orleans and served as Assistant Superintendent for Research and Development at the Louisiana Department of Education. He has published over *a Difference: Lessons Learned from a 10-year Study of School Effects* (1993, Teachers College Press) and *Advances in School Effectiveness Research and Practice* (1994, Pergamon). He currently has two books in press: *The International Handbook of School Effectiveness Research* (co-edited with David Reynolds) and *Mixed Methods and Mixed Models Studies in the Behavioral and Social Sciences* (co-written with Abbas Tashakkori). He serves as the series editor for *Readings on Equal Education, Volumes 13-17.*

ANNE WELLS is director of admissions and student services, University of Louisville School of Dentistry. She is also a doctoral student in Administration and Higher Education at the University of Louisville. Her academic and professional interests focus on affirmative action, admissions, career planning, and financial aid issues in higher education.

SECTION I.

DESEGREGATION LITIGATION
IN THE SCHOOLS

CHAPTER 1

INTRODUCTION TO SECTION I: THE STUBBORN PROBLEM OF RACIAL ISOLATION

Richard Fossey

Volumes 13 and 14 of *Readings on Equal Education* comprise a forty-year retrospective on the implications of *Brown v. Board of Education* on American education. In a series of essays edited by Charles Teddlie and Kofi Lomotey, various authors reviewed the impact of this historic decision on schools, colleges, and universities.

In many ways, this volume is a natural extension of Teddlie and Lomotey's work. Like its predecessors, it focuses on the nation's efforts to desegregate American public education in accordance with the Supreme Court's mandate in *Brown*. However, this book's theme is narrower than the earlier volumes. Specifically, volume 15 concentrates on recent legal developments in the struggle to desegregate the nation's education system.

This volume is organized in two parts. The second section, which will be introduced in chapter 8, explores recent legal developments in higher education. The first section, for which this chapter serves as an introduction, concentrates on desegregation in the nation's public schools.

This section begins with an analysis by Richard Fossey that describes the pervasive racial isolation in the nation's inner-city schools, a problem that stubbornly persists in spite of 40 years of desegregation litigation.   A majority of African Americans continue to attend schools that are predominantly non-white, he writes, and their academic achievement continues to lag behind the white population.

Fossey contends that the desegregation strategies of the past 40 years have failed to improve life opportunities for many African Americans. It is time, he argues, for educators to shift their focus from statistics on racial balance to the serious problems of inner-city schools: mismanagement and corruption, poor-quality staffs and curriculum, adversarial collective bargaining, and the crisis of the African American family.

In the following chapter,   Richard Fossey and Elizabeth Kemper discuss the implications of *Sheff v. O'Neill*, the Connecticut Supreme Court's 1996 ruling on racial isolation in the Hartford schools. At the time *Sheff* was decided, only 5% of the Hartford district's 22,000 students were non-Hispanic white, while many of the surrounding suburban districts were more than 90% non-Hispanic white. Connecticut's highest court declared this racial isolation to be illegal, introducing the possibility that some sort of cross-district desegregation plan might emerge for Hartford and more than 20 surrounding suburbs.

Federal courts have rejected cross-district desegregation plans unless it can be shown that school district boundaries were deliberately drawn to segregate school children by race. Intentional desegregation of this type can rarely be proven in northern cities, where African American-dominated urban districts like Cleveland and Detroit are racially segregated islands of poverty surrounded by affluent, mostly white suburban school systems.

In *Sheff*, the Connecticut Supreme Court relied on a state constitutional provision, not the federal constitution, when it declared the Hartford system to be illegally segregated. Thus, *Sheff* raises the possibility that the court might ultimately order some sort of cross-district desegregation plan for the Hartford metropolitan area. Nevertheless, at the time this volume goes to press, no such plan has been implemented, and it is not yet clear whether *Sheff's* desegregation remedies will be more bold than the ones previously developed by federal courts.

Next, Ralph Mawdsley examines the Supreme Court's recent desegregation decision in *Missouri v. Jenkins*, in which a federal court attempted to reverse the flow of white flight in the Kansas City metropolitan area. In spite of a massive financial investment in the Kansas City School District by the school district and the state of Missouri, student outcomes in the mostly African American district did not markedly improve, and white enrollments did not increase.

In chapter 5, Christine Rossell, an eminent desegregation researcher and theorist, reports on desegregation outcomes in Savannah, Georgia, and Stockton, California. Her study of these two communities supports the conclusion that voluntary desegregation plans, coupled with well-designed magnet school options, do a better job of retaining white students in a desegregated district than a race-based mandatory student assignment scheme.

Rossell's essay is extremely useful for pinpointing which desegregation strategies are most likely to achieve racially integrated school environments. Unfortunately, it does not suggest a way to reverse the decades-old migration of white families out of urban school systems. Rossell has identified a way to slow white flight in some school settings, but the formula for luring white families back to inner-city schools in large numbers remains elusive.

Finally, in chapter 6, Gary Mathews and Robin Jarvis pro-vide an historical perspective to desegregation efforts in Baton Rouge, Louisiana, where the school district has been mired in desegregation litigation for more than 40 years. As the authors relate, the Baton Rouge school district was first sued in 1956 for operating segregated schools. Unfortunately, it was not until 1981 that a comprehensive court-ordered desegregation plan was put into effect. That plan improved racial balance in the school district for a number of years, but by the early 1990s, demographic changes and poor achievement levels for African American students led school leaders to ask for a major modification to the 1981 order.

Mathews and Jarvis describe the process whereby the federal court's 1981 order was modified in 1996, by consent of all the parties to the litigation. They explain the pedagogical justification for a host of programmatic changes designed to improve educational outcomes for the district's black students. Their narrative also conveys an understated sense of urgency, for as they relate, Baton Rouge has been slowly but steadily losing white students for a period of more than 20 years.

It is coincidental but fortuitous that these essays are appearing shortly after two impressive contributions to desegregation scholarship were released. In 1996, Gary Orfield and Susan Eaton's work, *Dismantling Desegregation*, was published. In 1997, the Harvard Project on Desegregation issued its somber study on the status of school desegregation in the United States. Both works raise alarming questions about the nation's commitment to integrated education and its success in bringing it about. Indeed, both pieces argue that the nation is losing ground in the long struggle to implement *Brown's* promise of desegregated schools.

In many ways, the chapters in Section I of this book are in harmony with the themes raised by Orfield and Eaton and by the Harvard Project on Desegregation. Although some of the authors are upbeat--Rossell and Jarvis and Mathews, in particular--readers may find it difficult to read this volume's first six chapters without a sense of disquietude. An underlying theme of all these chapters is the quiet but seemingly irreversible flight of white students from urban schools. Together, these essays constitute a challenge to educators, courts, and policy experts to develop new strategies for achieving racial integration in American classrooms, a goal that remains elusive as the nation nears the twenty-first century.

References

Orfield, G. and Eaton, S. E. (1996). *Dismantling Desegregation: The Quiet Reversal of Brown v. Board of Education*. New York: Free Press.

CHAPTER 2

DESEGREGATION IS NOT ENOUGH: FACING THE TRUTH ABOUT URBAN SCHOOLS

Richard Fossey

Forty years ago, in *Brown v. Board of Education* (1954), the Supreme Court declared that racial separation of African American and white school children must end. Tragically, in spite of hundreds of court orders, efforts of the U.S. Justice Department, the NAACP, and legions of fair-minded educators, hundreds of thousands of African American and Latino children go to school in racial isolation. Demographic trends suggest that racial isolation will grow worse, not better, in the years to come.

Facing the truth: Most African American Children Attend Racially Isolated Schools

Overwhelming evidence is all around us. In many of the nation's urban districts — Cleveland, Detroit, New Orleans, and Washington, DC, to name a few — student enrollment is 80 percent or more African American:. In Los Angeles, the nation's second largest district, only 13% of the students are non-Hispanic white. In Miami, the nation's fourth largest district, the figure is 16% (Council of Great City Schools, 1994). According to a recent

5

study by the Harvard Project on School Desegregation, two-thirds of the nation's minority students attend predominately non-white schools (Applebome, 1997). As Gary Orfield and Susan Eaton (1996) wrote in their recent book, *Dismantling Desegregation*, the nation's schools are rapidly heading toward the *Plessy v. Ferguson* era of "separate but equal, " when segregated schools were taken for granted in many states and upheld by the courts.

Racial isolation of minority school children does not convey the worst aspects of their condition. Although many school districts try to hide the facts, educational outcomes in urban districts, where racially isolated African Americans and Latinos go to school, are appalling. On-time graduation rates in virtually all the racially isolated urban districts hover around 50% (Fossey, 1996), refuting claims that African American dropout rates are going down and are approaching dropout rates for the general population (NCES, 1995). Standardized test scores are low in urban districts, and a high percentage of children read below, often far below, grade level.

Although African American children start their educational lives with the academic potential of their white classmates, their academic performance seems to decrease the longer they stay in school (Lomotey & Fossey, 1997, citing Parham & Parham, 1989). While the gap in achievement levels between whites and African Americans has decreased in recent years, white children still outperform African American and Hispanic-American youth at all age levels and in all subjects.

Indeed, if the purpose of education is to enable our young people to earn a decent living and take their place in the nation's civic and political life, then surely the *Brown* experiment has so far been a failure for the African American population. A recent U.S. Census Bureau report indicates that more African American families, not less, have been sinking below the poverty line in recent years (Bennett, 1995). Thirty-nine percent of African American families with children lived in poverty in 1993, up from 32% in 1969. In California, to cite one more stark statistic, 40% of African American men in their twenties are caught up in the criminal justice system - either in prison, paroled from prison, or on probation (Butterfield, 1996).

Facing the Truth: Desegregation Efforts Have Often Failed

Stacks of research papers, scholarly articles, and books have been written about desegregation in the 44 years since the Supreme Court ruled in *Brown v. Board of Education.* Yet none have pinpointed an effective strategy for insuring that all African American children will attend racially diverse schools and achieve good educational results. Perhaps the leading desegregation theorists are Boston University's Christine Rossell and Gary Orfield of Harvard. Both have made important contributions to our understanding of this difficult subject; yet neither has found the formula for solving the crisis of urban schools.

Gary Orfield has written an impressive series of books and articles, culminating in the co-authored book, *Dismantling Desegregation* (Orfield & Eaton, 1996), in which he sounded the alarm about growing racial isolation in the nation's schools. Orfield advocates cross-district desegregation plans as one means of attacking the common pattern of a largely African American urban district surrounded by a ring of affluent, almost all-white, suburban districts (Eaton & Orfield, 1996, pp. 131-135).

Cross-district desegregation plans are operating in some metropolitan areas, but nothing like the kind of plan that would be needed to bring racial balance to such cities as Boston, Detroit, or Washington, DC. In *Milliken v. Bradley* (1974), the Supreme Court flatly rejected judicial imposition of a cross-district desegregation plan in the Detroit metropolitan area unless it could be shown that suburban district boundaries had been intentionally drawn for the purposes of segregation.

Until the Supreme Court changes its view, which does not seem likely, federal courts are prohibited from imposing desegregation plans that cross district boundaries, absent some evidence that local authorities drew district lines to segregate children by race. The Detroit plan, which the Court vetoed in *Milliken,* would have involved more than 50 districts and three-quarters of a million school children. The Court questioned the feasibility of such an undertaking, which would have diminished the authority of numerous local governments, affected taxing powers, and created a transportation and logistics nightmare.

Even if a court had the authority to order mandatory cross-district desegregation, it seems questionable whether such a plan could be effectively implemented on a large scale. Take Boston, for example. For more than 25 years, the Massachusetts legislature has funded METCO, a voluntary desegregation plan that allows 3,000 African American children from Boston to attend predominantly white schools in about three dozen surrounding suburban towns. That works fine. But could 30,000 African American children be accommodated by the suburbs, or could 30,000 white children be persuaded to enroll in Boston schools? It seems highly unlikely that the families of Wellesley, Brookline, Concord, and Dover — some of the wealthiest communities in New England — could be induced to take their children out of highly acclaimed local public schools and transport them to the troubled Boston school district.

Christine Rossell advocates magnet schools as a way of achieving voluntary desegregation of urban schools without forced busing. Her book, *The Carrot or the Stick for School Desegregation Policy* (1990), presents strong evidence that the establishment of high-quality magnet schools will lure white families to schools in African American neighborhoods, thus achieving desegregation without forcing unwilling families to bus their children to school.

However, a recent report by the U. S. Department of Education questions the value of magnet schools as a desegregation strategy (Hendrie, 1996). In fact, some evidence suggests that magnet schools and specialty schools can themselves be instruments of segregation. Moore and Davenport (1990), found that magnet and specialty schools were often over-represented by white students, while African American and low-income families were confined to nonselective, and often inferior performing, schools.

The East Baton Rouge Parish, Louisiana, school district provides an example of the way special school programs can segregate children by race. The district, which had been operating under a court-imposed desegregation order since 1981, maintained a highly regarded gifted and talented program for many years, one that was credited with helping to maintain white student enrollment. In 1995, it was revealed that 20% of the district's white middle school students were enrolled in these self-contained special programs, where they were insulated from the general school population (Pack, 1996). However, only one out of 50 African American middle schoolers had been identified as gifted and talented. In short, it was discovered that a program that had been intended to promote desegregation, was in fact a tool of segregation.

Moreover, although magnet schools and specialty schools have sometimes reduced or slowed "white flight" from urban schools, they have not reversed the long-term national trend toward racial isolation. In spite of all the strategies that have been used over the past 40 years to implement *Brown*, more and more African American children face the prospect of going to different schools than white children. That is a simple fact.

Besides metropolitan desegregation plans and magnet schools, some desegregation strategists have simply argued for more money for racially isolated urban schools. Without question more money is needed in many inner-city districts, where school facilities are on the verge of falling down, up-to-date texts can't be found, and computers and other educational aids are in short supply.

But money is not always the problem in our troubled urban schools. New Jersey's racially-isolated urban schools are funded at a high level, and yet the state has taken over three of them due to mismanagement or corruption (McLarin, 1994). The chronically under-performing Hartford schools are funded above the state average (How Hartford schools fare, 1995), and District of Columbia schools receive massive amounts of federal aid. Kansas City schools received more than a billion dollars in additional support specifically to aid desegregation. Yet only about half of Kansas City high school students graduate on time (Orfield and Eaton, 1996), and lavish investments in programs and facilities did not lure white students from the suburbs.

Gary Orfield has offered an interesting insight into why court-ordered desegregation plans with large financial components often failed to improve racially-isolated school systems. "In [many] court-ordered cases," Orfield observed, "the desegregation remedies were basically a result of a political battle between school districts who were trying to get as much money as possible for their favorite programs and the state governments who were trying to spend as little as possible for as few years as possible." As a result, Orfield wrote, "The victims of segregation often seemed lost in the shuffle" (Feldman, Kirby & Eaton, 1994, p. 5).

In short, three generations of African American students have been through the public schools since *Brown v. Board of Education*. On average, their educational attainment has not been satisfactory, and hundreds of thousands of African Americans have not experienced an integrated school environment. It is now time to fundamentally rethink the way we try to implement this landmark decision.

Facing the Truth: Urban Schools Have Massive Problems

First, of all, we must reaffirm our commitment to *Brown v. Board of Education.* Without question, this decision is one of the nation's premier moral statements of the twentieth century. We must never retreat from *Brown's* guarantee of equal educational opportunities for all, and we must continuously search for ways to bring African American children into the mainstream of public education and the national life.

At the same time, we must admit that thousands of African American children go to school in racial isolation every day, as if *Brown* had never been decreed. And it seems inevitable, given demographic projections and the present legal and political climate, that this will continue to be the case for some time to come. A core question for American educators, then, is this: How can we help African American children in Detroit, Philadelphia, Washington, New Orleans, and Cleveland to become economically self-sufficient citizens, even if they never sit in a classroom with a white child?

This is not the same thing as saying that African American children do not need to sit next to white children to learn. We know for a fact, even if the Supreme Court had not told us so, that an integrated classroom setting is beneficial for all children — be they white, Latino, or African American.[1] As Gary Orfield has pointed out, there is nothing in the American experience to suggest that racially segregated schools will ever be equal to integrated schools so long as profound inequalities exist in the rest of society (Orfield & Eaton, 1996, p. 361).

Nevertheless, most African American children do not sit next to white children at school, and many never will. To implement the spirit of *Brown*, we must shift our focus from statistical reports on racial balance in our schools. We must confront the fact that African American children who attend segregated schools are handicapped by more problems than racial isolation, and we must begin to attack those problems.

Corruption and Mismanagement

To begin with, we should face the fact that many urban districts where African American children are concentrated are afflicted with mismanagement, corruption, and various forms of employee abuse. For example, in 1993, New York City delayed opening schools in order to inspect them for the presence of asbestos, after it was discovered that many of the district's original asbestos inspection reports had been falsified (Marks, 1993). Earlier that year, the New York City district had published a report that chronicled fraud and corruption by some of the city's custodians (Flamm, Loughran & Keith, 1992; Sack, 1993). According to newspaper articles, the District of Columbia schools hired hundreds of employees with criminal records (Report: DC schools employ hundreds, 1995), had difficulty keeping an accurate account of its enrollment (Schmidt, 1995), and had issued lucrative contracts to unqualified individuals. Nor are these problems limited to New York and Washington, DC. In May 1995, *PrimeTime Live*, an ABC television news show, reported on wrongdoing and bureaucratic bungling in several of the nation's large urban districts. The Chicago school district constantly battles graft and corruption, as do many other urban districts.

Regardless of what desegregation or school reform strategy we implement, African American children will not receive the education they deserve until all of their schools are staffed by honest and conscientious employees. Yet we have done little to make this goal a reality.

Unskilled Teachers and Lackluster Curriculum

Second, a great many of the educators who staff our urban schools are incompetent, uninspired, or indifferent. Linda Darling-Hammond, who wrote about her early teaching experience in Camden, New Jersey, described an urban teaching environment that is not atypical. As a new teacher, Darling-Hammond "found a crumbling warehouse high school managed by dehumanizing and sometimes cruel procedures, staffed by under-prepared and often downright unqualified teachers, an empty book room, and a curriculum so rigid and narrow that teachers could barely stay awake to teach it" (1996, p. 7). Perhaps a quarter of the teachers hired each year are under prepared for their assignments, "and they are assigned disproportionately to schools and classrooms serving the most educationally vulnerable children" (p. 6). Frequently, our best teachers avoid the inner-city schools or transfer out of them as fast as they can.

Many of the teachers and staff who remain behind experience "burnout" (Dworkin, 1987). Too often, urban administrators practice sloppy recruiting procedures (Murnane, et. al, 1990) and simply refuse to document and address poor teaching practice. Susan Moore Johnson's classic case study, "The case of Edna Wiley," (1978) is an almost unbelievable description of one school system's tolerance of a tenured teacher's bizarre and dysfunctional behavior over a period of many years.

Hand-in-hand with the problem of under-prepared teachers is the "backwardness of curriculum policy" in schools for the poor (Darling-Hammond, 1996, p. 7) — in other words, the schools that many African American children attend. "Because of the capa-cities of their teachers," Darling-Hammond wrote, "most classrooms serving poor and minority children continue to provide students with significantly less engaging and effective learning experiences."

Several scholars have written convincingly about the need for "culturally relevant teaching methods" when teaching African American children (Ladson-Billings, 1994; Delpit, 1995). Indeed, we now have good scholarship on this topic. But a new curriculum, even a culturally relevant curriculum, will not increase learning in an environment where skilled teachers and motivated students are in short supply. In such environments, Richard Elmore wrote, "[s]trict curriculum mandates would seem to hold little promise of increasing student learning, except to reinforce adult influence against a hostile or indifferent clientele, or possibly to tell teachers whose knowledge and skill were low what to teach" (1987, p. 70).

Governance Problems

Many inner-city school districts have serious governance and leadership problems. In too many cities, school board members are driven, not by the needs of children, but by racial and ethnic politics (Applebome, 1996), patronage, and naked political ambition (Harris, 1996).

To bring more professionalism to urban school boards, various governance structures have been tried. In Boston, the city replaced a system of elected school board members with members appointed by the mayor. Some cities have tried to decentralize power in order to reduce school boards' mischief-making ability.

In order to discourage patronage, several states limit school boards' authority over the hiring process.

Thus far, however, we have found no sure-fire remedy for unprofessional school boards. Dallas provides an example of how intractable this problem seems to be. In 1980, a local magazine described the Dallas school board as "the worst elected governmental body that Dallas has ever seen" (Bradley, 1992, p. 11, quoting *D Magazine*). Ten years later, the Texas commissioner of education said that the Dallas school board's system of governance was "an inhibitor of student performance" (p. 12). In 1996, the Dallas board was in the news again, receiving national coverage about its turmoil and racial tensions (Applebome, 1996).

In addition to dysfunctional school boards, many inner-city school systems are shackled with ineffective executive leadership. Urban school superintendents seldom keep their positions for more than two or three years (Orfield & Eaton, 1996). Often they arrive at a school system touting a "brand-new" school reform plan. Too often, these executive educators resign their posts before they can be held accountable for results, frequently forced from office by a capricious school board (Parker, 1996).

Collective Bargaining

We must also acknowledge the role collective bargaining has played in making many urban school systems dysfunctional. This problem should not be overstated; most of the nation's school systems are unionized, and a unionized teaching force has not brought insurmountable problems to affluent, suburban districts (Nelson, Rosen, & Powell, 1996). Nevertheless, in the inner cities, teachers have contributed in various ways to a deteriorating learning environment.

First, the unions have fought tenaciously against a host of school reform initiatives, some of which would undoubtable improve urban schools. Teacher associations have opposed — in state legislatures and court rooms — charter school, postsecondary school options, teacher testing programs, school choice, and numerous other reform proposals (DeMitchell & Fossey , 1997). In 1997, to cite one recent example, a Boston teacher's union threatened to strike when school leaders attempted to increase the school day's instrucitonal time by fifteen miutes.

Second, teachers' unions frequently insist on rigid and byzantine work rules in collective barganing agreements. These rules generally provide favored status to senior teachers and promote job protection, but they often hamstring efforts to improve the school environment. For example, a seiority-based teacher transfer rule — which teachers strongly advocate — can hamper school district efforts to attract the best qualified job candidates. As Murname and associated pointe ut (1991), such a rule requires districts to offer vacant teaching positions to senior teachers already employed in a school district before offering those jobs to outside applicants. By the time that a district's senior teachers have ahs an opportunity to review and reject open positions, the most attractive outside candidates will have accepted jobs from other disticts, districts that were able to make job offers early in the recruiting session.

Finally, and perhaps most distubingly, the teachers' unions often continue to cling to an adversarial model of labor relations, one desinged for coal mines and steel mills. Although teachers' unions are beginning to show some signs of change, particuarly at the national level (DeMitchell, in press), local union leaers often approach labor issues as if school boards and teachers are hereditary enimies. In one urban district after another, this adversarial philosophy has undermined collegialigy, sit-based management initiatives, and team efforts at problem solving. Without question, the atmosphere of enmity that often accompanies collective bargining in the inner cities has contributed to the decline of the nation's urban schools.

Breakdown of the Two-Parent African American Family

We must also realize that our desegregation efforts are seriously undermined by the deteriorating condition of the African American family. Nationwide, almost one child in three is now born to an unmarried mother; but among African Americans, 70% of children are born to unmarried women (Popenoe, 1996, p. 34; Moynihan, 1996, p. 227, citing the National Center for Health Statistics). The rise in births to unwed mothers has skyrocketed in the African American community, more than tripling over the course of 30 years.

Changing the racial mix in inner-city schools will not improve life opportunities for African American children unless this disastrous social trend is reversed. As Blankenhorn (1995) pointed out, "[F]atherhood privileges children, providing them with a father's protection, financial resources, cultural transmission, and day-to-day nurturing" (p. 25). Indeed, one commentator noted: "There is a mountain of scientific evidence showing that when families disintegrate children often end up with intellectual, physical, and emotional scars that persist for life ..." (Karl Zinmeister, quoted in Moynihan, 1996, p. 149).

Desegregation specialists and the education community as a whole have said almost nothing about fatherless African American children. Perhaps this is understandable, given our poor understanding of the problem and our lack of a solution. Policymakers cannot explain how the biological family disintegrated so quickly in the United States, especially among African Americans. And most agree that state- and federal-level policies will have little impact on the problem. Even Blankenhorn, who has written most extensively on "fatherless America," admits that his proposals, largely consisting of community-based efforts, are "limited, speculative, and fragmentary" (1996, p. 233).

Nevertheless, education policy makers and researchers should at least admit that the meltdown of the two-parent African American family is the most serious educational problem that African American children have. We can tinker with court-imposed desegregation plans or invest resources in all kinds of programs for "at risk" youth, but if the two-parent family fails to re-emerge in the inner cities, educational outcomes for African American children are not likely to improve.

Conclusion

Three generations of African American children have passed through the nation's public schools since *Brown v. Board of Education* was decided more than 40 years ago. No one can say that *Brown's* bright promise has been fulfilled. Indeed, the condition of African American children, particularly in cities, has gotten worse.

What then should we do? First, we must admit that the majority of African American children attend schools that are predominantly non-white, and that this state of affairs is likely to continue for many years to come. Absent some miraculous change in the political, legal, and economic environment, hundreds of thousands of African American children will never experience *Brown's* promise of a desegregated schooling experience.

Second, we need to abandon the pretense that urban school districts are functioning systems that can deliver equal educational opportunities if relatively simple interventions — cross-district desegregation plans, magnet schools, better court supervision, more money, etc. — are put in place. We need to see urban schools for what many of them are — not healthy organisms with a few minor ailments — but dysfunctional educational environments suffering from mismanagement, unqualified staffs, political gridlock, and lackluster leadership. Except for the specialty schools that cater to elite families, many urban school systems are failing to educate African Americans, and failing badly. In some nonselective middle schools and high schools in these systems, public education is on the verge of collapse.

Of course confronting reality is not the same as changing reality. Without ceasing efforts to achieve desegregation, we must attack the many problems that afflict inner city schools: corruption, mismanagement, adversarial labor relations, poorly-trained and uninspired educators, and the breakdown of the two-parent family. This is a monumental task. There are many political obstacles; and the right course of action will not always be clear.

We must begin, however, by facing the truth. *Brown's* promise has been broken in the inner cities and may not be fulfilled in our lifetime. The challenge before us then is this: how can African American children receive better educational opportunities in schools where they will never see a white child?

Notes

1. For a comprehensive review of the research on the effects of desegregation on elementary and secondary students, consult Schofield (1996). Based on this review, Schofield concludes that desegregation has had a positive but modest effect on reading skills of African American children, but that mathematics skills seem unaffected. She also cites evidence that desegregation has favorably influenced adult outcomes for African Americans, such as college graduation rates and income.

Schofield also makes the important point that even if no specific benefits could be attributed to *Brown v. Board of Education*, the abolition of a "governmental sanctioned 'badge of inferiority'" was an important achievement in intergroup relations (p. 100).

References

Applebome, P. (1996, June 27). Bitter racial rift in Dallas board reflects ills in many other cities. *New York Times*, p. 1.

Applebome, P. (1997, April 8). Schools see re-emergence of "separate but equal." *New York Times*, p. A10.

Bennett, C.E. (1995). The black population in the United States. Washington D.C.: Bureau of the Census.

Blankenhorn, D. (1995). *Fatherless America: Confronting our most urgent social problem.* New York: Basic Books.

Bradley, A. (1992, April 29). Under state order, Dallas tries to clean up its act. *Education Week*, p. 11.

Butterfield, F. (1996, February 13). Study finds disparity in justice for blacks. *New York Times*, p. A8.

Council of Great City Schools (1994, September). *National Urban Education Goals: 1992-1993 Indicators Report.* Washington, DC: author.

Darling-Hammond, L. (1996). The right to learn and the advancement of teaching: Research, policy, and practice for democratic education. *Educational Researcher 25*, 5-17.

Delpit, L. (1995). Other people's children: Cultural conflicts in the classrooms. New York: The New Press.

DeMitchell, T.A. (in press). The reinvented union: A concern for teaching, not just teachers. *Journal of Personnel Evaluation in Education.*

DeMitchell, T. A., and Fossey, R. (1997). *The limits of law-based school reform: Vain hopes and false promises.* Lancaster, PA: Technomic Publishing Company.

Dworkin, A. G. (1987). *Teacher burnout in the public schools.* Albany, New York: State University of New York Press.

Elmore, R. F. (1987). Reform and the culture of authority in schools. *Educational Administration Quarterly 23*, 60-78.

Feldman, J., Kirby, E., & Eaton, S. E. (1994). *Still separate, still unequal: The Limits of Milliken II's Educational Compensation remedies.* Cambridge, MA: Harvard Project on School Desegregation.

Fossey, R. (1995, October 25). Corrupt, mismanaged and unsafe schools: Where is the research? *Education Week,* p. 31.

Fossey, R. (1996, October). High school dropout rates: Are we sure they are going down? *Phi Delta Kappan*, pp. 140-144.

Fossey, R. (1993). Site-based management in a collective bargaining environment: Can we mix oil and water? *International Journal of Educational Reform 2*, 320-324.

Flamm, S. R., Loughran, R. A., and Keith, L. (1992, November). *A system like no other: Fraud and misconduct by New York City school custodians.* New York: New York City Office of the Special Commissioner of Investigation.

Harris, J. (1996, December 14). Rein in the local school boards. *New York Times,* p. 23.

Hendrie, Caroline (1996, November 13). Magnet's value in desegregating schools is found to be limited. *Education Week,* p. 1

How Hartford schools fare (1995, April 13). *Hartford Courant,* p. A15.

Johnson, S. M. (1978). The case of Edna Wiley. Harvard Graduate School of Education, teaching case (typewritten).

Ladson-Billings, G. (1994). *The dreamkeepers: Successful teachers for African American children.* San Francisco: Jossey-Bass.

Lomotey, K. & Fossey, R (1997). The unkept promise of *Brown v. Board of Education*: How can its vision be fulfilled? In DeMitchell, T.A. & Fossey R. *The limits of law-based school reform: Vain hopes and false promises.* Lancaster, PA: Technomic Press. pp 165-181

Marks, Peter. (1993, August 8). Asbestos tests were faked, officials say. *New York Times*, p. 37.

McLarin, K. J. (1994, July 23). New Jersey, denouncing local management, prepares to take over Newark's schools. *New York Times*, p. 10.

Moore, D. R. & Davenport, S. (1990). School choice: The new improved sorting machine. In W. L. Boyd & H. J. Walberg (Eds.) *Choice in public education: Potential and problems*, pp. 187-224. Berkeley, CA: McCutchan.

Moynihan, D. P. (1996). *Miles to go: A personal history of social policy.* Cambridge MA: Harvard University Press.

Murnane, R., Singer, J., Willett, J., Kemple, J & Olsen, R. (1991). *Who will teach? Policies that matter.* Cambridge, MA: Harvard University Press.

National Center for Education Statistics. (1995, October). *Digest of Education Statistics 1995.* Washington, DC: author.

Nelson, F.H., Rosen, M., Powell, B. (1996). *Are teacher unions hurting American education?* Milwaukee, WI: Institute For Wisconsin's Future.

Orfield, G. and Eaton, S. E. (1996). *Dismantling desegregation: The Quiet Reversal of Brown v. Board of Education.* New York: Free Press.

Pack, W. (1996, January 9). Proposed changes anger some parents. *The Advocate,* p. B1.

Parham, W. & Parham, T. (1989). The community and academic achievement. In G. Berry & J. Asamen (Eds.), *Black students: Psychosocial issues and academic achievement* (pp. 120-137). Newbury Park, CA: Sage.

Parker, P. (1996). Superintendent vulnerability and mobility. *Peabody Journal of Education 71,* 64-77.

Popenoe, D. (1996). *Life without father: Compelling new evidence that fatherhood and marriage are indispensable for the good of children and society.* New York: Free Press.

PrimeTime Live. (1995, May 3). *Reading, writing and rip-off.* ABC News.

Rossell, C. H. (1990). *The carrot and the stick for school desegregation policy: Magnet schools or forced busing.* Philadelphia: Temple University Press.

Schofield, J. W. (1996). Review of research on school desegregation's impact on elementary and secondary students. In K. Lomotey & C. Teddlie (Eds.), *Readings on equal education, Vol 13. Forty years after the Brown decision: Implications of school desegregation for U. S. education* (pp. 157-175). New York: AMS Press.

Schmidt, P. (1995, May 3). Council moving to gain more say over D.C. schools. *Education Week,* p. 1.

Time for Teaching (1997, September 8). *Boston Globe,* p. A14.

CHAPTER 3

THE HARTFORD DESEGREGATION CASE: USING THE STATE CONSTITUTION TO FIGHT RACIAL ISOLATION IN URBAN SCHOOLS

Richard Fossey and Elizabeth A. Kemper

In *volume* 13 of Readings on Equal Education, an essay appeared on the policy implications of a desegregation case that was making its way through the Connecticut state court system. In this case, styled *Sheff v. O'Neill*, 17 school children from the Hartford metropolitan area sued the state of Connecticut, arguing that racial isolation in the Hartford school system violated the Connecticut Constitution. At the time the case went to trial, 92% of the Hartford school population was African American or Latino, while the surrounding school districts had school enrollments that were overwhelmingly non-Hispanic white.

Other lawsuits had attacked racially-isolated schools in the federal courts, but judicial precedent made most of these efforts futile. Federal courts will only desegregate schools if they find that children have been intentionally segregated by race. As Eaton and Orfield (1996) explained, federal courts distinguish between de jure and de facto segregation. De jure segregation results by law or deliberate act of school officials and is unconstitutional. De facto segregation results from housing patterns or other factors and is not remedial in the federal courts.

In *Sheff v. O'Neill*, the plaintiffs attempted to erase the distinction between de jure and de facto segregation. Abandoning all reliance on the U. S. Constitution, these children argued that racially isolated schools violate the Connecticut Constitution and must be desegregated, whether or not the racial isolation was the result of intentional government action. They asked the court to develop a regional school desegregation plan that would encompass more than 20 school districts.

The *Sheff* plaintiffs lost their case at the trial court level, but they won on appeal. In a 1996 decision, the Connecticut Supreme Court ruled that racial segregation of Hartford school children violated the state constitution. In the court's view, it was immaterial whether their segregation was de facto or de jure. Regardless of the reason, desegregation was harmful and unconstitutional and must be remedied. In this landmark decision, the Connecticut Supreme Court cleared the way for metropolitan desegregation plans, plans that could cross district boundaries to achieve better racial balance in schools.

Sheff will surely be a major milestone in the nation's long journey toward desegregated public schools. Forty years after *Brown v. Board of Education* decreed an end to segregated schools, *Sheff* is a fresh attempt to make *Brown*'s promise a reality for thousands of African American and Hispanic school children. If other state courts interpret their respective constitutions in harmony with *Sheff*, the decision may mark the beginning of a fresh effort to desegregate schools on a regional basis.

Background of the *Sheff* Case

Hartford school children are mostly African American or Hispanic. Like inner-city school children across the nation, they attend racially isolated schools that are surrounded by suburban, largely white school systems. In 1993, 93% of Hartford's students were African American or Hispanic. Meanwhile, most of the surrounding suburban districts had student enrollments that were 90% non-Hispanic white. In Connecticut as a whole, 80% of the state's minority students were enrolled in 18 districts;

while 136 of the state's 166 districts had minority enrollments of 10% or less (Pierce, 1993).

Remarkably, racial isolation in Hartford schools had gotten worse over the years, in spite of the fact that the state of Connecticut had an exemplary record for fighting race discrimination. Indeed, more than 30 years before *Sheff* was filed, Connecticut education leaders had recognized that school children in some Connecticut cities were becoming increasingly isolated by race; and they had taken a number of steps to address the problem (Integration proposals over 30 years, 1995).

In spite of these efforts, however, the plight of children in Hartford had dramatically deteriorated. In 1970, the school system was 71% white, and 32% of 9th graders dropped out of school or transferred to other districts before graduation. Twenty years later, 93% of the district's enrollment was African American or Hispanic; and 55% of its 9th graders failed to graduate with their Hartford classmates (Christensen, 1993). In 1993-1994, only 11% of Hartford students scored adequately on all three parts of state mastery tests, compared with 48% statewide. Almost three-quarters of Hartford's students lived in poverty in one of the nation's most affluent states (How Hartford fares, 1995). In 1988, 67% of Hartford children were born to unwed mothers, up from 10% in 1960 (Christensen, 1993).

Sheff v. O'Neill: The Trial Court Denies Relief

In April 1989, 17 schoolchildren from the Hartford area sued the state of Connecticut in an attempt to end the racial isolation of Hartford schools. Plaintiffs were represented by the Connecticut Civil Liberties Union, and consisted of 15 African American, Hispanic, and white Hartford school children and two white school children from the neighboring town of West Hartford. Milo Sheff, an African American student from Hartford, was the lead plaintiff and Connecticut Governor William O'Neill was the first-named defendant.

In their complaint, the children asked trial court judge Harry Hammer to develop a regional desegregation plan that would change the racial composition, not only of the Hartford school system, but of 21 surrounding suburban districts as well. They wanted Judge Hammer to redraw district boundaries to achieve racial balance or to order some other action to bring about racially balanced schools on a regional basis.

Although the *Sheff* plaintiffs submitted extensive evidence and testimony to support their case, their legal theory was simple. The Connecticut Constitution, they argued, guaranteed Hartford school children a minimally adequate education. This they were not receiving, as evidenced by scores on state mastery tests. Educational inequalities between Hartford's minority students and suburban white students were the result of state educational policies that had permitted de facto segregation of Hartford and surrounding suburbs. The state was constitutionally obligated to desegregate the districts on a regional basis, the plaintiffs maintained, regardless of how it had come about. Even if the segregation had resulted by accident or by forces outside the state's control, the plaintiffs contended that the Connecticut Constitution compelled the court to develop a remedy. The remedy they proposed was a cross-district desegregation plan that would encompass all the school districts in the metropolitan Hartford region.

Unfortunately for the plaintiffs, however, these arguments did not persuade the trial court. In a 1995 decision, Judge Hammer ruled that racial isolation of Hartford schools was not caused by state action, but was the result of residential segregation and other factors beyond the state's control. Quoting a federal court decision, Judge Hammer concluded that "racially balanced municipalities are beyond the pale of either judicial or legislative intervention;" and he granted judgment in favor of the state (*Sheff v. O'Neill*, memorandum of decision, 1995).

Judge Hammer's decision was immediately appealed, and the Connecticut Supreme Court directed the judge to supplement his opinion with written findings of fact and conclusions of law. Judge Hammer complied, and on June 27, 1995, he issued a supplementary opinion in which he outlined the reasoning and the evidence he relied on in making his original decision.

First, Judge Hammer's fact findings show that he was influenced by Connecticut's long history of local control in the field of education. Although he noted that Connecticut education had always been a colonial or state government responsibility, a tradition of local control could be traced back to the early eighteenth century. The judge was clearly reluctant to redraw school district boundaries or change school attendance patterns, a development that would alter a practice of local school governance spanning almost three centuries.

Second, Judge Hammer was favorably impressed by the state's long history of combating racial segregation. Judge Hammer found that Connecticut had actively promoted school desegregation for many years. Connecticut was one of only seven states that had spent its own funds on school desegregation programs without being under court order. Since 1966, the state had contributed financial and technical support for Project Concern, a voluntary interdistrict transfer program designed to promote school desegregation in the state's urban areas. According to the Judge, Project Concern was one of the longest continually operated desegregation programs of its type in the United States.

Third, Judge Hammer was not persuaded that racial isolation was responsible for substandard school conditions in Hartford. He ruled that poverty, not racial isolation, was the principal cause of low academic achievement in the Hartford school system.

Finally, Judge Hammer expressed pessimism about the value of cross-district desegregation plan as a means of attacking racial isolation in Hartford. In the judge's opinion, meaningful integration could only be achieved by building affordable suburban housing for the purpose of breaking up urban ghettos and by making urban schools more attractive to suburban families. In other words, the plaintiffs' proposal for a court order directing Hartford and suburban districts to reconfigure district lines or take some other mandated action to achieve racial balance simply would not work.

The Plaintiffs Appeal: Judge Hammer is Reversed

Judge Hammer's decision, with its bleak conclusions about school desegregation efforts, was appealed to the Connecticut Supreme Court. The case was argued in September 1995; on July 9, 1996, the Connecticut Supreme Court reversed.

According to the state's highest court, the Connecticut Constitution places an affirmative duty on the legislature to provide Connecticut school children with substantially equal educational opportunities.   When the state's public school systems become racially isolated, the court reasoned, some children are deprived of equal educational opportunities. This, the court ruled, is a violation of the state constitution.

In addition, the court made clear that a constitutional violation occurs whenever racial isolation exists, regardless of whether it results from intentional legislative action. The state's affirmative duty to provide substantially equal educational opportunities makes it unnecessary to inquire whether inequality results from intentional state misconduct. If the legislature fails, for whatever reason, to remedy a substantial inequality in educational opportunity, the Connecticut Constitution is violated.

Moreover, the court continued, the Connecticut Constitution contains a specific provision that protects citizens against segregation. In the court's view, this provision is neutral regarding state intent.   Thus, the Connecticut legislature is obligated to remedy segregation whenever it occurs, without regard to whether it exists in de jure or de facto form.

Having given its interpretation of Connecticut constitutional law, the court outlined a three-step process for analyzing the *Sheff* plaintiffs' claims.   First, plaintiffs must present a *prima facie* case showing that disparities in educational opportunities are not *de minimus*, that they jeopardize the fundamental right to receive an education that the Connecticut Constitution guarantees. Second, once a *prima facie* case has been made, the state must respond by showing that the disparities are incident to a legitimate state policy. If the state's justification is acceptable, a third test applies. Here the state must also demonstrate that the disparities in educational opportunities are not so great as to be unconstitutional.

Applying the three-part test, the Connecticut Supreme Court ruled that the plaintiffs had made a *prima facie* case that the racial isolation of the Hartford school system jeopardized their fundamental right to an education. However, the court also ruled that the state had justified the racial isolation as a consequence of a state policy to assign students to schools in the communities where they live. In the court's view, such a policy advances the goal of local control and community accountability, particularly in Connecticut, where the state had pursued other efforts to improve racial diversity in public schools.   For example, the court pointed out, the state had supported voluntary plans for improving interdistrict racial diversity, including funding support for magnet schools that would attract students across district lines.

Nevertheless, the court concluded that the state had not met the third test of its three-part constitutional analysis. In spite of the fact that the state had legitimate reasons for assigning students to their home districts, the disparities in educational opportunities — disparities resulting from racial isolation — were so great as to be unconstitutional.

Here the court cited cold statistics. During the 1991-1992 school year, 92% of Hartford school children were African American or Latino. In the 21 towns surrounding Hartford, only 7 had minority populations above 10%. Despite state efforts to improve that picture, it seemed evident that Hartford school children would be even more racially isolated in the years to come.

The court buttressed its ruling with a brief discussion on the critical value of racially diverse school environments. "It is crucial for a democratic society," the court wrote, "to provide all its schoolchildren with fair access to an unsegregated education" (p. 1289). The state's economy, its cultural fabric, and its material well-being all depend on skilled workers and educated citizens. "Finding a way across the racial and ethnic divide [in public education] has never been more important than it is today" (p. 1290).

In short, the Connecticut Supreme Court ruled that the children of metropolitan Hartford have a constitutional right to substantially equal educational opportunities, a right that was violated by the overwhelming racial isolation of the Hartford school system. Departing from federal precedent, the court emphasized that its ruling in no way depended on a finding of intentional discrimination by the state. Regardless of how racial isolation occurs, it violates the Connecticut constitution and must be remedied.

Significantly, the Connecticut Supreme Court did not specify what the remedy should be. Rather, it directed the trial court to issue a declaratory judgment consistent with the supreme court's ruling and to retain jurisdiction in case the Connecticut legislature failed to craft a remedy to cure the constitutional violation. It seemed clear at the time, however, that whatever the ultimate remedy would be, it would likely involve the significant movement of children across school district boundaries in order to achieve racial diversity in Hartford and the 21 other districts in the Hartford metropolitan area.

Reaction to the Decision

In response to the Connecticut Supreme Court's decision, Governor John G. Rowland appointed a twenty-two member panel to explore the options for desegregating the Hartford schools. Panel members included the state NAACP president, several state legislators, the Hartford school superintendent, and several lawyers from Hartford-area suburbs. The Governor was immediately criticized for failing to appoint a voice for the Hartford Latino community and for failing to have sufficient representatives from suburban towns that might be affected by the *Sheff* decision.

Many had assumed that *Sheff* would lead to some sort of mandated cross-district bussing plan, but Governor Rowland played down this idea from the start. The Governor made clear that he favored voluntary measures to desegregate the Hartford schools, including expanded opportunities for Hartford's minority children to attend suburban schools. "The real solution to better schools is still, in my opinion, more discipline, more parental involvement, and school choice responds to a lot of those issues," the Governor said in a radio interview (Judson, 1996, p. 4).

Nor was the public in favor of cross-district bussing as the means of complying with *Sheff's* desegregation mandate. In November 1996, several school board elections were held in the Hartford metropolitan area. In general, candidates who opposed forced bussing won those elections (Stansbury, 1996), sending a message that the voters were not in favor of this option.

In January 1997, Governor Rowland's panel presented 15 recommendations for improving Connecticut schools and reducing racial isolation (Green, 1997). In addition to an interdistrict school-choice plan, the panel recommended the establishment of regional magnet schools and charter schools, expanded pre-school programs, region-coordinated school construction programs, and additional funding to districts that have high numbers of disadvantaged students.

Plaintiffs were disappointed by the panel's recommendations, particularly its lack of strong guidelines for attacking racial isolation in the Hartford schools and surrounding towns. Suburban school authorities, on the other hand, expressed concern about any plan that would encourage out-of-district students to enroll in their schools. Suburban schools are already full, many school leaders said; they simply had no room for Hartford school children (Green & Brown, 1997).

In an effort to comply with the Connecticut Supreme Court's *Sheff* mandate, Connecticut lawmakers reviewed several legislative proposals during the 1997 legislative session. One bill linked school construction money to integration goals. Another sought to give the state more power over failing school systems, including the right to manage finances and change union contracts. The third bill focused on school management issues. None proposed to force suburban school districts to accept Hartford school children or to require suburban children to be transported to Hartford schools.

However, realizing that they were under a mandate by the Connecticut Supreme Court to address the plight of Hartford's school children, Connecticut lawmakers did take aggressive action. During the 1997 legislative session, the Connecticut Assembly passed a law authorizing the state takeover of the Hartford schools. By a vote of 27 to 9 in the Senate and 135 to 7 in the house, the legislature dissolved the Hartford Board of Education and replaced it with a panel of seven state-appointed trustees. "Desperate times call for desperate measures," Connecticut Senate Presidents Kevin B. Sullivan observed. "For children and teachers in Hartford these are desperate times" (Green, 1997).

By the end of the legislative session, the Connecticut Assembly took other action to improve school conditions in Hartford and comply with the Connecticut Supreme Court's *Sheff* decision. The legislature preserved and slightly expanded a voluntary bussing program in Hartford, funded some new regional schools, and directed the State Department of Education to develop a five-year plan to eliminate inequalities between Connecticut school districts (Keating, Lender, Daly, & Bernstein, 1997).

Conclusion and Implications

Sheff v. O'Neill is an important decision in the sense that a state court, disregarding federal precedents, recognized a state's constitutional obligation to end racial isolation in public schools regardless of how that isolation may have come about. By ignoring the distinction between de facto and de jure segregation, the Connecticut Supreme Court made cross-district desegregation remedies legally possible within the boundaries of its jurisdiction. If other state courts follow the Connecticut Supreme Court's lead and interpret their respective constitutions in a similar way, we may see cross-desegregation plans in other jurisdictions, plans either mandated or permitted by the judiciary. If so, the battle for desegregated schools will shift, just as school-finance litigation has shifted, from the federal to the state courts.

It should be noted, however, that although *Sheff* made cross-district desegregation possible, it did not make it inevitable. During the legislative session following the *Sheff* decision, the Connecticut legislature resisted the implementation of a cross-district desegregation plan. Instead, it passed legislation authorizing a state takeover of the Hartford school system and implemented other measures that fall short of a metropolitan desegregation scheme. It remains to be seen whether the Connecticut Supreme Court will deem these measures to be sufficient.

Even if *Sheff* ultimately results in a cross-district desegregation plan for metropolitan Hartford, the decision will not be a panacea for the problems of racially isolated schools. It has been more than forty years since the Supreme Court declared an end to school segregation in *Brown v. Board of Education*. In spite of the fact that federal courts have struggled to improve educational opportunities for African American children during all this time, the condition of African American children in the inner cities has gotten worse, not better (Lomotey & Fossey, 1997).

As the twentieth century closes, urban schools face a crisis of racial isolation, mismanagement, corruption, and dysfunctional school leadership. In the inner cities, the two-parent family is rapidly disappearing, along with job opportunities, and community infrastructures (Fossey, Chapter

2). *Sheff v. O'Neill* may marginally improve this picture by providing some inner-city school children with opportunities to attend schools in the suburbs. By itself, however, the decision seems unlikely to achieve what the federal courts have so far failed to bring about — equal educational opportunities for all children, regardless of color.

References

Christensen, J. (1993, March 15). Wicker watch: Connecticut Governor Wicker's plan to integrate schools across the state. *National Review.*

Eaton, S. E. & Orfield, G. A. (1996). Brown v. Board of Education and the continuing struggle for desegregated schools. In C. Teddlie & K. Lomotey (Eds.), *Readings on Equal Education, Vol 13. Forty years after the Brown decision: Implications of school desegregation for U. S. education.* New York: AMS Press, 117-138

Fossey, R. (1996). The Hartford desegregation case: Is there a judicial remedy for racially isolated inner-city schools? In C. Teddlie & K. Lomotey (Eds.), *Readings on equal education, Vol 13. Forty years after the Brown decision: Implications of school desegregation for U. S. education* (pp. 157-175). New York: AMS Press.

How Hartford schools fare. *Hartford Courant*, April 13, 1995, p. A15.

Green, R. (1997b, June 5). Mixed reviews for legislature's response to *Sheff* decision. *Hartford Courant*, p. A10.

Green R. (1997b, April 17). State to take over city schools: Desperate times call for desperate measures." *Hartford Courant*, p. A10.

Integration proposals over 30 years. (1995, April 13). *New York Times*, Section B, p. 6.

Keeating, C., Lender, J., Daly M., & Bernstein (1997, June 5). *Hartford Courant.*

Lomotey, K. & Fossey, R. (1997). School desegregation: Why it hasn't worked and what could work. In C. Teddlie & K. Lomotey (Eds.), *Readings on equal education, Vol 14. Forty years after the Brown decision: Social and cultural effects of school desegregation* (pp. 401-420). New York: AMS Press.

Peirce, N. (1993, February 28). A governor gleefully tackles income tax, school disparities. *Dallas Morning News*, p. 5J.

Table of Legal Cases
Brown v. Board of Education, 347 U.S. 483 (1954).
Milliken v. Bradley, 418 U.S. 717 (1974).
Sheff v. O'Neill, 678 A.2d 1267 (Conn. 1996).
Sheff v. O'Neill, CV89-0360977S, Memorandum of Decision (Judicial District of Hartford, April 12, 1995).
Sheff v. O'Neill, CV89-0360977S, Statement of Facts (Judicial District of Hartford, June 27, 1995).

CHAPTER 4

MISSOURI V. JENKINS: AN OVERVIEW

Ralph D. Mawdsley, J.D., Ph.D.

Introduction

Missouri v. Jenkins represents an eighteen-year odyssey through the federal courts. During that time period, reported federal decisions addressing the merits of the case include four by the district court for the Western District of Missouri (1978, 1984, 1985, 1987)), four by the Eighth Circuit Court of Appeals (1986, 1988, 1993a, 1993b), and two by the United States Supreme Court (1990, 1995). Remarkably, while the judicial membership of the Eighth Circuit and the Supreme Court changed during this period, the same federal district court judge, Judge Russell Clark, presided over all trial-level proceedings.

The lawsuit, first brought in 1977 by the Kansas City, Missouri School District (KCMSD), the school board, and the children of two school board members, alleged that the State of Missouri, eleven surrounding suburban school districts, and the federal Departments of Transportation (DOT), Health, Education and Welfare (HEW), and Housing and Urban Development (HUD) had created and perpetuated a system of racial discrimination in the schools of the Kansas City metropolitan area. Although nominally

33

joined as a defendant by the State, KCMSD continued to cooperate with the other plaintiffs in "a friendly adversary relationship" (110 S. Ct 1651, 1667 (Kennedy, J., concurring)) to implement the changes ordered by the district court.

This lengthy litigation can be separated into two separate and distinct phases. The first phase dealt with the funding of the desegregation of KCMSD and culminated with the case's first trip to the Supreme Court in 1990. The second phase, addressing implementation of the court ordered desegregation plan, was the subject of the case's second trip to the Court in 1995.

The Cost of Desegregating KCMSD: Who Pays, How Much, and By What Means?

The cost of remedies ordered by the district court in this case has been truly staggering. Following a 64-day trial that involved over 140 witnesses, included 2,100 exhibits, and produced 10,000 pages of depositions, Judge Clark ordered an extensive number of remedies that included restoration of KCMSD to the highest classification (AAA) awarded by the State, reduction in class sizes, improvement in educational opportunities by developing student-centered programs, implementation of a substantial capital improvements plan to upgrade the deteriorating facilities at KCMSD, initiation of a state-funded effective schools program that included substantial cash grants to local schools, and commission of a study on magnet school programs. By the time this case made its second appearance before the Supreme Court in 1995, maintenance of KCMSD at the highest State level had cost in excess of $220 million, capital improvements had reached more than $540 million, and a comprehensive magnet school and capital improvement program had cost in excess of $448 million (115 S.Ct. at 2042-44). These costs are even more remarkable when compared to Judge Clark's original estimate that the total cost of desegregation would be only about $88 million over three years, with $67.6 million allocated to the state and $20.1 million to KCMSD (639 F.Supp. at 43-44).

This allocation of costs was the basis for the first round of appeals. Following the trial, actions against all defendants except KCMSD and the State of Missouri were dismissed. The court specifically found that the eleven suburban districts surrounding KCMSD were autonomous and, although they had been the beneficiaries of white flight, had committed no intentional acts discriminating on the basis of race, thus leaving only KCMSD and the State as having failed to eradicate the vestiges of the former state-mandated dual school system. In addition, Judge Clark ruled that, because the suburban districts had not participated in the segregation, they could not be part of an interdistrict remedy, involving, among other aspects, interdistrict busing. On appeal, the Eighth Circuit upheld the remedies ordered by the district court, the dismissal of all parties except KCMSD and the state, and the finding of no interdistrict segregation. However, the court reversed and remanded on the allocation of costs. Since both KCMSD and the state were "constitutional violators," (807 F.2d at 686) the costs should be equally shared. The Supreme Court refused *certiorari* (484 U.S. 816 (1987)) and, on remand, Judge Clark faced the dilemma of how to allocate costs.

The original order allocating approximately 80% of the costs to the State had been based on two Missouri constitutional provisions which limited local property tax rates without voter approval and which required property tax rates to be rolled back where property was assessed at a higher valuation. The effect of these two provisions was that KCMSD could not raise tax rates without voter approval, something that had not happened since 1969 (110 S. Ct. at 1656, n. 5), and could not obtain any revenue increase as a result of increases in the assessed valuation of real property.

Following remand, Judge Clark used an apportionment analysis comparable to that in tort liability comparative negligence to set the liability of KCMSD at 25%. He quickly realized that with the state constitutional limitations the school district would not be able to meet its share of the expenses for desegregation. Injunctions issued in two successive years against enforcement of the state constitutional rollback provision generated a total of $10.5 million of new revenues for KCMSD. However, with the rapidly mushrooming costs associated with capital improvements (by 1991-92, the anticipated expenses for capital improvements had gone from $52.8 million to $187.4 million and involved the renovation of approximately 55 schools, the closure of 18 facilities, and the construction of 17 new schools) (Id. at 1657-58; 672 F. Supp. at 405) and the implementation of a magnet school program (set at $142.7 million for 1991-92), costs far exceeded the school district's revenue generating capacity. Thus, Judge Clark took the unusual step of ordering that the KCMSD property tax levy be raised from $2.05 to $4.00 per $100 of assessed valuation.

Among the features of the magnet school plan that set costs skyrocketing were a performing arts middle school, a technical high school offering programs from heating and air conditioning to cosmetology and robotics, as well as high schools with air conditioned classrooms. In addition, the plan called for a 25-acre farm with an 104-person capacity air-conditioned meeting room, a 25-acre wildlife area for science study, and a 2,000-square-foot planetarium. Other features included a model United Nations wired for language translation, radio and television studios with an editing and animation lab, a temperature controlled art gallery, a 3,500 square-foot dust-free diesel mechanics room, and 1,875 square-foot elementary school animal rooms for use in a zoo project (110 S. Ct. at 1676-77 [Kennedy, J., concurring]).

The authority of a federal district court to order a tax levy was the sole issue on this case's first trip to the Supreme Court. Prior to reaching the Supreme Court, the Eighth Circuit upheld the tax levy, but required that in the future the district court should not set the property tax rate itself but should authorize KCMSD to submit a tax levy to the state tax collection authorities and should enjoin the operation of state laws hindering KCMSD from adequately funding the remedy (855 F.2d at 1314).

The Supreme Court affirmed the Eighth Circuit's holding concerning future authorizations for tax levies, but reversed that court's affirmation of the district court's direct ordering of a tax levy. Holding that the district court had "abused its discretion in imposing the tax itself" (110 S. Ct. at 1663), the Supreme Court determined that Judge Clark should have required KCMSD to levy property taxes at a rate adequate to fund the desegregation remedy and enjoined state tax provisions preventing KCMSD from exercising this power. The Supreme Court addressed two substantive questions concerning desegregation and state taxing authority: the function of local taxing authorities; and the power of a federal court to order a tax levy in excess of state law limitations.

Reasoning that a federal district court in exercising equitable power has an obligation to respect "the integrity and function of local government institutions, (the Court found that)

> (a)uthorizing and directing local government institutions to
> devise and implement remedies not only protects the func-
> tion of these institutions but, to the extent possible, also

places the responsibility for solutions to the problems of segregation upon those who have themselves created the problems (Id.).

Concerning the State's argument that a federal court's order to levy taxes should be limited by state-imposed limitations on local taxing authority, the Court held that

the KCMSD may be ordered to levy taxes despite the statutory limitations on its authority in order to compel the discharge of an obligation imposed on KCMSD by the Fourteenth Amendment. To hold otherwise would fail to take account of the obligations of local governments, under the Supremacy Clause, to fulfill the requirements that the Constitution imposes on them. (Id. at 1666).

However, four justices (Kennedy, Rehnquist, O'Connor and Scalia), while concurring in the judgment, disagreed strongly with the majority opinion over "taxation imposed by the unelected, life-tenured federal judiciary...." (Id . at 1667). These four partial dissenters objected to the nature of the exercise of judicial power.

The exercise of judicial power involves adjudication of controversies and imposition of burdens on those who are not parties before the Court. The order at issue here is not of this character. It binds the broad class of all KCMSD taxpayers. It has the purpose and direct effect of extracting money from persons who have had no presence or representation in the suit. For this reason, the District Court's direct order imposing a tax was more than an abuse of discretion, for any attempt to collect the taxes from the citizens would have been a blatant denial of due process... A judicial taxation order is but an attempt to exercise a power that has always been thought legislative in nature. (Id. at 1671 [Kennedy, J., concurring]).

As a warning to the district court judge, Justice Kennedy on behalf of the three other justices, observed that in all of the desegregation cases heard by the Supreme Court, "no order of taxation has ever been approved," (Id. at 1678) and, at the very least, the district court must establish a record that it "gave due consideration to the possibility that another remedy among the wide range of possibilities would have addressed the constitutional violations without giving rise to a funding crisis." (Id . at 1677-78). This warning presaged the sequence of events that was to lead to this case's second appearance before the Supreme Court in 1995.

Implementation of Court-Ordered Desegregation:
Can a District Court Exceed Its Authority to Fashion a Remedy?

With the Supreme Court's decision upholding the district
court's taxation power, the parties set about the task of complying
with what a justice in the Eighth Circuit referred to as "the most
ambitious and expensive remedial program in the history of
desegregation." (19 F.3d 393, 397 [8th Cir. 1993] [Bean, J.,
dissenting]). Because of the inability of KCMSD to meet the
annual costs of desegregation either through its regular budget or
through its authority to tax, costs which by 1995 approached $200
million per year, the State of Missouri was forced to bear the brunt
of the increasing costs under the operation of a joint-and-several
liability fashioned by the district court. The friendly, adversarial
relationship between KCMSD and plaintiffs permitted the school
district to pursue ever more expensive programs, many of which
are identified above, and which the Supreme Court characterized
as "facilities and opportunities not available anywhere else in the
country."(115 S. Ct. at 2045).

The underlying problem for the second appeal to the Supreme
Court was the same as for the first, namely the absence of any
interdistrict segregation, which had resulted in a judicial remedy
being limited only to KCMSD. With a student population in
KCMSD that was 69% African-American, 24% white, 5%
Hispanic, and 2% Asian, the district court was prevented by its
own finding of no interdistrict segregation from ordering mandatory interdistrict distribution of students and refused to order
additional intradistrict reassignments because they would "increase
the instability of the KCMSD and reduce the potential for desegregation" (639 F. Supp. at 38). Thus, if KCMSD were to improve
"the quality and quantity of the educational services (it) offer(ed),"
(Id. at 26) a remedy would have to be fashioned that "maintain(ed)
and hopefully attract(ed) non-minority student enrollment (in
KCMSD schools)." (Id. at 38).

Two benchmarks for determining quality of education were
improvement in the KCMSD rating by the Missouri State Department Elementary and Secondary Education from AA to AAA and
raising the achievement level of school children in the district (for
reading scores of elementary children to the national norms and for
secondary students to a passing level for the BEST test from 51%
to a 90 to 95% rate) (Id. at 24-26). Attainment of the AAA rating

was achieved by the 1977-78 school year at a cost of $220 million. (115 S. Ct. at 2043). Among the changes were: hiring 22 librarians and purchasing additional media and library resources; hiring 54 specialists to provide elementary teachers with planning time during the school day; hiring 102 additional specialists to teach elementary art, music, and physical education; hiring 18 new elementary and secondary counselors; and hiring 183 additional teachers to reduce class sizes in K-3 grades to 22, in 4-6 grades to 27, and in secondary to 125 students per teacher per day (639 F. Supp. at 26-30).

While the outcome of satisfying the State's AAA rating was fairly easily achieved by increasing expenditures of sufficient money, the expenditure of considerable sums of money did not improve student achievement. In approaching the problem of low student achievement scores, Judge Russell Clark was influenced both by the necessity of raising academic achievement lowered by the effects of segregation and operating successful learning experiences that would attract non-minority enrollment from surrounding school districts. (Id . at 31).

To accomplish these goals the judge approved a two-prong plan. In the first prong, he ordered implementation of a multi-faceted remedial program which included:

- summer school programs for students who would otherwise have been retained;
- expansion of all-day kindergartens throughout the school district;
- implementation of an after-school tutoring program;
- establishment of early childhood language development programs;
- provision of State funds for the 25 schools with 90% or more black student enrollment to purchase instructional and curricular materials proposed by school advisory committees;
- implementation of a comprehensive plan that converted every senior high, every middle school, and one-half of elementary schools into magnet schools; and,
- provision of staff development for administrative personnel and teachers on such subjects as fair and equitable discipline and transportation. (Id. at 30-35).

The second prong of Judge Clark's plan to increase student achievement was to order a salary assistance plan for KCMSD employees. This prong, which by 1995 was to cost $200 million, became the basis for the second trip to the Supreme Court. (115 S. Ct. at 2044). Initially ordered only for teachers, the salary assistance was extended by the district court in 1990 to include all but three employees of KCMSD. In 1992, the American Federation of Teachers sought additional salary increases to be paid as desegregation expenses. The State opposed the salary increases, arguing that "funding for salaries was beyond the scope of the District Court's remedial authority" (Id. at 2045). In essence, the State claimed that low salaries did not "flow from any earlier constitutional violations by the State." [11 F.3d at 767). In addition, the State argued that it had achieved a partial unitary status with the remedial quality education programs and therefore the programs should no longer be funded by the State.

Perhaps not surprisingly, Judge Clark rejected the State's arguments. Judge Clark reasoned that the increases were necessary not only "to implement specialized desegregation programs intended to improve educational opportunities and reduce racial isolation, "but also "[to improve] the desegregative attractiveness of KCMSD" (Id. at 766, 777). Because Kansas City, Missouri was part of the national urban market, any roll-back of the salary increases would adversely affect the ability of KCMSD to hire and retain qualified personnel. Judge Clark did not respond to the legal arguments regarding partial unitary status, and, instead, simply ordered the State to continue to fund the quality education programs.

The State appealed to the Eighth Circuit, which upheld the salary increases as an appropriate desegregation remedy. The issue, as the court saw it, was not that low teacher pay is a constitutional violation, "but rather the systemic reduction of student achievement and white flight which require as part of the remedy quality education programs and magnet schools." (Id. at 767). Under this reasoning, despite the establishment of successful quality education programs, partial unitary status was not appropriate because the record did not provide evidence that the vestiges of past discrimination had been eliminated to the extent practicable.

On appeal, the Supreme Court reversed in a 5-4 decision. Writing for the majority, Chief Justice Rehnquist disagreed with three assumptions that had undergirded efforts by the district court to desegregate KCMSD: attraction of non-minority students from outside KCMSD; across-the-board salary increases in pursuit of desegregative attractiveness; and use of national norms as the test to determine whether KCMSD had achieved unitary status.

Prior to analyzing the scope of the district court's authority to fashion a desegregation remedy, Justice Rehnquist reviewed the standards in earlier desegregation cases, *Swann v. Charlotte Mecklenberg Board of Education* (1971), *Milliken v. Bradley I* (1974), and *Milliken v. Bradley II* (1977), to demonstrate that federal district courts do not have unlimited power to fashion remedies. *Milliken II* established a three-part test to determine limits to judicial remedies: the nature of a desegregation remedy must be determined by the nature and scope and violation of the constitutional violation; a remedy must be designed to restore victims to the position they occupied but for the discrimination; and a remedy must take into account that restoring state and local authorities to the control of local school districts is a vital national tradition. (*Milliken II*, 433 U.S. 267, 280-81).

The scope of a judicial remedy must address alleged constitutional violations in one or more of the areas of student assignments, faculty, staff, transportation, extracurricular activities, and facilities. (*Green v. School Board of New Kent County,* 1968). Since *Milliken II*, the Supreme Court has identified three factors in *Freeman v. Pitts* (1992) that need to be considered before a district court permits a partial finding of unitary status in one or more of these areas:

[1] whether there has been a full and satisfactory compliance with the decree in those aspects of the system where supervision is to be withdrawn; [2] whether retention of judicial control is necessary or practicable to achieve compliance with the decree in other facets of the school system; and [3] whether the school system has demonstrated, to the public and to the parents and students of the once disfavored race, its good-faith commitment to the whole of the courts' decree and to those provisions of the law and the Constitution that were predicate for judicial intervention in the first instance. (503 U.S. 467, 491).

With regard to efforts by the district court judge to attract non-minority students from outside KCMSD, the Supreme Court found that the judge exceeded his authority by attempting to achieve indirectly what he could not achieve directly, namely limit white flight through mandatory interdistrict student transfers. The district court's remedy focusing on "desegregative attractiveness," rather than seeking to remove the racial identity of the various schools within KCMSD, set out to create a school district that was equal to or superior to the surrounding suburban school districts. However, as Chief Justice pointed out, "this *inter*district goal is beyond the scope of the *intra*district violation identified by the District Court (and thus) ... beyond the scope of its broad remedial authority." (115 S. Ct. at 2051, 2052 (emphasis in original)). As an added rationale, the Chief Justice noted that, however much increased expenditures spent on KCMSD under "desegregative attractiveness" makes that district more attractive to surrounding non-minority students, "the rationale is not subject to any objective limitation." (Id. at 2054). For example, excluding capital costs, the per pupil costs in KCMSD already greatly exceeded those for the suburban districts (from between $7,665.18 and $9,412 in KCMSD and from $2,854 to $5,956 in neighboring suburban districts) (Id.). Concerning the across-the-board salary increases, the Supreme Court found them also beyond the broad authority of the district court because they were "simply too far removed from an acceptable implementation of a permissible means to remedy previous legally mandated segregation." (Id. at 2055).

Finally, the district court order requiring the State to continue to fund quality education programs because student achievement levels were at or below national norms at many grade levels was not the appropriate test to be applied in deciding whether a previously segregated district had achieved partial unitary status. "The basic task of the District Court is to decide whether the reduction in achievement by minority students attributable to prior de jure segregation has been remedied to the extent practicable." (Id.) Since all parties agreed that improvement on test scores was not necessarily required for the State to acquire unitary status, the district court was directed to limit, if not eliminate, its reliance on that factor. As the Supreme Court observed in conclusion, "(i)nsistence upon academic goals unrelated to the effects of legal segregation unwarrantably postpones the day when the KCMSD will be able to operate on its own." (Id . at 2056).

When the final chapter is written on court-ordered desegregation, *Missouri v. Jenkins* may be seen as the Waterloo of that nationwide effort. After having spent in excess of $1.7 billion on KCMSD schools through the 1995-96 academic school year, the annual per-pupil expenditure had reached $9,412, "an amount exceeded by perhaps 40 of the nation's 14,881 school districts."

(*Time*, p. 41). The number of out-of-district white children enrolled at magnet schools peaked in 1995 at 1,476 (Id.), but with the ending of state-funded transportation into the district, the number of white students is declining. Judge Clark's judicial experiment had become the victim of its own success. The magnet schools designed to attract white students had become too expensive to operate and the possibility of closing one or more of the schools came under discussion.

Another unanticipated result of the KCMSD desegregation plan has been the effect of enrollment limits on African American students. With enrollment targets of 35% white students in magnet schools, African American students have found themselves turned away from the more popular schools. Clint Bolick, litigation director for the Libertarian Institute for Justice in Washington, predicted that *Jenkins* will mark the end of court-ordered desegregation within the next decade. The shortcoming of forty years of nationwide litigation in general, and *Jenkins* in particular, was making racial balance a goal, an effect that has led to preferences for whites and "turn[ed] *Brown* on its head." (Id. at 45)

Conclusion

Missouri v. Jenkins has had a tortuous eighteen-year odyssey through the courts, one that is not yet over. In two separate trips to the Supreme Court, the power of district court judges to fashion desegregative remedies has been circumscribed, but at no point has the Court declared that KCMSD's judicially mandated desegregation plan should be ended. Thus, the district court for the Western District of Missouri continues to oversee the most expensive desegregation plan in history. Increased tax levies ordered by KCMSD subsequent to the 1990 Supreme Court decision have not kept pace with the escalating costs of the plan and, therefore, the State of Missouri has had to bear the most significant portion of the cost. While the most recent Supreme Court decision has redirected the focus of the presiding district court judge in evaluating progress of KCMSD toward unitary status, the expensive remedies for quality education still remain in place.

Throughout the litigation, KCMSD has maintained friendly relations with the plaintiffs. The school district obviously benefitted significantly from the expensive and expansive programs and facilities which were paid for largely by the State of Missouri. Unfortunately for KCMSD, however, the district will be unable to maintain programs and facilities at the present level if state support is reduced. Thus, undergirding the legal issues of judicial remedies and unitary status is the practical problem of an educational program in KCMSD that may well collapse without the current level of state funding.

Someday a federal court will undoubtably rule that KCMSD has achieved unitary status and that supplementary state aid is no longer required. Even with that aid, student achievement in KCMSD had not risen to the level of student achievement in surrounding suburban districts. It remains to be seen what KCMSD's students outcomes will be when it is forced to operate with substantially less financial resources that it now enjoys. Ultimately though, those at risk may well be the 37,000 students in KCMSD who have been the beneficiaries of a state and local desegregation effort, but whose quality of education in the future could be negatively affected if KCMSD is determined by the courts to have achieved unitary status.

References
James S. Kunen (1996, April 29), End of Integration, *Time*, p. 38.

Table of Legal Cases
Freeman v. Pitts, 503 U.S. 467 (1992).
Green v. School Board of New Kent County, 391 U.S. 430 (1968).
Milliken v. Bradley I, 418 U.S. 717 (1974).
Milliken v. Bradley II, 433 U.S. 267 (1977).
Missouri v. Jenkins, 460 F. Supp. 421 (W.D. Mo., 1978).
Missouri v. Jenkins, 593 F. Supp. 1485 (W.D.Mo.,1984).
Missouri v. Jenkins, 639 F. Supp. 19 (W.D.Mo. 1985).
Missouri v. Jenkins, 672 F. Supp. 400 (W.D. 1987).
Missouri v. Jenkins, 807 F.2d 657 (8th Cir. 1986).
Missouri v. Jenkins, 855 F.2d 1295 (8th Cir. 1988).
Missouri v. Jenkins, 11 F.3d 755 (8th Cir. 1993).
Missouri v. Jenkins, 13 F.3d 1170 (8th Cir. 1993).
Missouri v. Jenkins, 110 S.Ct. 1651 (1990).
Missouri v. Jenkins, 115 S.Ct. 1038 (1995).
Swann v. Charlotte Mecklenberg Board of Education, 402 U.S. 1 (1971).

CHAPTER 5

THE FULFILLMENT OF *BROWN*: FROM THE OLD FREEDOM OF CHOICE TO THE NEW FREEDOM OF CHOICE IN FOUR DECADES

Christine H. Rossell

Introduction

Brown v. Board of Education of Topeka, Kansas (1954), stands at the very heart of the struggle to eliminate legalized discrimination in America. It also has achieved an unparalleled reverence in American political culture. J. Harvey Wilkinson, for example, a leading conservative of the Reagan Administration's Justice Department, writes:

> No single decision has had more moral force than *Brown*; few struggles have been morally more significant than the one for racial integration of American life (Wilkinson, 1979, p.62).

This chapter was originally published as "The Progeny of Brown: From the Old Freedom of Choice to the New Freedom of Choice in Four Decades" by C. H. Rossell, in *Urban Geography, 15* (5), pp 435-453.

The aftermath of the *Brown* decision, however, was a decade of massive resistance in the South. School districts and states refused to rescind their state laws or integrate their schools in any shape or form. After several shocking desegregation confrontations displayed on national television, the Office for Civil Rights increased the pressure on southern school districts to the point where many grudgingly implemented geographic zoning plans and freedom of choice plans in the mid-1960s. Most of these plans required every pupil to exercise a choice at the beginning of each school year, thus eliminating the automatic initial assignment of pupils to schools for their race. Few African American students changed schools and no whites did, however, so that by 1965 almost 94 percent of southern African American students were still in black schools.

In the North, the struggle was as much political as it was legal since northern school districts did not have state laws mandating school segregation. The outcome, however, was very much the same — the school districts did nothing or at most instituted a freedom-of-choice plan voluntary in nature, small in scope, and burdensome only to the African American children willing to travel long distances at their own expense in order to reap its benefits. In the North, these plans were called majority to minority transfer plans. Any student could transfer from any school in which his race was in the majority to any school in which his race was in the minority. Until the 1970s, transportation was not provided.

All of these voluntary transfer plans were quite acceptable so long as *Brown* remained the dominant Supreme Court decision on the issue of school segregation. *Brown* was essentially an antidiscrimination decision holding that assigning students to schools solely on the basis of race deprived the child of the minority group of equal educational opportunities.

Despite the moral force of *Brown*, current debates over race and schools owe their intellectual origins more to *Green v. New Kent County* (1968), than to *Brown*, because it was in *Green* that the Court decided that eliminating racial discrimination was not enough to establish a unitary system, that is, a school in which there were no white schools and no Negro schools, but "just schools." Indeed, the actual requirement was not just schools, but schools that were racially mixed to a greater degree than would occur merely as a result of ending discrimination.

Green thus marked the end of the period of "nondiscrimination" remedies and the beginning of the period of "affirmative action" remedies. Not only were the plans to be judged by their effects, but it was assumed a priori after *Green* that the most effective plan would be one that *required* black and white students to transfer from their formerly one-race schools to opposite-race schools. This conclusion was drawn on the basis of empirical observation by the Court that forbidding discrimination as *Brown* had required and allowing school districts to implement race-neutral assignment policies such as geographic zoning and voluntary transfer plans had not, as evidenced by the continued existence of all-black schools, dismantled the dual system of black and white schools.

By 1971 with *Swann v. Charlotte-Mecklenburg*, mandatory desegregation techniques such as pairing and clustering, satellite zoning, and contiguous rezoning were the only plans accepted in the South by courts when the old geographic zoning plans were challenged by plaintiffs. Many southern school districts desegregated before 1971, however, with court approved neighborhood school plans that involved at most some minor contiguous rezoning and many of these were never challenged. Indeed, this is the case with *Brown v. Board of Education*. Topeka, Kansas, the defendant school district in *Brown*, was allowed to desegregate with a neighborhood school plan and to this day has instituted no plan other than that.

Most geographic zoning plans were, however, challenged soon after the 1971 *Swann* decision and, as a result, mandatory reassignment plans were implemented all over the South and, after 1973, the North as well. Desegregation plans continued to evolve, however, so that by 1975 federal district courts were once again entertaining the notion that voluntary transfer plans might be acceptable. In three separate court decisions between 1975 and 1976, federal district courts approved voluntary transfer plans with incentives in the form of magnet schools in order to motivate the voluntary transfer of whites to formerly minority schools. These plans, implemented in Houston in 1975, and in Milwaukee and Buffalo in 1976, quickly achieved a national reputation as successes. By 1981, virtually all new plans were voluntary transfer plans, most of them with magnet programs. Thus, desegregation plans had come full circle in the space of three decades, from voluntary plans that were considered ineffective because no whites ever transferred to black schools, to voluntary plans that were now considered effective in comparison to the "ineffective" mandatory reassignment plans implemented from 1968 to 1981.

The Evolution and Impact of Desegregation Plans in Stockton, California, and Savannah-Chatham County, Georgia

The evolution of desegregation plans nationwide and their impact is exemplified by two cases that I compare over a 25-year time period from fall 1967 through fall 1992. These two districts, Savannah-Chatham County, Georgia and Stockton, California, represent important demographic differences in desegregating school districts: southern versus northern, formerly de jure segregated versus de facto, and a county-wide school system of 455 square miles versus a central city school system of 56 square miles.

There are also similarities. Despite the different origins of school segregation in each district, both were found to have been engaged in intentional segregation by courts that concluded that the existence of racial imbalance and differential school resources along racial lines was evidence of intentional discrimination necessitating a school segregation remedy. This occurred even though, at the time, both school districts had in place race-neutral assignment policies: geographic zoning, and voluntary transfer plans.   After the court rulings, both school districts desegregated initially with court-ordered mandatory reassignment "pairing" plans in the 1970s. (When two K-5 schools are "paired," all students go to one school for kindergarten through second grade and to the other school for grades three through five.)   Recently both school districts have received court approval to dismantle these plans and implement voluntary transfer plans. Thus, desegregation plans here, as in the rest of the U.S., appear to have come full circle.

Desegregation remedies began in the South where the segregation was most clearly a result of discrimination. In the pre-*Brown* South, white students, regardless of where they lived or their preferences, were forced to attend all-white schools and black students, regardless of where they lived or their preferences, were forced to attend all-black schools. Thus, every school district had two geographic zoning schemes — one for blacks superimposed on top of one for whites — and it is this that the court decisions have termed a "dual" school system. In 1962, *Stell v. The Board of Education for the City of Savannah and the County of Chatham et al.* (1963), was filed. Under the court-approved geographic attendance zone with freedom of choice, 18% of the black students in Savannah-Chatham County had voluntarily transferred to white schools and 72% of the white students were in schools with blacks by 1969 when the district was ordered to implement a mandatory reassignment remedy that desegregated all schools in compliance with *Green.*

By contrast, there never had been a dual school system in the North. Schools had only one geographic attendance zone around them and all students, regardless of their race, went to the school in their zone. Because there is considerable residential segregation in the U.S., however, race neutral assignment policies, the policy that *Brown* had mandated, did not eliminate school racial imbalance. Several states, among them California, New York, Connecticut, and Massachusetts, adopted laws that required school districts to have a specific level of racial balance in their schools regardless of its cause. It was in light of this state law that plaintiffs brought suit in 1975 in *Hernandez v. Stockton Unified School District,* Case No. 101016 (Superior Court of California, County of San Joaquin), demanding that the racial imbalance in the Stockton public schools be eliminated.

Although the Stockton Unified School District filed an immediate appeal of the state court's 1975 decision, it also implemented a desegregation plan for the senior high schools that fall. The Stockton School District lost its appeal of the state court's 1975 decision. It also implemented a desegregation plan for the senior high schools that fall. The Stockton School district lost its appeal, and in fall 1977 the elementary schools were paired and the attendance zones for junior and senior high schools were redrawn to further increase racial balance. Five K-6 elementary schools were exempted because they were already racially integrated.

White Flight

Of all forms of white response to school desegregation, white flight is probably the most important because it directly

affects interracial exposure, the ultimate goal of any desegregation plan. Statistical analyses of school districts show that the
greater the reduction in racial imbalance in a district, the greater
the white loss during the implementation year (Coleman, Kelly
and Moore, 1975; Frey, 1977; Rossell, 1978; Clotfel-ter,1979;
Farley, Wurdock, and Richards, 1980; Ross, Gratton, and
Clarke, 1982; Steel, Levine, Rossell, and Armor, 1993). A
greater reduction in racial imbalance is highly correlated with
greater white mandatory reassignments (Rossell, 1978).

Moreover, central-city school districts above 30-35%
minority with mandatory desegregation plans never regain the
lost whites (Coleman, 1977; Rossell, 1978; Armor, 1980; Farley,
Wurdock, and Richards, 1980; Ross, Gratton, and Clarke, 1982;
Smylie, 1983; Armor, 1988). Smylie (1983) and Ross, Gratton,
and Clarke, (1982) even found that county-wide school districts
with less than 35% minority enrollment, thought to be most
resistant to white flight, never recover the implementation year
white-enrollment loss. The few studies to compare white flight
in mandatory and voluntary plans have concluded that the
mandatory plans produce more flight in the period surrounding
implementation and that this disparity is never overcome
(Smylie, 1983; Welch and Light, 1987; Rossell, 1990a, 1990b).
These studies analyze district level data. It is important, however, to understand what happens at the school level, because
this is where white flight begins. When a mandatory reassignment desegregation plan is drawn, students of one race are
mandatorily reassigned to an opposite race school. They then
have the option of complying or leaving the school system.

Table 1 shows what happened in Savannah-Chatham
County, Georgia in 1970 and 1971, when whites were reassigned to formerly black schools and to integrated schools. In
1970 when the busing distance was very short and the schools
nearby, the white no-show rate was 28%. That is, 28% of the
whites reassigned to formerly black schools did not show up at
the school to which they were reassigned, although this varied
from as little as 8% to as much as 40% at the individual school.
In 1971 in response to the *Swann* ruling, more distant schools
were paired and the "no-show" rate increased to 42%, varying
from 10 to 71% at individual schools. Moreover, it was as great
when whites were assigned to integrated schools of approxi-

mately 50 and 60% black enrollment as when they were assigned to all black schools.

TABLE 1. White Enrollment Change for Elementary Pairings with Mandatory Reassignment Plans, Savannah-Chatham County, GA.

1970-1971	
Paired/clustered schools [a]	% White enrollment change

100% black schools	
Ellis/38th	-19%
Herty/Spencer	- 40%
Pulaski/Haven	- 31%
Sprague/Haynes	- 8%
Total loss rate 1970	-28%

1971-1972	
Paired/clustered schools [b]	% White enrollment change

100% black schools	
Low/Gadsden	-64%
Wh. Bluff/Florence	-35%
Hesse/Hodge	-46%
Heard/Anderson	-54%
Largo/DeRenne	-30%
Windsor/Jackson	-71%
Gould/Butler	-10%
Smith, JG./Henry	-57%
Port Wentw./Strong/Bartow	-34%
Bloomingdale/Pooler/Tompkins	-17%
Tybee/Howard/Hubert	-33%
Total loss rate	-41%
50-60% black schools [c]	
Thunderbolt/37th	-25%
Isle of Hope/Riley	-59%
Total loss rate	-49%
Total loss rate 1971	-42%

a - the black school is the last school named in the pair or cluster

b- the Penn. Ave./Whitney/Massey cluster is excluded from this analysis because the number of whites assigned to Massie is unknown.

c - resident whites not counted.

As illustrated by the bottom line of the top chart in Figure 1, the net effect on the district was an 8% reduction in white enrollment in 1970, a 15% reduction in 1971, and a 13% reduction in 1972.   Thereafter the school district's annual loss was about three percent a year until 1986 when it was announced that the mandatory plan would be dismantled.

Figure1. Enrollment Tends Savannah-Chatham County, GA
1968-1992

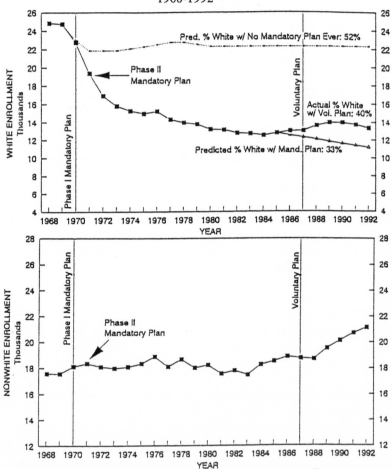

The social scientist's task is to determine how much of this decline is due to the mandatory reassignment plan and how much to normal demographic processes. Because there are only two years of pre-desegregation enrollment data, I cannot calculate a pre-desegregation trend and project it forward. Instead, I use another common technique to estimate what Savannah's enrollment would have been if no mandatory plan had ever been implemented. I compute the average percentage change in white enrollment for a "control" group of all districts that never implemented a mandatory reassignment plan but have demographic characteristics similar to those of Savannah. The control group districts are southern, county wide, and less than 70% white in 1968.[1] The annual change rate is applied to Savannah's 1969 enrollment and the enrollment is projected forward. These districts experienced in 1970 and 1971 a drop in white enrollment from implementing neighborhood-school, freedom-of-choice plans, but this was substantially less than that of Savannah-Chatham County. Moreover, the decline resulting from this change was temporary, and from 1974 on, despite a nationwide decline in the white birthrate, the white enrollment of these districts remained fairly constant because of white migration to the sunbelt. This "normal" trend if Savannah had not implemented its pairing plan is represented by the top line of the top chart in Figure 1.

Subtracting Savannah-Chatham County's 1986 white enrollment from that projected by this "normal trend" line indicates a loss of 9,727 white students from 1970 to 1986 due to the pairing plan. This is 82% of the total loss of 11,816 white students over this time period.

At the same time that Savannah-Chatham County was implementing Phase I of its pairing plan in 1970, the California Rural Legal Assistance (CRLA) was filing a discrimination lawsuit against the Stockton Unified School District on behalf of Victor Hernandez. There had never been a dual school system in Stockton, and all students, regardless of their race, attended their neighborhood school. Nevertheless, because of residential racial imbalance most schools were outside the state standard of plus or minus 15 percentage points of the district's racial composition. In addition, there were disparities between the white and minority schools in terms of academic achievement outcomes and some school resources.

The Stockton school segregation trial commenced in February 1974. The next fall the judge found the district guilty of intentional discrimination and ordered it to draw up a plan to desegregate the school system. The state court that made the decision, however, was careful to base it on a finding of intentional segregation in conformity with federal law. As a result, when a state referendum was passed in 1980 requiring state courts to abide by federal law in deciding school segregation cases — that is, to show intent to segregate in school board actions — the Stockton Unified School District had no obvious basis for appeal as did the Los Angeles Unified School District, which had been convicted only on a showing of racial imbalance in its schools. Nevertheless, the District appealed the decision and implemented a high school desegregation plan simultaneously.

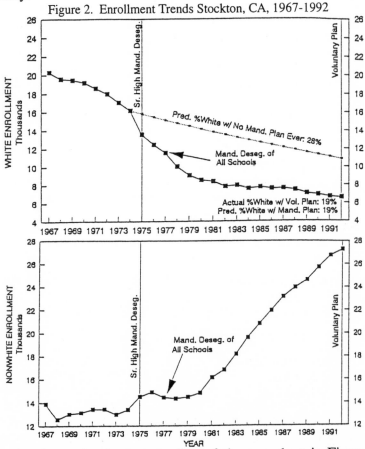

Figure 2. Enrollment Trends Stockton, CA, 1967-1992

As shown by the bottom line of the top chart in Figure 2, the senior high school plan was accompanied by a significant

14% drop in white enrollment. The district's white enrollment continued to decline, provoked further in fall 1977 by the implementation of an elementary pairing plan.

Table 2 shows the 1977 school loss rates for Stockton schools under the 1977 plan. The greatest white loss occurs at the earliest grades and the most minority schools with 67% of the white students failing to show up at the grade 1-3 schools in formerly 80-100% minority schools.[2]

TABLE 2. White Enrollment Change with Mandatory Reassignment Plan, Stockton United School District, 1977-1978

School type	Grades	% white enrollment change
Elementary Schools		
Paired > 80% minority	1-3	-67%
	4-6	-44%
	Total	-55%
Paired 50-79% minority	1-3	-32%
	4-6	- 8%
	Total	-21%
Paired white	1-3, 4-6	-2%
Predominantly white neighborhood	6	5%
Junior High Schools		
Minority neighborhood	7-8	-26%
White/mixed neighborhood	7-8	-5%
Senior High Schools		
Minority neighborhood	9-12	-31%
White/mixed neighborhood	9-12	-6%

Busing distance, neighborhood racial composition, and perceived school quality have more impact than school racial composition. The loss when whites were allowed to stay at their neighborhood school was only 2.2 %, even though these schools were projected to be roughly the same racial composition as the schools in minority neighborhoods. At the secondary level, we can see a similar pattern. The loss was five times greater when the schools that students were assigned to were in minority neighborhoods than when they were in white neighborhoods, although again all schools were projected to have about the same racial composition. Schools that were not paired at all actually had an increase in their white enrollment; this suggests that some of the white flight was to the exempted integrated schools rather than out of the district.

These data are consistent with other school level analyses such as Rossell (1988)[3] and Pride and Woodard (1985). These studies, and the analysis of Savannah and Stockton, suggest that whites in northern school districts, although coming out of a very different tradition, behaved much the same as whites in southern school districts. Approximately half of them refused to comply when their child was reassigned across town to minority neighborhood schools. In addition, these studies demonstrate that countywide districts are not immune from white flight (see also Rossell, 1978).

The white enrollment decline as a result of the mandatory reassignment plan in Stockton is estimated by first calculating to 1991 the district's "normal" trend — the average percentage white enrollment decline from 1968 to 1974 projected forward. This is the top line of the top chart in Figure 2. This loss rate was also compared to a control group of western, central city school districts of less than 70% white enrollment in 1968. It is very similar, with an average annual white enrollment decline from 1975 to 1991 of 2.2 % if the district had not implemented a mandatory reassignment plan. Although the white enrollment decline for the district has slowed in recent years to about the "normal" demographic decline, it has never recovered the initial loss it suffered. By the fall of 1991, the district had lost an estimated 4,383 white students, 32% of its total white enrollment decline, solely on account of desegregation.

Moreover, differential white enrollment losses at the individual schools in the pairs and triads continue to subvert the plan long after its implementation. Table 3 shows the white cohort change rate from fall 1989 to fall 1990 for first graders and fourth graders assigned to paired white schools, paired minority schools, and K-6 schools in Stockton. Because kindergarten students go to their neighborhood school, most students in Stockton have to change schools when they go to first grade. As shown in Table 3, when the first grade assignment is to the same neighborhood white school, there is no change or a 10% increase in the white enrollment over the previous year's kindergarten enrollment in comparison to a 19% loss when the first grade assignment is to a minority neighborhood school.

TABLE 3. White Cohort Change in Paired Schools, Stockton Unified School District, 1989-1990.

	White cohort % change
Kindergarten (1989) to first (1990)	
Paired schools	
First grade assignment to same white neighborhood	10%
First grade assignment to minority neighborhood from white kindergarten	-19%
K-6 schools	
First grade assignment to same fixed neighborhood school	0%

	White cohort % change
Third (1989) to fourth (1990)	
Paired schools	
Fourth grade assignment to minority neighborhood from third grade in white neighborhood	-29%
Fourth grade assignment to white neighborhood from third grade in minority neighborhood	49%
K-6 schools	
Fourth grade assignment to same mixed race neighborhood	-11%

The fourth grade assignment losses show even greater disparity. There is a huge gain in white enrollment when the fourth grade paired school is in a white neighborhood as whites return from the private schools to which they fled to avoid the earlier grade 1-3 minority school assignment. On the other hand, when white children leave a white primary school to go to a minority upper school, there is a loss of 29%. Thus, some white parents enrolled their children in private schools for grades 1-3 when the assignment is to a minority school, and put them back in their neighborhood school for fourth grade. In short, 15 years after the plan was implemented, many Stockton white parents continued to subvert the intent of the desegregation plan by refusing to accept transfers out of their neighborhood.

White Return

Stockton, California and Savannah-Chatham County, Georgia are fairly typical in the amount of white flight produced by their desegregation plans. They are less typical in that both voted to dismantle their mandatory reassignment plans and replace them with comprehensive, magnet-voluntary plans while still under court supervision.

On June 14, 1985, Judge Edenfield pronounced the Savannah mandatory reassignment plan a failure and ordered the district to revise it. On December 23, 1986, the Board of Education voted to dismantle the pairing plan and implement a voluntary magnet school plan in its place. The publicity surrounding the judge's order and the Board's decision appeared to have turned around the two-decade decline in white enrollment before the plan was actually implemented in fall 1987.

White-enrollment in Savannah-Chatham County increased by 4.5% over the seven years of the voluntary plan. The bottom line in the top chart in figure 1 is the expected white enrollment from 1987 to 1992 if the mandatory plan had continued, estimated from the average percentage decline from 1980 to 1984. This shows that by fall 1992 there are 2,000 more white students and 7% higher percentage white enrollment in the Savannah public schools than would have been predicted if the pairing plan had been continued.

In 1991, four years after Savannah, the Stockton Unified School District began the first stage of dismantling their mandatory reassignment plan under a settlement agreement reached with the plaintiffs. Secondary-school attendance zones were redrawn so that they were contiguous around a single school but maximized racial balance within that constraint. Another settlement agreement in 1992 ordered the dismantling of the pairing plan at the elementary level the subsequent fall. It is this phase, with the dissolution of the school pairings and the return to neighborhood schools, that marks a real change in the desegregation plan. The white enrollment decline in fall 1992 was 1.4%, about half what it had been the previous four years. Stockton had 120 more whites and a white percentage almost one point above what would have been predicted if the mandatory plan had continued. In Savannah, by contrast, there were 746 more whites in the first year of the voluntary plan than would have been predicted with the mandatory plan, although this first phase involved only a few unpairings and two magnets.

The difference in the impact of dismantling the mandatory plan in these two districts undoubtably is related to differences in their racial composition. As shown in the bottom charts of Figures 1 and 2, although both districts lost about 12-13,000 white students up to the time they implemented their voluntary plans, there is quite a difference in the growth of the minority population. The minority population in the Savannah-Chatham public schools grew very little during the mandatory reassignment plan, and the percentage white in Savannah only declined from 59% in 1968 to 41% in 1986. The Stockton minority enrollment, however, almost doubled from 13,893 in 1968 to almost 27,000 in 1991 and the percentage white over a slightly longer time period dropped from 59% to 20% as a result of both white decline and minority increase.

Thus, the problem in Stockton is that, with only three exceptions, no elementary school was projected to be more than 30% white with a return to neighborhood schools. Many whites do not consider that an attractive enough racial composition to warrant putting their children back in the public schools. Many of the white neighborhood schools in Savannah, by contrast, were projected to be 50 to 65% white with the return to neighborhood schools. Thus, unfavorable demographics in Stockton reduced the benefit, in comparison to Savannah, of returning to neighborhood schools.

School desegregation plans, however, should not be judged solely on how much or how little white flight they produce. All policy alternatives have costs and if this is the only criterion, the alternative chosen would always be "do nothing." A policy analyst must calculate both the benefits and costs of each alternative. These benefits and costs must be interpreted in terms of the instrumental goal of a desegregation plan. The instrumental goal is the exposure of the races to each other in integrated schools.

Measuring School Integration

Social scientists have typically measured school segregation or integration as the extent to which the races are evenly distributed among schools. This strategy was fueled by *Swann,* which held that the racial composition of the entire school district was a starting point by which to judge each school in the district. If a school district was 95% black, all schools should be 95% black.

The measure of racial imbalance typically used by social scientists is the index of dissimilarity, also called the Taeuber Index (Taeuber and Taeuber, 1965; Farley 1981; Farley, Wurdock, and Richards, 1980; Smylie, 1983; Van Valey, Roof, and Wilcox, 1977). The formula is:

$$D = \frac{1}{2} \Sigma \left| \frac{Wi}{W} - \frac{Mi}{M} \right|$$

where W is the number of whites, or any other ethnic or racial group, and M is the number of minorities or any ethnic or racial group.[4] The index of dissimilarity represents the proportion (or percentage if multiplied by 100) of minority students who would have to be reassigned to white schools, if no whites are reassigned, in order to have the same proportion in each school as in the whole school district.[5] The index ranges from 0 (perfect racial balance — no minority students need to be reassigned) to 100 (perfect racial imbalance — 100% of the minority students need to be reassigned, if no whites are reassigned, in order to have perfect racial balance).

Another common way of measuring the contact between the races is as interracial exposure — specifically, the proportion of white enrollment in the average minority child's school. This measure has been used in more recent studies of school desegregation to estimate the outcome of a plan (e.g. Farley,1981; Orfield, 1982; Ross, 1983, Rossell, 1978, 1979, 1985, 1990a, 1990b). The measure is calculated as follows:

$$Smw = \frac{\Sigma_k (Nkm)(Pkw)}{\Sigma_k (Nkm)}$$

where k stands for each individual school. Thus Nkm is the number (N) of minorities (m) in a particular school (k) and Pkw is the proportion (P) white (w) in the same school (k). Hence, the number of minorities in each school is multiplied by the proportion white in the same school. This is summed for all schools and divided by the number of minorities in the school system to produce the proportion white in the average minorities child's school. This can be used for blacks and whites in the equation. Since the proportion white in the average minority child's school increases with racial balance reassignments, but goes down as the white enrollment decreases, it measures the instrumental net benefit of desegregation reassignments.

Racial balance, by contrast, is an inadequate goal because it ignores the number of whites coming into contact with minorities. This becomes clearer if we consider a hypothetical segregated school system with six schools and the racial composition shown below.

	Minorities	Whites
	100	0
	100	0
	100	0
	0	100
	0	100
	0	100
Sum	300	300
% of Total	50	50

Virtually all supporters of school desegregation would prefer a plan that produced outcome A (below) with considerable racial balance and 245 white students remaining to outcome B, with perfect racial balance and 6 white students remaining.

	OUTCOME A		OUTCOME B	
	Minorities	Whites	Minorities	Whites
	50	20	50	1
	50	45	50	1
	50	40	50	1
	50	50	50	1
	50	45	50	1
	50	45	50	1
Sum	300	245	300	6
% of Total	55	45	98.1	1.9

Although outcome B has only one white in each school, it has a racial imbalance score of 0, that is perfect racial balance. It has very little interracial exposure, however, with only 2 % white in the average minority child's school.

Outcome A, by contrast, has more racial imbalance than outcome B, but greater interracial exposure with 44.2% white enrollment in the average minority child's school. Thus, if we have racial balance as our goal, we would be forced to choose the intuitively least desirable plan producing outcome B with 2% white enrollment in the average minority child's school. If we have interracial exposure as our goal, however, we would choose the intuitively most desirable outcome A with 44.2% white in the average minority child's school.

Desegregation Outcomes in Stockton and Savannah

When Savannah-Chatham County implemented its mandatory reassignment plan in 1970 and 1971, the percentage white in the average minority (black) child's school increased a total of 35 points as shown in Figure 3. However, as is typical of mandatory reassignment plans (see Rossell, 1990a, 1990b), the district immediately began to resegregate.

Figure 3.   Elementary Interracial Exposure Savannah-Chatham County, GA, 1968-1992

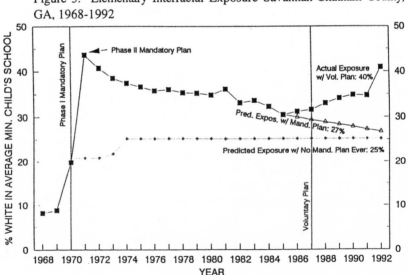

The predicted exposure with no mandatory reassignment plan is derived from the annual change in exposure for the control group school districts with the same characteristics: southern, county wide, and less than 70% white in 1968. When this annual change in exposure is applied to Savannah's 1969 exposure and is projected forward to 1992, we can see in the bottom line of Figure 3 that by that year there would have been only a two point difference between what the district would have achieved if the mandatory reassignment plan had continued and what it would have achieved if no mandatory plan had ever been implemented.

The implementation of the voluntary plan in 1987 and its announcement the year before increased interracial exposure solely by attracting whites back from private schools. By 1988, the increase in interracial exposure was due to a combination of attracting whites back from private schools and the success of the magnet programs in attracting whites to schools in black neighborhoods. The voluntary plan with magnet incentives has produced a level of interracial exposure at the elementary level that is 7 points higher than would have been predicted if the mandatory plan had continued.[6] This is the top line on the right of Figure 3. There is less change at the secondary level because the plan characteristics have changed less.

In the South, implementing a mandatory reassignment plan produced a benefit in interracial exposure because the school districts were operating under de jure segregation — all blacks went to black schools and all whites went to white schools regardless of where they lived. This is not the case in many districts in the North where voluntary transfer plans and long standing race neutral assignment policies based on residence had by 1968 produced a modest level of interracial exposure. Stockton Unified, for example, had almost 40% white in the average minority child's school in 1968 compared to 9% white in Savannah. By 1974 when the liability trial commenced, Stockton's level of interracial exposure had increased to 41%. From this height, unfortunately, there was only one direction to go — down.

Although the Stockton Unified School District became one of the most racially balanced school districts in the country when it desegregated its elementary and junior high schools in 1977

1974, the huge white flight produced by the plan overwhelmed the expected gain in interracial exposure.

Figure 4. District Interracial Exposure Stockton, CA, 1967-1992

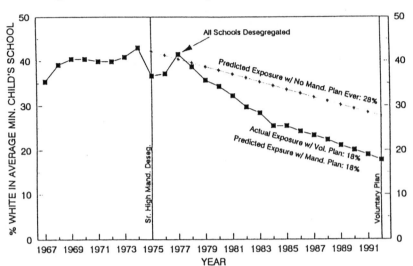

As Figure 4 indicates, by Fall 1979 interracial exposure was more than four percentage points *lower* than 1974, the year before desegregation began. By extending the average annual change in interracial exposure from 1970 to 1975 forward and adjusting it for the normal demographic decline in exposure observed in a control group of western, central city school districts less than 70% white in 1968, we can see in the top line in Figure 4 the level of interracial exposure expected in Stockton in the absence of a mandatory reassignment plan. In 1992 this is about 28% white in the average minority child's school — 10 points higher than the actual 1992 interracial exposure after 23 years of mandatory reassignment. In contrast to the South, the northern trend line without a mandatory plan shows a decline in interracial exposure after 1973, caused by the declining white birthrate and the increasing minority population.

Stockton's actual decline, however, is considerably greater than the control group because it is caused both by the "normal" decline in the percentage of white students and the white-flight or non-entrance produced by the plan. This analysis suggests that the district as a whole would have had more integration if it had simply continued with its pre-1975 voluntary transfer plan and minor contiguous rezoning.

In contrast to Savannah, the effect of the 1992 voluntary plan on interracial exposure in 1992 has been negligible. There is no difference between what would have been expected this year with the mandatory plan and what actually occurred with the voluntary plan. (Unlike Savannah, there is no difference in the effect of the plan between elementary and secondary levels.) In one sense, this is remarkable, since unlike the Savannah plan, the Stockton voluntary desegregation plan has no racial balance goals, a concession that the plaintiffs gave the 80% minority school district in return for extra resources (Milliken II relief) at the minority neighborhood schools.

Conclusion

The evolution of these two cases, *Stell v. Board of Education of the City of Savannah and the County of Chatham, et al.* and *Hernandez v. Stockton Unified School District, et al.*, and their plans illustrate how and why desegregation remedies have in many respects come full circle since *Brown*. Desegregation plans have evolved from freedom of choice with no racial balance goals and no busing to freedom of choice with racial balance goals, free transportation, and magnet incentives to motivate white transfer to schools in minority neighborhoods. In short, freedom of choice has become more effective, in part to avoid having to implement a mandatory reassignment plan, by adding incentives.

Moreover, the courts have accepted the argument of the potential effectiveness of voluntary plans with magnets. What appears to have changed since 1968 when the courts decided that the goal of a desegregation plan should be the elimination of one-race schools and that the voluntary plans were not doing this, is not the courts' willingness to approve ineffective plans, but their assessment after a decade of mandatory reassignment plans that voluntary plans might be more effective.

The growing belief that voluntary plans can work is founded on a number of remarkable social changes that *Brown* began four decades ago: (1) the overwhelming acceptance by whites of racial integration of the schools; (2) the overwhelming rejection by whites of "forced busing" to achieve this; (3) the public perception of continuing white flight from mandatory reassignment plans; and (4) the creation of magnet school plans that appear to provide an incentive for whites to act in accordance with both their self-interest and their support of integration.   Indeed, in approving the Savannah-Chatham County school district's voluntary plan based on magnets and majority-to-minority transfers, the court stated that "the law does not require that a desegregation plan be mandatory in any way, only that it be effective."   The court judged the voluntary plan to be potentially effective, in part because the prior mandatory plan was pronounced ineffective.

In essence the history of school desegregation illustrates the limits of government and judicial policy.   Because there is widespread agreement that government cannot arbitrarily discriminate against people on account of their race or other ascribed characteristic, the civil rights movement has been extraordinarily successful in protecting the civil liberties of black Americans, and the *Brown* decision is almost universally revered regardless of one's political affiliation.   There is, however, no widespread agreement that whites should be discriminated against — that is, have their freedom to choose taken from them —- in order to compensate black Americans for past discrimination.   Moreover, black Americans now resent having this freedom taken away from them as well.   Parent surveys in school districts considering desegregation show that the single most popular school desegregation strategy among minority parents is neighborhood schools and magnets.   The least popular, with about 30-40% support, is a mandatory reassignment plan (see Armor, 1991; Armor and Rossell, 1986a; 1986b; 1989; 1990a; 1990b; 1990c; 1991; Rossell, 1993).

What black Americans were asking for in 1954 was the freedom to go to their neighborhood school if they wanted to even if they were of the "wrong" race. *Brown* gave them that freedom, but could not protect them from prejudice and individual acts of discrimination.   As a result, somewhere along the way, liberal white America and its allies on the court got confused and started forcing blacks to go across town to schools chosen for them by paternalistic whites regardless of whether they wanted to go or even if in fact they wanted simply to go to their neighborhood school or another school that they them-selves chose. Today black Americans still want freedom and since the early 1980s, the courts have appeared to be willing to give them what *Brown* promised. As evidenced in Savannah, and to a lesser extent in Stockton, in this policy area, greater free-dom combined with incentives ultimately produce greater inte-gration. Even if this produces the same integration, however, freedom of choice can be justified on the grounds that it is the preferred policy alternative of a majority of parents, most impor-tantly, the parents whose rights this civil rights policy is sup-posed to be ensuring.

Notes

1. These data come from a national random sample of 600 U.S. School districts funded by the Department of Education. The annual percentage change for these districts is 1970, -7%; 1971, -5%; 1972 and 1973, no change; from 1974 to 1977 a 1% increase; and from 1978 on, no change. I use district case weights to estimate for the population of multi-school districts nationwide (Steel, Levine, Rossell, and Armor, 1993).
2. This analysis utilizes data on assigned enrollment provided by the district and takes into account most of the normal demo-graphic change.
3. Analyzing no-show rates, Rossell found busing distance and social class to be more important than percent minority in Los Angeles and as important in Baton Rouge.
4. It is calculated as follows: the whites in school 1 are divided by the whites in the school district. The minorities in school 1 are divided by the minorities in the district. The sums of these two calculations for school 1 are subtracted from each other and minus signs are eliminated. This is summed across all schools and divided by two. The measure can be used for any two racial groups.
5. It is also the sum of (1) the proportion of minority students who need to be reassigned to white schools, and (2) the propor-tion of white students who need to be reassigned to minority schools, in order to have the same proportion as in the whole school district. The specific proportions of each group adding up to the index are a function of racial proportions and prior segregation.

6.   Only the elementary index is presented here because the effect of the voluntary plan on exposure is clearer at this level where there are neighborhood schools.

References

Armor, D. (1980).   White flight and the future of school desegregation, in Walter G. Stephen & Joseph R. Feagan (Eds.), *School Desegregation: Past, Present and Future.* New York: Plenum Press: 187-226.

Armor, D. J. (1988).   School Busing: A Time for Change.   In P.A. Katz, and D.A. Taylor (Eds).   *Eliminating Racism.* New York: Plenum Press.

Armor, D. J. (1991).   Survey of Public School Parents in Worcester, Massachusetts.

Armor, D. J., & Rossell, C. H. (1986a).   Survey of Public School Parents in Yonkers, New York.

Armor, D. J., & Rossell, C. H. (1986b).   Survey of Public and Private School Parents in Savannah-Chatham County, Georgia.

Armor, D., and Rossell, C. H. (1989).   Survey of Public School Parents in Natchez, Mississippi.

Armor, D. J., & Rossell, C. H. (1990a).   Survey of Public School Parents in DeKalb County, Georgia.

Armor, D. J., & Rossell, C. H. (1990b).   Survey of Public School Parents in Topeka, Kansas.

Armor, D. J., & Rossell, C. H. (1990c).   Survey of Public and Private School Parents in Stockton, California.

Armor, D. J., & Rossell, C. H. (1991).   Survey of Public School Parents in Knox County, Tennessee.

Coleman, J. S. (1977). Population stability and equal rights. *Society*, 14, 34-36.

Coleman, J., Kelly, S., and Moore, J. (1975). *Trends in School Segregation, 1968-1973.*   Washington, D.C.:   Urban Institute.

Farley, R. (1981). *Final Report, NIE grant #G-79-0151.* Ann Arbor: The University of Michigan, Population Studies Center.

Farley, R., Wurdock, C. & Richards, T. (1980). School desegregation and white flight: An investigation of competing models and their discrepant findings. *Sociology of Education*, 53, 123-139.

Frey, W. H. (1977). *Central city white flight: Racial and nonracial causes.* Paper presented at the annual meeting of the American Sociological Association, September, Chi cago.

Orfield, G. (1982). *Desegregation of black and hispanic students form 1968 to 1980.* Washington, DC: Joint Center for Political Studies.

Pride, R.A., & Woodard, J.D. (1985). *The burden of busing: the politics of desegregation in Nashville Tennessee..* Knoxville, TN: the University of Tennessee Press.

Ross, J.M. (1983). The effectiveness of alternative deseg-regation strategies: the issue of voluntary versus mandatory policies in Los Angeles. Unpublished paper. Boston M.A.: Boston University.

Ross, J.M., Gratton, B., & Clarke, R.C. (1982). School deseg-regation and "white flight" reexamined: the issue of diff-erent statistical models. Unpublished Paper, Boston, M.A.: Boston University.

Rossell, C.H. (1993). Controlled choice desegregation plans: Too much control, not enough choice. A paper presented at the annual meeting of the New England Political Science Association.

Rossell, C. H. (1990a). The carrot or the stick for school desegregation policy. *Urban Affairs Quarterly*, 25, 474-499.

Rossell, C. H. (1990b). *The Carrot or the Stick for School Desegregation Policy: Magnet Schools or Forced Busing.* Philadelphia: Temple University Press.

Rossell, C. H. (1988). Is it the busing or the blacks? *Urban Affairs Quarterly*, 24, September: 138-148.

Rossell, C. H. (1985). Estimating the net benefit of school desegregation reassignments. *Educational Evaluation and Policy Analysis*, Vol. 7, 217-227.

Rossell, C. H. (1979). Magnet schools as a desegregation tool: the importance of contextual factors in explaining their success. *Urban Education*, Vol. 14, 303-320.

Rossell, C. H. (1978). Assessing the unintended impacts of public policy: school desegregation and resegregation. Report to the National Institute of Education. Boston: Boston University.

Smylie, M. A. (1983). Reducing racial isolation in large school districts: the comparative effectiveness of mandatory and voluntary desegregation strategies. *Urban Education*, 17, 477-502.

Steel, L., Levine, R., Rossell, C., and Armor, D. 1993. *Magnet Schools and Issues of Desegregation, Quality, and Choice.* (Final Report to the Department of Education) Palo Alto, CA: American Institutes for Research.

Taeuber, K.E. & Taeuber, A. (1965). *Negroes in cities.* Chicago, IL: Aldine.

Van Valey, T.L., Roof, W.C., & Wilcox, J.E. (1977). Trends in residential segregation: 1960-1970. *American Journal of Sociology,.* Vol. 82, 826-844.

Welch, F. and Light, A. (1987). *New evidence on school desegregation.* Washington, D.C.: U.S. Commission on Civil Rights.

Wilkerson III, J.H. (1979). *From Brown to Bakke: the Supreme Court and school integration.* New York, N.Y.: Oxford University Press.

Table of Legal Cases

Brown v. Board of Education of Topeka, Kansas, 347 U.S. 483 (1954).

Green v. New Kent County , 391 U.S. 430 (1968).

Hernandez v. Stockton Unified School District, Case No. 101016 (Superior Court of California, County of San Joaquin, 1975).

Stell v. The Board of Education for the City of Savannah and the County of Chatham et al., 220 F.Supp 667 (S.D.Ga., June 28, 1963); with most recent action 1994 W.L. 448677 (S.D. Ga., Aug. 12, 1994) (No. Civ. A. 1316).

Swann v. Charlotte-Mecklenburg, 402 U.S. 1 (1971).

CHAPTER 6

FORTY YEARS IN THE WILDERNESS: THE CONVOLUTED STORY OF THE EAST BATON ROUGE DESEGREGATION CASE

Gary S. Mathews and Robin Garrett Jarvis

For the citizens of East Baton Rouge Parish, desegregating the community's schools has not been an easy task. Instead, the journey toward desegregation in this community has been much like the trials and tribulations of the Israelites as they wandered in the wilderness after their emancipation from slavery in Egypt. For the Israelites, a journey that should have taken only eight days lasted 40 years due to their disobedience. For the citizens of this community, the path to desegregation has also lasted 40 years, and has brought with it considerable strife, pain, and discontent. The path from a completely segregated school system to the present consent decree is littered with failed attempts at voluntary desegregation as well as a court order fraught with problems.

The consent decree that the school district has negotiated with the plaintiffs in this case is a renewed attempt at voluntary desegregation by the East Baton Rouge community. This voluntary plan differs from earlier desegregation attempts by the district in that it melds the components of community based attendance zones

71

and school choice within the public school system. This chapter provides both an overview of this consent decree and its implementation as we travel the path of one community toward desegregation.

Background of the Case

As one of the longest running school desegregation suits in the United States, the case of *Clifford Eugene Davis, et al. v. East Baton Rouge Parish School Board, et al.* has had a tumultuous history. The case was originally filed on February 29, 1956, by a group of African American parents who opposed having their children bused to African American-only schools outside of their own neighborhood. These schools were some distance from the children's homes, and were already overcrowded (Shinkle, 1996, July 29). Of particular concern to the parents was one elementary school in their own area that was originally designated for African American students, but was redesignated, in 1942, for white students in order to make room for a growing white population in the area. These parents, their 39 children, and an attorney had already staged a march to this school on September 3, 1954, after the *Brown* decision, in an attempt to enroll there. They were not allowed to enter the school (EBR School Children, 1954, September 7).

In 1960, an order was issued by the federal district court located in Baton Rouge prohibiting the East Baton Rouge School Board from continuing to operate a racially segregated school system. The district court also ordered the school board to submit a desegregation plan. The board developed and submitted a "freedom of choice" plan that was approved by the court in 1963. This decision was appealed by the plaintiffs, and was reversed by the Fifth Circuit Court of Appeals. The Supreme Court subsequently refused to hear an appeal by the school board.

The case did not reappear in the courts until 1970. At that time, the school board submitted a "neighborhood zoning plan" to the district court. This plan was proposed to create further desegregation of the school system. The plan was approved by the court, and was not appealed by the plaintiffs. However, in 1974, the plaintiffs filed a motion with the district court requesting further relief. This request was made on the basis that the neighborhood zoning plan had failed to achieve the goal of complete and effective desegregation of the entire school system. The motion was denied by the district court, which subsequently ruled, in August 1975, that the school board was operating a "unitary" school system, and that the suit should be dismissed. As would be expected, this decision was also appealed by the plaintiffs, and the district court was once again reversed by the Fifth Circuit Court of Appeals (*Davis v. East Baton Rouge Parish School Board*, 570 F.2d 1260, 1978).

The next phase of litigation in this case occurred in 1979 when the Department of Justice intervened as a plaintiff in the litigation. A motion was then filed by the Justice Department seeking a partial summary judgment. The Justice Department argued that it had been clearly established as a matter of law that the East Baton Rouge Parish School Board was not operating a unitary school system. The undisputed facts used by the Justice Department in that motion included statistical data indicating the number of single race schools in the district as well as the number of minority students assigned to those single race schools.

Based upon information demonstrating that 67 of the system's 113 schools had a more than 90% one-race student population and that 78 schools had a more than 80% one-race student population, the district court issued a memorandum opinion on September 11, 1980 (*Davis v. East Baton Rouge Parish School Board*, 498 F.Supp. 580). This opinion granted the Justice Department's motion for partial summary judgment, and ordered the school board to submit a new plan for additional desegregation of the public schools. In its decision, the court also noted that 76 new public schools had been constructed since 1954, and that 73 of these had opened with student populations that were more than 90% one-race. In addition, the court also authorized the plaintiffs and the Justice Department to submit desegregation plans to be considered by the court.

Court Order of 1981

Following the court's ruling, the school board submitted a new desegregation plan. This plan proposed making every school in the district a "magnet" school of some kind. The plan was based on the school system's theory that each school would create and market a thematic magnet program that would attract students of the opposite race, thereby desegregating the schools. Each school would be expected to have at least a 25% white or African American student population by the end of the three-year program implementation. This plan was rejected by the district court on the grounds that the school system would be unable to guarantee that each of the magnet programs would be successful at attracting the targeted percentage of opposite race students (*Davis v. East Baton Rouge Parish School Board*, 514 F. Supp. 869, 873, 1981). The court also determined that the plan did not meet the school system's obligation to desegregate immediately, and that a three year period for implementation was too long.

The plan submitted by the Justice Department, and endorsed by the local plaintiffs, had as its major objective to minimize the number of racially identifiable schools by reassigning students through the pairing of predominantly white and predominantly African American schools. At the elementary level, this meant that one school in the pair would house grades K-3, while the other school operated grades 4-6. Students living in the attendance zones would attend one school until they finished 3rd grade, and then would transfer to the other school for the remainder of their elementary school years. The Court also rejected this plan, characterizing it as a "classic pair 'em, cluster 'em, and bus 'em" plan (*Davis v. East Baton Rouge Parish School Board*, 514 F. Supp. 869, 873, 1981).

On the last day of the trial, March 11, 1981, the court ordered the parties to conduct private negotiations in an attempt to reach an agreement about a desegregation plan. After intensive negotiations, the parties informed the court on April 15, 1981 that they had been unable to reach an agreement. The court responded that it had no alternative but to develop its own plan for the desegregation of the East Baton Rouge Parish schools. The court's plan was issued just two weeks later, on May 1, 1981 (*Davis v. East Baton Rouge Parish School Board*, 514 F. Supp. 869, 1981), and incorporated some concepts from each of the plans submitted by the parties in the suit as well as other provisions added by the court.

The court's plan was intended to achieve desegregation of the elementary schools during the 1981-82 school year through the closure of several older or smaller schools and the pairing or clustering of the remaining elementary schools. Due to constraints such as the geography of the school district and transportation difficulties, this plan left eleven essentially one-race elementary schools in the district. The court's original plan to desegregate the district's middle schools involved transforming most of these sites into single-grade or double-grade centers (*Davis v. East Baton Rouge Parish School Board*, 514 F.Supp at 881-82, 1981).

In response to a school board request, the court released an amended secondary plan for the 1982-83 school that desegregated East Baton Rouge's middle and high schools through establishing feeder patterns. This plan was to effectively eliminate all one-race middle schools and all but two one-race high schools. The district court's plan also included a majority-to-minority transfer policy as well as additional provisions regarding the board's construction of new schools and use of temporary buildings.

An appeal of the September 11, 1980 and May 1, 1981 court orders was filed by the school board. During the time that the appeal was pending, a change of administration in Washington prompted the school board to contact the Justice Department about attempting to reach a consent decree on an alternative plan. A desegregation expert, Christine Rossell of Boston University (1988, 1990, 1995), was hired at that time by the justice department to develop a magnet school plan similar to the board's earlier proposal that had been rejected by the court. This new plan eliminated the three year phase-in period, and imposed additional transportation requirements on the school system. The school board voted to reject this plan also.

On December 15, 1983, the Fifth Circuit Court of Appeals affirmed the orders of the district court. In doing so, the appellate court found that the school board had apparently located new schools in areas that would serve single-race attendance districts. The school system was also found to have continued to erect temporary buildings to relieve overcrowding in certain schools, generally those serving predominantly white neighborhoods, rather than redraw district lines to increase the enrollment in under-used school facilities in other neighborhoods. In its opinion, the Fifth Circuit stated "until it can show that all reasonable steps have been taken to eliminate remaining one-race schools, the board must in its pursuit of a unitary system respond as much as reasonably possible to patterns and changes in the demography of the parish" (*Davis v. East Baton Rouge Parish School Board*, 721F. 2d 1425, 1983).

Since 1981, the East Baton Rouge Parish School System has operated under Judge John Parker's court-ordered desegregation plan. Dozens of orders have been approved by the court approving modifications to various aspects of the plan, but the basic plan has remained. These modifications include the approval in May 1988 of a magnet school type plan called "Redesign" ("What efforts," 1996).

The goal of the Redesign program was to decentralize management in the school district creating site-based management teams at each school sites *(At the crossroads,* 1988). These teams were given the responsibility of developing educational programs within their schools which would meet the needs of their students and attract students from other schools. The Redesign program, while not proposed specifically as a desegregation tool, was expected to improve the racial mixtures in the schools because it allowed students to transfer to schools in which their race was the minority to participate in special magnet programs. Unfortunately, redesign was ultimately unsuccessful due in part to a lack of funding, and it therefore had little impact on integration in the district.

In December 1988, despite his earlier order to decrease the use of temporary buildings in the school system, Judge John Parker approved the installation of an additional 47 temporary buildings. At this time, he also instructed the board to develop a plan to eliminate the use of all temporary classrooms. Various schools in the district were also making extensive use of their auditoriums and closets as temporary classrooms to relieve overcrowding.

Community Disenchantment Grows

In the years following the imposition of the court-mandated desegregation plan, the Baton Rouge community became increasingly disenchanted with the school system. This dissatisfaction became resoundingly clear in 1994, when the East Baton Rouge Parish School Board developed the Community Schools and Capital Outlay Plan, its most recent desegregation initiative. The process of developing this plan began in 1990 when the board directed the school system staff to develop a capital outlay plan that would move the system closer to unitary status. A Desegregation Task Force was appointed by then school board President Eva Legard consisting of parents, teachers, administrators, and community leaders. This task force recommended that a new desegregation plan seek to establish home-based school attendance zones, build new school facilities in more centrally located areas, reduce the mandatory transportation times, and maximize the use of school feeder patterns.

Based upon these recommendations, the school board staff developed a proposal that reduced operational expenses, improved educational offerings to students, and reduced the number of one-race schools. This plan (East Baton Rouge Parish School Board, 1993) was later amended based upon recommendations by David J. Armor, who was hired as a desegregation expert at the suggestion of the plaintiffs after their review of the initial plan. On September 23, 1993, the East Baton Rouge Parish School Board voted 11-1 to submit the new Community Schools and Capital Outlay Plan to the district court. However, at the urging of the plaintiffs, the court refused to consider the plan until the school board was able to show that it had the financial ability to implement the plan if it was approved. In April 1994, the school board asked voters to approve a $215 million bond issue to fund the plan. The bond issue failed with a 63 percent "no" vote, a more than 11,000 vote margin, fundamentally killing any hopes of a new desegregation plan that called for taxpayer support.

Following this defeat, Judge Parker continued to indicate that the school system had a constitutional obligation to desegregate the schools, and that he expected the school district to develop a proposal to do so as quickly as possible. Judge Parker also continued to stress the importance of complying with his earlier orders requiring the school board to replace the temporary buildings with permanent facilities.

While the community's dissatisfaction had been evident for quite some time, the bond election defeat was a crushing blow to the school system. Since the 1981 desegregation plan, the school system had lost 18,749 white students and gained 9,083 African American students for a total student loss of 9,666 over the period (East Baton Rouge Parish School Board, 1996). This shift in student population was rapidly transforming the school system from a majority white system to a predominantly African American system. This change signaled the erosion of both middle class tax support and public confidence in the public school system.

Many of these white students were being lost to private schools in the community which, during the period from 1980 to 1990, had moved from educating 16 percent of the white school age population in the district to educating 36 percent of it. A very disturbing aspect of this trend was the tendency for teachers within the public school system to enroll their own children in private schools. According to a 1995 study (Doyle and Rice, 1995), 35.7 percent of East Baton Rouge Parish School System teachers sent all or some of their children to private schools. Among the country's top 100 largest cities, Baton Rouge ranked thirteenth in terms of the percentage of the system's teachers enrolling their own children in private schools. Considering these factors, the tax election defeat may not have been surprising to many of those involved. However, it did spell the beginning of the end for the incumbent board and the superintendent, Bernard Weiss.

In June 1994, the school board voted to end Weiss's superintendent contract effective December of that year. Following this action, five of the 12 board members decided not to run for re-election in the upcoming school board election to be held in November. With the newly formed group, Community Action for Public Education (CAPE), heavily supporting their opponents, four of the seven members running for re-election were defeated. In January 1995, nine new school board members joined the three remaining incumbents in a national search for a new superintendent and a new direction for the East Baton Rouge Parish School System. In August 1995, Gary S. Mathews began his tenure as the superintendent of schools in this troubled district.

Developing A New Desegregation and Education Plan

The task that faced the new superintendent and the school board was not an easy one. Years of desegregation failure, a history of broken promises, and what was perceived as "bad faith" implementation of the 1981 court order had produced a high level of mistrust on the part of the plaintiffs. In order to address some of these concerns, and to begin the journey toward a renewed attempt at desegregation in this district, the new administration took several steps which proved critical to their potential success. A new seven-member Executive Leadership Team was assembled that included both leaders from within the school district and administrators from Mississippi, Texas, and Florida, where the new superintendent had previously served in school administration. In addition, a new legal team was hired to handle the 40-year-old desegregation lawsuit.

To the members of this team, it was clear that to build trust with the plaintiffs, it would be necessary to use a "data-driven, research-based" approach in developing a new desegregation plan. Data used to develop the district's new desegregation plan clearly indicated that the school system was "broken." Poor test scores abounded throughout the district, but were especially alarming for African American children. Test data indicated that African American students in the district had scored below white students on every area of the Louisiana Educational Assessment Program during the seven year period between 1989 and 1995. Over this period, a 34.2 percentile point gap existed between the achievement of African American students and white students across grades two through nine on the California Achievement Test (East Baton Rouge Parish School Board, 1996).

Furthermore, analyses of school effectiveness indices conducted by Charles Teddlie and colleagues (1996) showed that 48 percent of the public schools in East Baton Rouge Parish were ineffective for the three year period from 1991 to 1994. Effectiveness status was determined from a statewide study in which student socioeconomic status and community type were used to predict student achievement on standardized tests. Ineffective schools were those that scored below the 95 percent confidence interval for their predicted score.

The highest percent of ineffective schools was found among the district's middle schools, with 53 percent being ineffective and only six percent being effective. Based upon these findings, Teddlie (1996) concluded that schooling in the East Baton Rouge Parish schools during the period from 1991 to 1994 had actually exacerbated the effects of poverty. This conclusion is clearly illustrated by the fact that five of the district's high schools which, due to their higher proportion of economically deprived students, were predicted to score below the state average on standardized tests, did even worse than expected. It was evident that these schools, and other like them, were only aggravating the educational disadvantages their students faced.

Statistics regarding suspension, expulsion, and dropout rates also demonstrated that the district was failing its African American students. During the 1992-93 school year, there were 7,476 suspensions in the East Baton Rouge Parish School System with 85 percent of these suspensions involving African American students (Fossey, 1995). African American students were also far more likely than any other race to be expelled from the district's schools, representing 91 percent of the expulsions in that same year. Over the period of the litigation, the school system had also done little to improve the graduation opportunities of its African American students. The cohort rate for on-time graduation of African American students in 1958 was 55 percent. By 1994, this rate had dropped to 50 percent. The cohort rate for *all* East Baton Rouge Parish public school students has stabilized at about 60 percent since 1987 (Fossey, 1995).

In addition to these problems, the new administration was also faced with increasing racial isolation in many of its schools, which was occurring in spite of the district court's 1981 court order. As of the 1995-96 school year, 30 of the school system's 102 sites were still one-race schools with 90 percent or more of their student populations being of the same race (East Baton Rouge Parish School Board, 1996). This was due to white flight from the district's schools as well as demographic changes within the individual school attendance zones since 1981. As a result of these factors, a court order that had intended to desegregate the schools had resulted in the mandatory reassignment of African American students from their neighborhood schools to other predominantly African American schools.

Facing these unsettling conditions, the new administration utilized the results of a parent survey conducted in July 1993 as well as information from the Savannah-Chatham County and other school districts (Rossell, 1995) to begin developing a new plan for education and desegregation in the East Baton Rouge Parish Public School System. According to the results of a parent survey (East Baton Rouge Parish School Board, 1993, p.30) of 600 African American and 600 white parents, 80 percent of both groups strongly supported a return to neighborhood schools and the use of magnet school programs to achieve desegregation.

The most popular magnet themes with white parents were computers, math/science, accelerated programs, and composition writing. For African American parents, the most popular magnet programs were computers, math/science, accelerated programs, and extended day. At the secondary school level, both African American and white parents expressed the greatest interest in magnet programs emphasizing college prep and the medical/health professions.

The survey also provided estimated participation rates for each type of magnet program as well as for majority to minority transfer programs. These data were used in the district's desegregation proposal as the basis for the projected voluntary transfer figures, and the projected program and school enrollments. In addition to this information, results of surveys of both Baton Rouge voters and district administrators (School System Perception Inventory, 1995) indicated that both of these groups also supported a return to a community/neighborhood school plan.

A New Desegregation and Education Plan
for the East Baton Rouge Parish School System

The long-awaited new desegregation plan was released to the public and the plaintiffs on April 12, 1996. The plan's goal was to reduce segregation in the system through the "redrawing of attendance zones for schools, the provision for voluntary transfers to magnet and regular schools, and the relocation of gifted programs to predominantly African American schools" (East Baton Rouge Parish School Board, 1996, p. 1). Major components of the plan included community/neighborhood attendance zones, an extensive magnet program, and a resource equity program. The plan included a phase-in period of three years with the elementary school changes being made for the 1996-97 school year, the middle school and high school changes in 1997-98.

The reconfigured attendance zones were designed by the school board staff not only to enhance integration in the district while maintaining community schools, but also to reduce transportation times and distances for students to the greatest extent possible, and to make maximum use of the existing facilities. The proposed magnet program was intended to be a primary tool for integrating predominantly African American schools in inner city areas with programs ranging from gifted and scholastic to visual and performing arts academies. The underlying assumption in this proposal was that these programs could be utilized not only as an incentive to encourage white students to voluntarily transfer to predominantly African American schools, but also to enhance the resources and status of these schools.

In addition to these two components, an extensive resource equity plan was also proposed in the new desegregation plan to provide for a more equitable distribution of material resources throughout the district. This plan included the centralization and management of state funds for textbooks to the school system's Division of Operations and Budget Management, thus discontinuing the practice of utilizing textbook funds for discretionary purposes. Expenditures of these funds also required the approval of each site's School Improvement Team and the appropriate executive director.

The new resource equity plan also included a long-range program to increase the availability and use of technology. For the 1996-97 school year, $200,000 was dedicated to funding a pilot technology program in approximately 20 at-risk schools. Half of these schools were to be funded by the school system, while the other half were to funded by a business consortium. According to the new desegregation plan, "initial priorities for funding will be given to the 59% of the inner-city, historically African American schools which now fall below the EBRPSS average pupil-to-computer ratio of 16:1" (East Baton Rouge Parish School Board, 1996, p.49).

The resource equity plan also sought to equalize supplementary funding to individual schools by providing those schools that have difficulty generating additional independent funding with district office staff to assist with grant writing, fund raising, and other income generating projects. This part of the plan also included a change in the standard for inclusion in Title I funding, lowering the previous requirement of 75 percent of the school's student population eligible for the free or reduced lunch program to 50 percent. This change was proposed to allow nonparticipating elementary schools that were below the median level to begin to receive Title I funds, thus providing additional supplementary funding to these schools.

In addition to these major provisions, the *New Desegregation and Education Plan* (East Baton Rouge Parish School Board, 1996) also included reforms of the gifted and talented, special education, and middle school programs in the district, the adoption of an *Effective Schools Model* based on the work of Ron Edmonds, and the establishment of School Improvement Teams at each school site. Also included in the plan were revisions in the district's Pre-Kindergarten program to make these classes more accessible to at-risk populations, and to coordinate services between the various providers (i.e., Head Start, Title I, Early Childhood Block Grants, etc.). Extended time programs for at-risk children were included in the plan in the form of extended day and extended school year programs at those schools where a need existed.

While the plan required approximately $10.4 million in additional spending over a four-year period, mostly on inner-city majority African American schools, it did not require any new taxes from the community. Instead funding for the program was expected to come from savings in transportation costs estimated at $1 million per year, and a new energy conservation program. In addition, the system planned to utilize a portion of its $8 million in reserves to fund the plan, if necessary.

The school system argued that a community school based plan which provided for voluntary transfers would bring about more long term integration than had resulted from the 1981 court order. This assertion was based on the findings of several large-scale, national studies which indicate that voluntary desegregation plans result in more integration than do forced assignment plans (Rossell, chapter 5, this volume; 1995, 1990; Rossell & Armor, 1996)

Overcoming Mixed Reactions

The district's proposal met with mixed reactions from the public. While many parents were pleased that their children would now be able to attend school closer to their homes, and with other children in their neighborhood, others were upset that their children would be relocated to new schools by the plan. In large part, parents of children participating in the district's gifted and talented programs were disturbed that these programs would be moved to inner-city predominantly African American schools. They were also alarmed that the criteria for these programs would be revised to allow for greater participation by students of both racial groups.

Alvin Washington, president of the local NAACP chapter, expressed initial satisfaction with parts of the program including the provision of preschool programs for at-risk students. However, he had some concern about the plan's goal of reducing the number of one-race schools in the district from 30 to nine stating in a newspaper interview, "We'll have to see if that is actually going to happen — because all of this stuff is on paper" (Shinkle, 1996).

Jensen Holliday, a leader of CAPE, the group largely responsible for the election of nine of the 12 school board members, expressed immediate support for the plan. He added that "he and other CAPE members are 'convinced that for the first time in the history of this desegregation suit, all 12 board members are doing what they can to get us out from under this desegregation suit and at the same time enhance the education product'" (Shinkle, 1996).

Brace Godfrey Jr, president of the local group 100 Black Men of Metro Baton Rouge, voiced his excitement with the plan, saying that he was especially happy with the plan's support for inner-city schools and magnet programs (Shinkle, 1996). After holding five televised public forums to gain community input on the plan and making minor revisions to the plan, the East Baton Rouge Parish School Board voted on April 30, 1996 to send the *New Desegregation and Education Plan for the East Baton Rouge Parish School System* to the litigants.

While there continued to be numerous objections to the desegregation plan adopted by the school board, these were all but forgotten with the release, on May 30, 1996, of the U.S. Justice Department and NAACP's recommendations for revisions of the plan (Bad Plan, 1996). These changes included carving out 13 one-race African American schools, thus giving up any hope of ever integrating these schools, and continuing mandatory cross-town busing through the establishment of 13 school pairs at the elementary and middle school levels. Under the plaintiffs' plan, these pairs would function at the elementary level by allowing kindergartners and first graders to attend their home school, then having second and third graders attend one school in the pair, and fourth and fifth graders attend the other. At the middle school level, sixth and seventh graders would attend one school in the pair, while eighth graders would attend the other. This revision would require many students to travel far from their home for one school year, and then return to their home school the following year, further alienating many parents and community members. In addition, the revised plan relocated some magnet programs and established several others.

Suddenly support for the school board's plan increased rapidly. Within three days of the release of the plaintiffs' plan, community support for the school board's plan included some of the most prestigious African American groups and leaders in town. In reacting to the Justice Department's proposal, Alvin Washington, the local NAACP president noted that acceptance of the changes by the school board was not a requirement for the two sides to reach an agreement (Dunne, 1996, June 1). The president of the local chapter of 100 Black Men, Brace Godfrey, noted that while the black community in Baton Rouge owed a great debt to the Justice Department for their efforts over the period of the case, it was time to let the community do what it believed to be best for the children. Additionally, he indicated that it was possible that a coalition of black leaders from the community would go to Washington to meet with justice department officials to ask them to back the school board plan (Dunne, 1996, June 2).

Support also came from members of the local NAACP's Education Committee. Clara Glasper, a member of this committee and a retired school system administrator, noted that the black community had rallied behind the school board's plan after the release of the U.S. Justice Department's modifications. In addition, she stated that several members of the local NAACP had sent a letter and petition to Franz Marshall, the Justice Department's attorney, asking him to support the school district's plan (Dunne, 1996, June 2). Religious leaders also expressed support for the school board with Reverend Charles Smith, pastor of a local African American church and president of the Fourth District Baptist Association, expressing the concerns of many in the community that mandatory assignments had not worked under the 1981 court order, and probably would not work now (Dunne, 1996, June 2).

Area teacher groups also expressed public support for the school board's plan. David Lovely, president of the East Baton Rouge Federation of Teachers, expressing everyone's sentiment, stated simply "it's time to end the quarrel." With this support, the East Baton Rouge Parish School Board voted on June 2, 1996 to reject the revised plan proposed by the plaintiffs, but expressed hope that the plaintiffs would join with the school board to present a united front to convince U.S. District Judge John Parker to approve the board's plan (Bad plan, 1996).

Rebuilding Trust In A Troubled Community

With this vote, the negotiations began among the parties to reach a consent decree. By this time, the deadline of July 1, 1996 for approval of a new plan to be implemented during the 1996-97 school year was rapidly approaching. However, there was a history of mistrust to be overcome. The school system's attempts to portray the district's problems honestly had done little to alleviate the plaintiffs' belief that "this is East Baton Rouge Parish." There were forty years of history, fifteen under the last court order, to be addressed. Thus, while the players may have changed, the plaintiffs argued, the place had not.

Especially problematic for the plaintiffs, as they came to the negotiating table, was a whole list of concerns, including:

- temporary buildings had increasingly been added at predominantly white schools, thereby thwarting desegregation;
- racially-identifiable facilities were evident in the distinct differences in the appearance and equipping of white vs. African American schools;
- gifted programs with a disproportionate percentage of white students had excluded African Americans;
- disproportionate percentages of African American students, especially African American males, placed in special education classes;
- the school board's failure to fund special programs geared to promote desegregation, including the failed Redesign program which, for large measure, had existed on paper only;
- the perception that the court's order of 1981 was not faithfully carried out by some school system administrators who were thought to "sabotage" the orders, even "coaching" parents about how to circumvent school assignment rules; and
- the perceived insensitivity of past school boards and administrations to the academic and cultural needs of African American students in the public schools.

While the new administration of the school system was attempting to alleviate many of these concerns through its "research-based, data-driven" approach, their efforts had, in large part, only confirmed many of the plaintiffs' negative perceptions of the district. In the final months of the negotiations, it was evident that it would be necessary to verify everything to gain the cooperation of the plaintiffs. Several meetings were held that addressed particular concerns of the plaintiffs.

In order to gain the trust and cooperation of the plaintiffs, school authorities demonstrated that the school system had properly estimated the costs of the 30+ magnet programs, and could provide the recurring revenue needed to fund over $20 million in improvements called for in the school district's desegregation plan. In addition, the school system spelled out the intent of the new magnet programs through narrative descriptions of each magnet program's purpose. It also provided details about student interaction plans that provided for the intermingling of magnet and non-magnet students through the school day. These plans included dispersing magnet and non-magnet classrooms throughout the school buildings so that classes would be indistinguishable. The interaction plans were based on similar plans stipulated by the U.S. Department of Justice in *Stell and U.S. v. Board of Public Education for the City of Savannah and the County of Chatham, et al.* (1989). The school system provided schedules of these interaction opportunities to the plaintiffs, and had them explained by the principals and staff who were responsible for their implementation.

After two months of final negotiations, and 28 days after the original deadline set by the superintendent of schools for implementation in the coming school year, the parties involved in the 40-year struggle known as *Davis, et al. vs. East Baton Rouge Parish School Board, et al.* were joined together in a new consent decree on July 29, 1996. According to Franz Marshall of the U.S. Justice Department, this "voluntary desegregation" agreement broke new ground for the federal government. In his statement to the local newspaper, *The Advocate*, Marshall remarked "We view the settlement as an experiment. We will watch it closely to determine how it is working before applying it in any other situations" (Dunne, 1996, August 1).

The final settlement agreed to by the litigants in this case closely reflected the School District's original proposal. However, there were several modifications including, most substantially, a cost of $21.2 million over a 4 year period as opposed the district's proposal of $10.4 million over the same time (Dunne, 1996, August 1). The consent decree also required the school district to reduce the number of racially identifiable schools from 67 to 53 by the end of the third year of implementation (Dunne, 1996, August 1). In addition, the district was required to reduce the number of temporary buildings by one-third at the end of the fifth year of implementation, and by 75 percent at the end of the eighth year (Dunne, 1996, August 1). Finally, the consent decree requires court supervision of the school district's efforts for at least five more years. At the end of the five year period, the plaintiffs and the school board can jointly request that the school system be declared unitary. The school district cannot make this request on its own until after the eighth year of implementation of the consent decree (Dunne, 1996, August 1).

Conclusion

As this chapter goes to press, the East Baton Rouge School District is beginning its second year of implementation of the new consent decree. While in some ways, the year got off to a rocky start, there have also been numerous positive outcomes for the community and the school district.

In order to meet the enrollment changes expected at the elementary school sites, it was necessary to move 67 temporary buildings from one site to another throughout the district. Due to the late approval of the consent decree, only one month before the scheduled first day of school, it became impossible to have all of the temporary buildings in place for the beginning of the school year. In schools where the buildings were not in place for the first day of school, principals set up temporary teaching stations as needed, and moved classes once the buildings became available (King, 1996). In some cases, the temporary buildings were not on site and ready for occupancy until mid-October.

As expected, the school system did suffer a drop in enrollment with the implementation of the consent decree. While the district had projected student losses for the first year of implementation, the actual losses totaled 1,833 students, twice the expected number. The additional student loss was attributed by school officials to the late approval of the consent decree, and confusion about school attendance zones that resulted from the lengthy negotiations. This reduction in student enrollment translated into a total loss of about $2.3 million in state funds. However, according to Charlotte Placide, Associate Superintendent for Budget and Operations, this funding reduction was offset by the hiring of fewer additional teachers in the first few days of school which resulted in a $1.7 million savings for the school system. As a result, the drop in student enrollment had a total budget loss impact of approximately $50,000 (Dunne, 1996).

On the positive side, the school system has reduced by six the number of racially identifiable schools in the district. At the elementary level where the new consent decree was implemented in 1996, the number of racially identifiable schools has been reduced by four. In addition, at the middle school level, where the new plan is being implemented in the 1997-98 school year, there was a two-school reduction in this area during the 996-97 school year. Considering that the consent decree requires the district to reduce the number of racially identifiable schools by 14 over the next three years, the district appears to be making good progress toward this goal.

In addition, there has been a 123 percent increase in participation in Boy Scouts by East Baton Rouge Parish School students. For African American students, the increase has been 315 percent. Tom Varnell, President of the Istrouma Area Council of Boy Scouts has attributed this increase directly to the new desegregation plan. It should be noted that according to the Harris poll, students who have participated in scouting are more likely to graduate from high school than are their non-participating counterparts.

Finally, a school district that was overwhelmingly rejected by the community when it attempted voter approval for a bond issue in April 1994, received a 75 percent approval for the renewal of three taxes in January of 1997. Although East Baton Rouge voters typically approve tax renewals, it must be noted that their approval rating in this instance was considerably higher than for the 61 percent yes vote cast for renewals requested in 1994 (King, 1997). This high approval rating was seen by many on the school board and within the district administration as a thumbs up from voters on the changes being made throughout the system.

While the first year of implementation was laden with both positives and negatives, the school system and the community are beginning to work together toward the goal of desegregation. While there is still much distance to be traversed, it appears that the East Baton Rouge Parish community and its school district may finally be making progress toward the promised land of unitary status.

References

At the crossroads: East Baton Rouge Parish school redesign plan into the next century. (1988, March 11). Baton Rouge, LA: East Baton Rouge Parish School System.

Bad plan makes board plan shine. (1996, June 4). *The Advocate,* p. 6B.

Doyle, D. & Rice, A. (1995). *Where connoisseurs send their children to school.* Washington, D.C.: The Center for Education Reform.

Dunne, M. (1996, June 1). NAACP clarifies position on schools. *Saturday State-Times/Morning Advocate*, p. 1A, 4A.

Dunne, M. (1996, June 2). Black leaders back plan. *Sunday Advocate*, p. 1A, 12A.

Dunne, M. (1996, August 1). School board sends plan to federal court. *The Advocate*, p. 1A, 8A.

Dunne, M. (1996, October 2). EBR school enrollment down 1,833: Biggest losses noted in elementary grades. *The Advocate,* p. 1B, 2B.

EBR school children to start new term: Vacation time ends. (1954, September 7). *Morning Advocate,* p. 1A, 6A.

East Baton Rouge Parish School Board. (1993, October). *Community schools and capital outlay plan presented to U.S. District Court, Middle District of Louisiana.* Baton Rouge, LA: Author.

East Baton Rouge Parish School Board. (1996, April 12). *A new desegregation plan and education plan for the East Baton Rouge Parish School System.* Baton Rouge, LA: Author.

Edmonds, R. (1979). Effective schools for the urban poor. *Educational Leadership*, 37, 15-27.

Fossey, R. (1995). *African American students in East Baton Rouge Parish: How have they fared in desegregated schools?* Unpublished manuscript, Louisiana State University College of Education, Baton Rouge.

King, K. (1996, August 15). Some t-buildings won't be in place for Sept. 3. *The Advocate,* p. 1A, 4A.

King, K. (1997, January 19). Voters renew school taxes. *Sunday Advocate*, p. 1A.

Rossell, C.H. (1988). Is it the busing or the blacks? *Urban Affairs Quarterly, 24,* 138-148.

Rossell, C.H. (1990). *The carrot or the stick for school desegregation policy: Magnet schools vs. Forced Busing.* Philadelphia: Temple University Press.

Rossell, C.H. (1995). Controlled choice desegregation plans: Not enough choice, too much control? *Urban Affairs Review, 31*(1), 43-76.

Rossell, C.H. (1995). The convergence of Black and White attitudes on school desegregation issues during the four decade evolution of the plans. *The William and Mary Law Review*, 36(2), 613-663.

Rossell, C.H. (1996). The effectiveness of school desegregation plans, 1968-1991. American Politics Quarterly.

School system perception inventory. (1995, August 7). School Services, Inc.

Shinkle, P. (1996, July 29). Original plaintiffs find both success, disappointments. *The Advocate*, pp. 1A, 7A.

Shinkle, P. (1996, April 13). Initial reactions mixed; NAACP likes parts of plan. *The Advocate*, pp. 7A.

Teddlie, C. (1996, April). *School effectiveness indices, East Baton Rouge Parish public schools, Academic years 1991-92, 1992-93, 1993-94.* Unpublished manuscript, Louisiana State University College of Education, Baton Rouge.

What efforts have been made by the EBR School Board to satisfy the federal court before the development of the preliminary draft under discussion this weekend? (1996, April 13). *The Advocate*, pp. 7A.

Table of Legal Cases

Davis v. East Baton Rouge Parish School Board, 570 F.2d 1260 (5th Cir. 1978).

Davis v. East Baton Rouge Parish School Board, 514 F. Supp. 869,873 (M.D. La. 1981).

Davis v. East Baton Rouge Parish School Board, 498 F. Supp. 580 (M.D. La. 1980).

Davis v. East Baton Rouge Parish School Board, 514 F. Supp. 869 (M.D. La. 1981).

Davis v. East Baton Rouge Parish School Board, 514 F.Supp. at 881-82 (M.D. La. 1981).

Davis v. East Baton Rouge Parish School Board, 721 F. 2d 1425 (5 Cir. 1983).

Stell and U.S. v. Board of Public Education for the City of Savannah and the County of Chatham, et al., 888 F. 2d 82 (11th Cir. 1989).

SECTION II.

DESEGREGATION LITIGATION
IN HIGHER EDUCATION

CHAPTER 7

INTRODUCTION TO SECTION II: THE CONFLICT BETWEEN COMPETING VIRTUES

Richard Fossey

In the previous six chapters, authors analyzed recent desegregation lawsuits involving American public schools. This section shifts the field of view from elementary and secondary education to the nation's colleges and universities, where litigation concerning race and educational opportunities is having a profound impact on higher education.

In Chapter 8, Edward P. St. John provides a historical perspective on efforts to desegregate higher education in the South. Historically black colleges and universities (HBCUs) were founded after the Civil War, first by white church groups and then by Southern states, as they began constructing the "separate but equal" era in the late nineteenth and early twentieth centuries. Even after the Supreme Court's decision in *Brown v. Board of Education*, states continued to maintain two systems of public universities — one for white students and a separate, poorly supported system for African Americans.

As St. John relates, the federal government began assuming a major role in promoting equal educational opportunities at the college level during the 1960s. Federally funded student aid

95

programs that began in this period contributed to an increase in minority college enrollments. In the next decade, the Supreme Court's decision in *Adams v. Califano* gave the federal government a mandate to pursue the desegregation of public colleges and universities.

St. John explains that the federal philosophy toward higher education desegregation in the 1970s was based on two parallel goals: 1) providing remedies for past segregation policies in public colleges and universities, and 2) strengthening the role of HBCUs in state systems of higher education. This philosophy was reflected in the federal desegregation guidelines that were issued by the US Department of Health, Education and Welfare in 1977.

St. John argues that recent court cases have reshaped federal policy toward higher education desegregation in recent years. Based on an analysis of recent litigation in Alabama, Louisiana, and Mississippi, he concludes that the federal courts are focusing on the desegregation of HBCUs rather than their development as viable institutions with a distinct and long-term mission. In other words, the courts seem more interested in expanding white enrollments in HBCUs rather than enhancing their status as predominantly black institutions.

In chapter 9, St. John and Don Hossler follow St. John's historical review with recommendations for pursuing desegregation in a legal environment that places more emphasis on the system-wide desegregation of public colleges and universities and less on the development of HBCUs. In this environment, St. John and Hossler advise, HBCUs may need to think about developing a dual mission — building programs that will attract white students to their campuses while retaining their traditional focus on educating African American students. For many HBCUs, the authors suggest, the best way to increase white enrollments is to establish high-demand academic programs that will attract part-time white students. In some instances, HBCUs that created such programs have been able to increase white enrollments, while retaining their mission of serving African American students.

St. John and Hossler conclude their essay with some thoughts about achieving better integration at historically white colleges. They suggest that an increase in need-based student aid may attract more minority students to traditionally white campuses. In addition, financial incentives to encourage these institutions to recruit more minority students may also be helpful.

In chapter 10, the focus shifts from desegregation of colleges and universities to the controversial issue of affirmative action. In this chapter, Ann Wells and John Strope provide an overview of *Podberesky v Kirwin* (1994), in which the Fourth Circuit Court of Appeals struck down a scholarship program for African Americans operated by the University of Maryland at College Park (UMCP). The authors take the reader through the history of this litigation, which spans a four-year period, and explain the Fourth Circuit's legal analysis.

As Wells and Strope relate, Daniel Podberesky, a college student of Hispanic origin, sued UMCP, arguing that the Banneker scholarship program violated his constitutional right to equal protection by excluding him on account of his race. UMCP admitted that its scholarship program was intentionally discriminatory, but argued that it had a "compelling interest" in maintaining it. Specifically, UMCP contended that the program was necessary to overcome the effect of past discrimination by the university.

In a 1994 opinion, the Fourth Circuit reversed a lower court decision and held the scholarship program to be unconstitutional. According to the appellate panel, UMCP had no compelling reason to award scholarships exclusively to students of one race. UMCP appealed the decision to the Supreme Court, supported by amicus curiae briefs filed by numerous colleges, universities, and civil rights groups. The Supreme Court declined to hear the appeal, however, thereby allowing the Fourth Circuit's opinion to stand.

Chapter 11 is an essay by Lino Graglia, one of the nation's leading critics of affirmative action in education. In a review of federal case law, Graglia argues that the judiciary has perverted the original aim of *Brown v. Board of Education* and the Civil Rights Act of 1964, substituting the racial preferences of affirmative action for the simple concept of equal opportunity without regard to race.

Graglia then goes on to identify and attack the major policy arguments in favor of affirmative action. Proponents contend that the policy is necessary because traditional college admissions criteria –– standardized test scores, grades, and the like —

are "culturally biased." But this, Graglia contends is not true. He cites evidence indicating that standard admissions criteria predict a minority student's academic success with a fair amount of accuracy.

Nor, in Graglia's view, can affirmative action be justified as the means for counteracting the "under-representation" of minority students in education. Higher education institutions are not meant to be representative institutions, Graglia argues, but institutions that select entrants based on ability and interest in an area of study. Moreover, Graglia contends that African Americans are "over represented" rather than under represented in higher education, once IQ scores are taken into account. Citing evidence from Herrnstein and Murray's *Bell Curve* (1994), Graglia contends that an African American in the bottom 10 percent of a college or university's IQ range has a far better chance of being admitted than a white applicant with the same IQ score.

In Graglia's view, affirmative action has had a pernicious effect on higher education, admitting minority students to study who are not as qualified as their classmates. Graglia believes that affirmative action has contributed to racial tensions on campus, and he predicts the day will come when affirmative action will be eliminated from the nation's higher education institutions.

In chapter 12, Monique Weston Clague criticizes the *Podberesky* decision. Minority-targeted scholarships, she argues, are not "an exercise in racial spoils." Rather they are "educationally sound" strategies for increasing the numbers of minority students on college campuses and for ensuring that these students are successful.

In addition, Clague makes an important link between race-targeted scholarships — the focus of *Podberesky* — and ongoing efforts to desegregate higher education in the South. She points out that increasing the number of minority faculty members at the nation's colleges and universities was one of the focal points in *U.S. v. Fordice*, the long-running litigation involving the desegregation of Mississippi's public universities. Increasing the number of minority faculty members depends, Clague observes, on increasing the pool of minority students in undergraduate and graduate programs. She persuasively argues that minority-targeted scholarship programs, like the one the Fourth

Circuit struck down at UMCP, are exactly the kinds of programs that will ultimately lead to a larger presence of African American scholars on college faculties.

This volume's final chapter is Virginia Davis Nordin's provocative essay on the policy implications of *Podberesky* and *Hopwood v. State of* Texas, the 1995 Fifth Circuit decision striking down a race-biased admissions process at the University of Texas School of Law. Both decisions, Nordin maintains, strike at the heart of academic freedom, which includes an institution's right to determine who shall be admitted to study. She points out that colleges and universities have recognized the value of student diversity for many decades — diversity based on geography, intellectual interest, and even race.

In addition, Nordin argues that *Podberesky* and *Hopwood* fundamentally misunderstand higher education's role in the larger society. In *Podberesky*, the Fourth Circuit ruled that UMCP's efforts to attract out-of-state minority students was not narrowly tailored to meet the goal of improving Maryland's minority participation in higher education. In *Hopwood*, the Fifth Circuit ruled that the University of Texas Law School could not justify a minority-targeted admissions program on a history of segregation in Texas secondary and elementary schools. According to Nordin, both decisions failed to grasp the relationship between higher education and the larger society. Consequently, these courts delivered a major and unnecessary setback to legitimate university policy when they ruled that state universities could not fashion affirmative action policies to address discrimination beyond their boundaries

Nordin concludes with some reflections about the future of affirmative action in higher education. If the Supreme Court ultimately adopts the reasoning of *Hopwood* and *Podberesky*, she believes that minority participation in higher education will likely diminish, particularly at the nation's flagship universities. In her view, some sort of affirmative action is justified in college admissions and scholarship decisions, if minority students are going to achieve adequate opportunities to participate in higher education.

When all six essays are considered together, they illustrate one central theme about the recent lawsuits concerning race and equal opportunity in higher education. In most of these cases, a conflict emerges between two competing values — values that most Americans accept as worthy and good. In *Hopwood* and *Podberesky*, for example, federal courts endorsed the constitutional principle that universities should not make important decisions about students based on their race. This is the philosophy that Lino Graglia so persuasively espouses. Nevertheless, the philosophy conflicts with another moral view — that efforts should be made to ensure equal access to previously under represented groups. It is this philosophy that is articulated most clearly in Monique Clague and Virginia Nordin's chapters.

In the HBCU litigation that St. John and Hossler examined, the tension between competing virtues is equally apparent. On the one hand, most Americans would endorse the principle that no college or university should cater to a particular race or ethnic group. On the other hand, many would agree that the HBCUs serve an important function in addressing the educational needs of African American students and should be given some place in the overall scheme of higher education.

On the whole, the nation's academic leaders and policy makers have been reluctant to address these tensions. With regard to affirmative action, many colleges and universities have been content to follow some form of the practice, without wrestling with the moral implications of racial preferences or examining its impact on their academic missions. Likewise, academia has reconciled itself to the permanent presence of publicly funded HBCUs; and it has done so without confronting the irony of open segregation in higher education, perhaps the most stringently anti-racist sector in our society.

The following six essays do not resolve these tensions, but they serve the useful purpose of highlighting them. Perhaps, in weighing the conflicting views that are expressed in the following pages, the reader will achieve some new insight about the struggle to bring equal educational opportunities to everyone seeking to participate in higher education, without regard to race.

CHAPTER 8

HIGHER EDUCATION DESEGREGATION IN THE POST-*FORDICE* LEGAL ENVIRONMENT: AN HISTORICAL PERSPECTIVE

Edward P. St. John

Ironically, at the time when the first complete round of desegregation litigation has been concluded, with *Knight v. Alabama* (1995) and *Ayers v. Fordice* (1995), historically black colleges and universities (HBCUs) are again confronted by a crisis. Precisely when their historic role should be celebrated, HBCUs are again faced with fundamental questions about their future, if not challenges to their survival. Given the long history of struggle to provide African Americans with opportunities to attend colleges and universities in the United States, it is more than a little ironic that some advocates for HBCUs (e.g., Barnes, 1993; Brown and Hendrickson, 1997) have argued that the future of these institutions is now threatened by the very court decisions that were intended to promote equal opportunity to attend. Given that the recent *Ayers* and *Knight* decisions, the two state desegregation cases fully litigated in the post-*Fordice* legal environment, have focused on the desegregation of HBCUs as the last issue to be litigated in the midsouth, it now seems an appropriate time to ponder the implications of this new legal environment for future development of HBCUs.

Indeed, the caution used in the examination of the *Fordice* decision (Carter, 1992) by desegregation advocates in *Adams* states[1] (those states that settled under federal guidelines) seems well founded. States that settled with the federal government under *Adams* guidelines developed desegregation plans that included both an emphasis on desegregation of the state system and the continued development of historically black colleges, dual goals that made it possible to build alliances in the construction of state plans. However, in the post-*Fordice* legal environment, HBCU-development and system wide desegregation have taken a back seat to a new intent: removing the vestiges of de jure segregation to promote student choice. In the process of settling under this new criterion, the *Adams*-era consensus-building goals were virtually overlooked.

This chapter sets the stage for untangling some of the complex legal and policy issues confronting states and HBCUs, as they begin to contend with fundamental issues related to the continued development of HBCUs and system wide desegregation in this new legal environment. To untangle the complex legal and policy issues confronting HBCUs and those in policy positions who are concerned about the future of these vital institutions,[2] this chapter reviews the history of the major public policy and legal decisions leading to the current crisis. From this review, it is readily evident that (1) crisis conditions are not new for HBCUs; and (2) HBCUs simply have not received equal treatment under the law. Based on this historical perspective we then critically examine recent developments in the legal environment focusing on the ways the legal and policy discourses have been reframed as a result of recent court decisions.

An Historical Perspective

The evolution of the legal and policy context influencing the development of HBCUs and system wide desegregation is examined in the following section. At a time when a major change in the legal context has recently emerged, it is important to place this development in an historical perspective.

Separate, But Equal?

While there was some history of higher education for African Americans prior to the Civil War, there were no colleges founded for them. After the Civil War, however, the first wave of black college founding began in earnest. In a sense, the change that made formal education for African Americans possible was Abraham Lincoln's Emancipation Proclamation, issued during the Civil War. Motivated by the war, there was no advanced planning for education of African Americans. Rather, the war itself had to be settled in favor of the Union before the education of African Americans could surface as a political issue.

While at first glance it may seem strange to raise questions about education for African Americans at the time of the Emancipation Proclamation, when we ponder this issue in relation to other events at the time, it becomes an obvious question. While the nation was enmeshed in a Civil War, testing whether the Union would survive, its Congress was also debating the first major federal program for higher education, the *Land Grant Act of 1862*. Clearly parallel policy discourses were taking place. On the one hand, the Union engaged in a war with the rebellious southern states, a war that motivated the timing of the emancipation of the slaves. On the other, both houses of Congress were debating the creation of state institutions to promote the technical and economic development of the states. Yet the issue of education for the newly freed African Americans was not explicitly considered. Was it simply assumed that African Americans would have access? Or was the education of African Americans a nonissue?

After the Civil War, most southern colleges resisted following the pattern of development of colleges in the rest of the United States. Before the Civil War, the south was "isolated and dominated by slavery -- [it] was developing a uniquely regional way of life" (Stetar, 1989, p. 239). And after the Civil War, colleges in the south further resisted the development of a research emphasis and instead tacitly emphasized cultural solidarity (Stetar, 1989).

Further complicating the situation, many northern colleges resisted admitting African Americans and integrating dormitories in the late ninetheenth century (Wechsler, 1989). Indeed a debate emerged in the higher education and philanthropic communities about integration versus separation, a debate symbolized by the positions of DuBois and Washington. Unfortunately, before *Plessy v. Ferguson,* there was little opportunity for African Americans to attend public institutions, especially in the south. However, by the early twentieth century Harvard's Charles Eliot supported Booker T. Washington's philosophy of segregated black colleges over DuBois' talented tenth argument (Wagoner, 1989), symbolizing a near consensus around separation. But was there ever a chance for equality within a policy framework that promoted separation?

Providing higher education for African Americans did become a public policy issue after the Civil War. The post-Civil War period was a period of founding of HBCUs, but mostly by missionary groups from the north. A "racial uplift" argument emerged in the south, among freed slaves and northern missionaries:

> It was supposed axiomatically, in other words, that the former slaves would be active participants in the republic on an equal footing with all other citizens. Education, then, according to the more liberal and dominant segments of missionary philanthropists, was intended to prepare a college-bred leadership to uplift the black masses from the legacy of slavery and the restraints of the postbellum caste system. (Anderson, 1989, p. 656)

As late as 1926-27, three-fourths of the African Americans attending higher education attended private southern black colleges (Anderson, 1989), many of which had been founded by northern missionaries.

Later states in the south began to develop dual state systems of higher education with separate institutions for whites and African Americans. Frequently the new public black colleges were located near the older public colleges and universities, institutions that were exclusively for European Americans. This pattern of founding separate HBCUs proximate to public white institutions continued into the post-*Brown* period in the midsouth (i.e., Southern University of New Orleans and the University of New Orleans).

The *Land Grant Act of 1890* provided funds for HBCUs, as states began de jure systems, indicating federal support for policies that promoted separation even before *Plessy v. Ferguson.* But with the presence of missionary colleges, states were slow to invest in public institutions for African Americans (Anderson, 1989). Thus, from the very beginning a pattern emerged: (1) higher education for African Americans was not explicitly considered in the public policy process until after the issue of separation had been resolved; and (2) African Americans did not receive equal treatment in the construction of the new public policies.[3]

The Supreme Court's *Plessy v. Ferguson* decision in 1898 validated the legal framework of separation in higher education that had evolved in both northern and southern states. Even in former Union states (e.g., Ohio, Missouri, West Virginia, and Kentucky) separate systems of public higher education developed. In the deep south, there eventually was an attempt to build public colleges and universities for African Americans. By the middle 1930s nearly half of the African Americans enrolled in HBCUs were in public institutions (Anderson, 1989). However, some of the border states lacked the will to build duplicate systems and they soon became the battleground for the efforts to desegregate state systems.

Information on educational attainment by African Americans in the United States was not routinely collected during the first half of the twentieth century. However, available evidence suggests substantial inequities in enrollment opportunity existed and persisted through this period (Teddlie and Freeman, 1996). In fact, "equality of opportunity" had not yet emerged as a central issue for activists, as the focus was on providing opportunity. Ironically a larger percentage of African Americans attended college in some of the states with separate systems, than in states where African Americans were permitted to enroll in mainline institutions. In some parts of the country, African Americans had less opportunity in part because de facto segregation of public schools also created unequal preparation.[4] Thus, in spite of the inherent problems with separate but equal, there were reasons why some African Americans advocated for the separate systems. Available evidence (e.g., Darden, Bagakas, and Marajh, 1992; Darden and Hargett, 1981) can be interpreted to mean that African Americans were better off in states with a history of segregated systems because higher percentages of African Americans are enrolled in many of these states.[5]

Public policy during this period essentially maintained this system of unequal opportunity. Evidence from *Adams v. Richardson* and other cases indicates that states did not treat the two systems equally (Marcus, 1981; Stuart, 1974; Williams, 1988; Willie, 1979). Federal policy was also alarmingly quiet on the topic of inequity in education in the near century of separate but equal. Federal land grant funds continued to be distributed within this dual — and historically unequal (Anderson, 1989) — system through the present. Thus, the basic inequities in higher education policy persisted throughout the first half of the twentieth Century, a situation reinforced by the Supreme Court, as well as by state and federal policies on higher education.

Equal Opportunity Delayed

In the 1954 *Brown v. Board of Education*, the Supreme Court established a new precedent and standard for judging local and state systems of education. This decision, however, had more influence on the desegregation of public schools than on higher education (Teddlie and Freeman, 1996). It was not until the Supreme Court's *Adams v. Califano* decision in 1977 that the federal government had a mandate to pursue higher education desegregation (Williams, 1988). However, the goals of promoting equality opportunity emerged and began to take shape in higher education public policy more than a decade before *Adams.*

At the federal level, the *Higher Education Act of 1965* (HEA) created a structure for promoting equal opportunity. First, under Title IV, the HEA established a structure for federal student aid programs. The HEA not only reauthorized the federal National Direct Student Loan and College Work Study programs, but it also created the Guaranteed Student Loan (GSL) and Equal Opportunity Grant (EOG) programs. These programs provided funding for needy students to attend college. As funding for the federal grant program grew in the 1960s and 1970s, the number and percentage of minority students attending also increased (Teddlie and Freeman, 1996). These developments, coupled with the emergence of economic arguments that student aid had a more substantial return, as measured by equal opportunity to attend, than did subsidies to institutions (Hansen and Weisbrod, 1969; Committee on Economic Development, 1973), fostered further movement toward federal policies that promoted equal opportunity. In particular, the 1972 HEA reauthorization focused on the goals of equal opportunity (Gladieux and Wolanin, 1976).

The cornerstone of the 1972 legislation was the Basic Educational Opportunity Grant (now Pell) program. In part because institutions redirect funds from the Supplemental Educational Opportunity Grant program (the new name of the EOG program) to middle-income students (St. John and Byce,

1982), it became difficult to measure the effects of the Pell program. While well-designed studies have consistently found student aid influenced enrollment by low-income students (Jackson, 1978; Leslie and Brinkman, 1988; McPherson and Schapiro, 1991; Manski and Wise, 1983), there have been lingering doubts about the effectiveness of aid (Hansen, 1983; Hearn, 1993). This ambiguity helped create a window for some of the new critics of equal opportunity in the 1980s (e.g., Bennett, 1986, 1987; Finn, 1988).

Second, the HEA also created the federal developing institutions program under Title III. In the early 1960s, black college advocates called attention to the plight of HBCUs, describing them as out of the mainstream and advocating for an investment in their development. These arguments had a substantial influence on the authorization of Title III (Jacobs and Tingley, 1977). While the Title III program has changed substantially over time (St. John, 1981), it has continued to emphasize HBCU development throughout its history. Evaluations of Title III have been ambiguous. For example, one major study indicated that student aid (under Title IV) may be a more effective way of promoting enrollment by low-income students than the large institutional subsidies provided through Title III (Jackson, 1977; Weathersby, et al., 1977). Nevertheless, the Title III program has continued to have the political support it needed to be reauthorized every four or five years.

Thus, the federal government had a well established role in promoting equal opportunity and institutional development of HBCUs even before *Adams*. The *Adams* regulations have been described as follows:

> As a result of the *Adams v. Califano* decision, DHEW issued desegregation guidelines in July, 1977 and received court approval for them in February, 1978 (*Federal Register*, 1977). The Title VI guidelines identify four major elements that must be reflected in state higher education desegregation plans: (1) restructuring dual systems; (2) increasing Black enrollment at predominantly white institutions and increasing White enrollment at traditionally Black institutions; (3) increasing "other race" faculty, administrators, nonprofessional staff, and trustees; and (4) reporting and monitoring requirements.

In order to "disestablish the structure of the dual systems," the Office of Civil Rights' guidelines required in each state desegregation plan: (1) "definitions of the mission of each state college and university on a basis other than race"; (2) "specific steps to eliminate educationally unnecessary program duplication among traditionally black and traditionally white institutions in the same service arena"; (3) "steps. . . to strengthen the role of traditionally black institutions in the state system"; and (4) "prior consideration to placing . . . new . . . degree programs. . . at traditionally black institutions." The guidelines also suggest specific actions. These include reassigning duplicative instructional programs from one institution to another, mounting jointly conducted academic programs, adding new "high demand" programs at traditionally Black institutions, and merging institutions or branches of colleges and universities. (Williams, 1988, p. 9)

Through these regulations, the federal government develop-ed a process for remedying de jure segregation under the *Adams* decision. These guidelines established HBCU development and system wide desegregation as parallel goals. Two goals were embedded in the new regulations: desegregation of state systems and institutional development of HBCUs. These new goals closely paralleled the established federal roles of promoting equal opportunity with student aid (HEA Title IV) and promoting HBCU development with direct subsidies (HEA Title III).

However, during the early 1980s, new critics began to argue that the dual goals of HBCU development and desegregation could be contradictory goals, that promoting HBCU development could inhibit their desegregation (Ayers, 1982; Baxter, 1982). These arguments, along with the claims that the current system of higher education in Mississippi was promoting student choice, seem to have influenced the Circuit Court in the original *Ayers* decision. While the subsequent Supreme Court *Fordice* decision overturned some aspects of the *Ayers* decision, it upheld the use of student choice as a criterion in judging desegregation plans.

The Post-Fordice Environment

The Supreme Court's *Fordice* decision rejected the Circuit Court decision that the state system of higher education in Mississippi was desegregated because both African American and

European American students have the freedom to choose to attend either HBCUs or traditionally white institutions, instead holding them to the standard of remedying vestiges of de jure segregation. However, given that the Supreme Court upheld other aspects of *Ayers*, the federal standards established under *Adams* were no longer the criteria used to guide the selection of remedies. To construct a workable legal meaning of this new framework, we need to look at the decisions in the three states that have been settled since *Fordice*.

First, in Louisiana, the litigants in *United States v. Louisiana* settled out of court. The agreement included: new community college in Baton Rouge, administered jointly by Louisiana State University and Southern University; funding for major new programs at the HBCUs; race-based scholarships to promote other-race enrollment in both HBCUs and PWIs (predominantly white institutions); and an emphasis on other-race recruitment. The factor that seems to have influenced a settlement in Louisiana was that the court appeared to be supportive of creating a single governing board, a position that was resisted by historically black colleges (Spikes and Meza, 1996). The compromise also stops short of creating a state-wide system of community colleges, thus down-playing the system wide desegregation goal (because the community college system would have promoted access across the state).

In Louisiana, institutional interests clearly won out in the political struggle over the goal of system-wide desegregation. The judge's proposal for a state community college system, which had been circulating prior to the settlement was eliminated in the Louisiana litigation settlement agreement. The prospect of a statewide board over both the Louisiana State University and Southern systems, another component of the proposal circulated by the judge, was rejected by the HBCUs. Rather than advocating a separate and autonomous state community college system with a mandate for promoting access, a single community college in Baton Rouge, jointly controlled by the LSU and Southern systems, was created as part of the political compromise. The broader question of access across the state went unaddressed.

Second, the new *Ayers* decision in Mississippi included: funds for new programs at HBCUs, new admissions standards at HBCUs, and race-based scholarships. The access arguments made by the plaintiffs (e.g., Blake, 1991) seem to have been ignored by the court in the final decision. While there are concerns that the decision threatens the future of HBCUs in the state (Brown and Hendrickson, 1997), the case was not appealed by the litigants. The prospect of merger or closure of HBCUs was a pervasive issue in this case (Teddlie and Freeman, 1996), a factor that could have deterred further appeals.

Third, in Alabama, the *Knight* decision included both an endowment fund to support new program development in the HBCUs, and funds for other-race scholarships in HBCUs. These were among the remedies to the mission issue (i.e., removing the vestiges of de jure segregation in the missions), which was decided in favor of the plaintiffs. This case was also not appealed. The prospect of merger was also a central issue in this case, as litigants on both sides wanted to maintain the identity of their institutions.

The *Knight* decision clearly gave the HBCUs some freedom in the way they constructed their new academic programs. However, the decision stopped substantially short of meeting the aspirations of HBCU advocates who had proposed graduate programs and other major new developments. The endowment created by the court provided seed funds for new program development, but no clear mandate to move to the doctoral degree granting status that had been sought. Therefore *Knight* was a mixed success for HBCUs. Further, the issue of system-wide access, settled under the 1991 decision, had not been appealed and was not reviewed in this most recent decision.

These decisions have some commonalities. First, all of them focused on program development in HBCUs *as a means of promoting desegregation.* This represents a shift from the implicit equal treatment of the two goals in the *Adams* guidelines (e.g., Williams, 1988). The HBCU-development and system-wide desegregation goals have been sublimated to the goal of desegregating HBCUs, especially in Alabama and Mississippi. Second, in all three states the traditionally white institutions were considered desegregated, to have overcome the vestiges of de jure segregation. Third, all three decisions made use of other-race student aid in spite of the fact that race specific aid has not been upheld in other federal court decisions (Janschik, 1994a, 1994b). And the recent *Hopwood v. Texas* decision (1996) casts doubt on whether race-based scholarships are legal. In sum, in the post-*Fordice* environment a new standard seems to be emerging, one that places a greater emphasis on factors that appear to influence student choice (i.e., student aid) and less emphasis on access (a method of promoting system wide desegregation) and HBCU development for their own sake.

Interestingly, the U.S. Department of Education recently handed back a plan by the Ohio Board of Regents to continue its desegregation efforts. The grounds for rejecting the proposal included a lack of emphasis on HBCU development, as indicated in published quotes by ED officials:

> "The draft proposals that we reviewed do not include any specific commitments to make positive change at Central State [Ohio's HBCU]," Mr. Pierce wrote. In an interview, he was even more forceful: "It's obvious to me that there's been no real attention paid to that university by the Board of Regents." (Healy, 1996, p. A22)

Given the recent round of federal court decisions, it is questionable whether the U.S. Department of Education's position on HBCU-development would prevail if it were litigated under the new legal standards. To understand this issue, we need to examine how the new federal court decisions in the midsouth have essentially reframed the legal debate about desegregation.

Reframing Desegregation

The post-*Fordice* legal and policy environment seems to have a different set of embedded assumptions than the environment in which the *Adams* decisions[6] were made and implemented. Further, these new values seem driven by a different standard of evidence about cause and effect than had been used in the *Adams* guidelines. The implications of these developments are more easily understood if they are viewed in a context of other changes in theory and research on higher education policy. Below we examine two ways of framing desegregation policy, the pre- and post-*Fordice* frames, before suggesting an alternative approach.

The Pre-Fordice Frame

In the 1970s when the *Adams* decisions were rendered, there was a broad liberal consensus about higher education policy in the United States (St. John, 1994; Slaughter, 1991). Most higher education officials who made arguments before Congress used human capital arguments to justify their appeal for new programs and funding (Slaughter, 1991). And the assumption that there were both individual and social returns from the public investment in higher education, an integral concept in human capital theory (Becker, 1975), was commonly accepted by both conservatives and liberals (St. John, 1994). At the time, arguments between the two political perspectives pertained to the extent to which returns accrued to individuals and society, and the extent to which individual investments should be subsidized.

In retrospect, federal higher education policy in the 1980s was based loosely on the human capital construct. In particular the emphasis on equal opportunity in the HEA Title IV programs was based on human capital arguments and research (Gladieux and Wolanin, 1976). And research on the effects of student aid conducted in the early 1970s consistently supported the claim that prices had an influence on the opportunity to attend college (Jackson, 1977, 1978; Manski and Wise, 1983). Further, early studies that attempted to assess the relative effects of institutional subsidies (which suppress tuition) and student aid (which subsidize the direct costs of students with financial need) consistently concluded that student aid was a more cost-efficient approach to public finance (National Commission on the Financing of Postsecondary Education, 1973; Jackson, 1977; Weathersby et al., 1977). However, these econometric studies had limited influence on state finance policies.

Interestingly, public support for institutions did not waver substantially in the 1970s, in spite of claims by economists that student aid was more effective. State support for public higher education remained steady, except in periods of tax revenue shortfalls (Hines, 1993; St. John, 1994). And at the federal level, the HEA Title III program continued to enjoy steady Congressional support. In fact, when eligibility for some colleges began to run out, an advanced program was created to ensure their long-term funding(St. John, 1981).

Thus, there was an old set of generally accepted beliefs that seemed to guide public policy in higher education through the 1970s. There was a dual emphasis on both student aid and institutional aid. Liberals tended to use growth of the gross domestic product as a general indicator of return on public investment, but argued against using any more precise measures, such as the rate of tax revenue return (e.g., Kramer, 1993). Similarly, the *Adams* decision seemed to carry forward this general logic, assuming public support for HBCU development to be integral to desegregation.

The Post-Fordice Frame

The new legal and policy context for higher education places a greater emphasis on the linkage between remedy strategies and student outcomes, a pattern evident in the *Ayers* and *Knight* decisions. These decisions are parallel to the breakdown in the old consensus about higher education policy. In federal policy, new conservative arguments about waste and excess now have more influence on state and federal funding than do new liberal arguments constructed to defend these programs (St. John, 1994). In this environment there seems to be an emphasis on assessment and other forms of empirical evidence (Pascarella and Terenzini, 1991). In the post-*Fordice* era, the old beliefs about the weak linkage between strategy and outcome are breaking down under a new standard of evidence. Liberals are now confronted with a need to prove their heralded strategies (i.e., HBCU development) resulted in specified outcomes (i.e., desegregation). This new standard of evidence changed the nature of the policy discourse.

This emphasis on measurable outcomes and ideologically driven interpretations is quite evident in the most recent round of court decisions about higher education desegregation. On the one hand, the courts seem driven by a numeric approach to desegregation, i.e., the link between potential remedies and desegregation in HBCUs. On the other, the courts have shifted their emphasis on access (and the desegregation of historically white campuses of state systems) to the desegregation of HBCUs. These shifts also appear to have been influenced by the new conservative arguments. This new lens is inherently critical of liberal claims and uses evidence to build arguments to support new conservative claims. This prescriptive was evident in the *Hopwood* case (Janscik, 1994b), as it has been in recent desegregation cases.

A central issue in the new federal court decisions about higher education is the explicit linkage between HBCU development and numeric desegregation in HBCUs. In other words, rather than value HBCU development because of its promise to overcome past inequities (the pre-*Fordice* perspective), the courts are not treating HBCU development as a means of desegregation. Patterns of desegregation of HBCUs in *Adams* states (i.e., the numbers of European Americans enrolled in HBCUs in these states) became the major source of evidence considered by the courts, especially in Alabama and Mississippi. In this context, the courts were essentially considering which HBCU-development strategies had previously resulted in numeric desegregation in HBCUs. This attitude differs fundamentally from the U.S. Department of Education's position (i.e., their rejection of Ohio's plan because it did not sufficiently promote HBCU development [Healy 1996]).

These new conditions are troubling, especially for those of us who still value desegregation in public education. In the pre-*Fordice* environment, desegregation policy, like other areas of higher education public policy, seemed to ignore evidence about effects in favor of generally-held liberal, progressive assumptions. In the post-*Fordice* environment, in contrast, desegregation policy seems more oriented toward empirical evidence, but seems to have an inherent interpretive bias. Those who advocate the development of HBCUs and the desegregation of state systems are faced with a choice of either adhering to old liberal claims which tend to be difficult to support empirically in the courtroom,[7] or building a better evidentiary case.

A Concluding Reflection

As we take a step back and reflect critically on the shifting ground of desegregation policy in higher education, three issues stand out as the dust settles on the post-*Fordice* legal environment. First, the focus of the desegregation litigation has shifted to desegregation of HBCUs. This is a perplexing development. On the one hand, I continue to think that desegregation is an important goal in all social institutions and communities. On the other hand, I think there is still an important mission of service for HBCUs. Therefore, from my point of view at least, caution is needed in the rush to meet this new desegregation policy goal in HBCUs. Yet, while I cannot advocate that this new social goal should be resisted by HBCU advocates, I concur with those interested in enhancing the mission of the HBCUs about the need to engage in the new policy discourse. Indeed, the development of HBCUs, especially development that preserves and enhances their historic mission, should be on center stage in the post-*Fordice* policy discourse.

Second, the issue of system-wide desegregation in higher education has almost fallen off the table in the post-*Fordice* policy discourse. This is troubling indeed. If the past few decades of oscillation in minority enrollment reveal anything at all, it should be that the issue of equal opportunity is not yet settled. Indeed, the mere fact that in the 1980s the neoconservative argued (a) that student aid did not make a difference and (b) cut federal student aid, causing (c) declines in minority participation rates (St. John, 1994), illustrates that system-wide desegregation is still an important policy issue.

Third, HBCU development has also diminished as an explicit goal in desegregation litigation. This means that the advocates of HBCUs face an increasingly uphill battle. These advocates must contend with is the fact that federal courts have explicitly linked HBCU development with desegregation. Remedies aimed at promoting development of HBCUs were assessed based on the extent to which they promoted desegregation. This would not be as troubling as it now seems if system-wide desegregation had not fallen off the table in the desegregation policy discourse. The fact is that historically white institutions do not have to rationalize their development plans based on their potential effects on desegregation. If equal opportunity had been a goal of public policy during the past 100 years, then HBCU development would not be an important issue, indeed most HBCUs probably would not have been created in the first place.

In conclusion, this historical analysis of the emergence of the post-*Fordice* legal environment suggests that advocates of HBCU development and of system-wide desegregation need to adopt more critical-empirical approaches. On the one hand, analytic studies conducted by advocates of these goals need to recognize the critical nature of the current period of social policy in the United States. Indeed, more explicit recognition of the plight of HBCUs and of the declining of state and federal support for system wide desegregation is needed. On the other hand, analytic studies on both sides of these issues need to build a well-reasoned empirical case if they are to carry weight in this new policy environment. The fact that the federal courts are making use of empirical studies and reasoning may open a new doorway for reform-minded higher education policy analysts and reform advocates who are concerned about the future of HBCUs.

There should be little doubt from the history of separation that the creation of HBCUs was an artifact of resistance by Americans of European heritage to the integration of freed slaves into the historically white American system of education (Anderson, 1989;

Johnson, 1996). American higher education has reentered a period of resistance to the new social mandate to equalize opportunity, as evidenced by the *Hopwood* decision (1996) and the recent vote on affirmative action by the citizens of California. In this troubling context, it would be short-sighted to loose sight altogether of the aims of system wide desegregation and HBCU development.

Notes

1. In this text, the general term *Adams* refers to the sequence of Supreme Court decisions that defined the federal role in desegregation (i.e., *Adams v. Califano, Adams v. Richardson, and Adams v. Weinberger.*

2. We use this term "vital" because we agree with those who argue that HBCUs have a crucial role to play in higher education (e.g., Allen, 1991; Fleming, 1984).

3. My thesis is that there was an obvious inequity between slaves and slave owners at the time, an inequity that has never been fully and adequately addressed as part of public policy deliberations on higher education.

5. De facto segregation has never been litigated in higher education. However, the resegregative effects of new conservative state and federal finance policies may provide a basis for such litigation (St. John, 1997).

6. This is not my position. I still think that goals of equity and desegregation have merit, but my bias may keep me from seeing what is really happening. The position one takes on separate but equal during this prior period would in some way be linked to the position taken on current issues. Given the extent to which the future of historically black colleges is being threatened by the new wave of desegregation decisions, those of us who hold old liberal beliefs need to continue to examine our beliefs (e.g., Hossler, 1997; St. John, 1997).

7. There was a series of *Adams* decisions (i.e., *Adams v. Califano* [1977], *Adams v. Richardson* [1973], and *Adams v. Weinberger* [975]).

8. We are not arguing that there is not evidence of segregation. Quite the contrary, the courts have ruled there was de jure segregation. However, the old attitude about the supposed effects of remedies was not seriously considered by the courts. In other

words, the courts, especially in *Knight*, essentially assessed whether the addition of new programs at HBCUs would increase European American enrollment.

References

Allen, W. R. (1991). Introduction. In W. R. Allen, E. G. Epps, and N. Z. Haniff (Eds.) *College in black and white: African American students in predominantly white and in historically black public universities* (pp. 1-14). Albany, NY: State University of New York Press.

Anderson, J. D. (1989). Training the apostles of liberal culture: Black higher education, 1900-1935. In L.C. Goodchild and H.S. Wechsler (Eds.) *ASHE Reader on the History of Higher Education* (pp. 47-79). Needham, MA: Ginn Press. (Reprinted from: J.D. Anderson, *The Education of Blacks in the South, 1860-1935*).

Ayers, Q. W. (1982). Desegregation or debilitating higher education. *Public Interest, 69(Fall)*, 100-116.

Barnes, E. (1993). Higher education gains for African Americans erode following dismissal of *Adams*, observers say. *Black Issues in Higher Education,* 10(3), 14-19 & 32.

Baxter, F. V. (1982). The affirmative action to desegregated institutions of higher education: Defining the role of the traditionally black college. *Journal of Law and Education, 11(1)*, 1-40.

Becker, G. S. (1975). *Human capital: A theoretical and empirical analysis, with special reference to education.* Second Edition. New York: National Bureau of Economic Research.

Bennett, W. F. (26 November 1986). Text of Secretary Bennett's speech on college costs and U.S. student aid. *Chronicle of Higher Education*, p. A20.

Bennett, W. F. (18 February 1987). Our greedy colleges. *New York Times*.

Blake, E. (1991). Is higher education desegregation a remedy for segregation but not educational inequality?: A study of the *Ayers v. Mabus* desegregation case. *Journal of Negro Education,* 60(4), 538-65.

Brown, M. C., and Hendrickson, R. M. (1997). Public historically black colleges at the crossroads: The *United States v.Fordice* and higher education desegregation. *Journal for a Just and Caring Education*, 3(1).

Carter, D. (1992). Former *Adams* states take cautious attitude toward *Fordice* decision. *Black Issues in Higher Education*, 17(9), 16-19.

Committee on Economic Development. (1973). *The management and financing of colleges*. New York: Committee on Economic Development.

Darden, J. T., Bagakas, J. G., and Marajh, O. (1992). Historically black colleges and the dilemma of desegregation. *Equity & Excellence*, 25(2-4), 106-112.

Darden, J. T. and Hargett, S. (1981). Historically black colleges and the dilemma of desegregation. *Integrated Education*, 19(3-6), 48-53.

Finn, C. E. (1988). Judgement time for higher education: In the court of public opinion. *Change*, (July/August), 35-38.

Fleming, J. (1984). *Blacks in college: A comparative study of students' success in black and white institutions.* San Francisco: Jossey-Bass.

Gladieux, L. E. and Wolanin, T. R. (1976). *Congress and the colleges*. Lexington, MA: Heath.

Hansen, W. L. (1983). Impact of student financial aid on access. In J. Froomkin (ed.) *The crisis in higher education* (pp. 84-96). New York: Academy of Political Science.

Hansen, W. L. and Weisbrod, B. A. (1969). *Benefits, costs, and finance of public higher education*. Chicago: Markham.

Healy, P. (1996, June 29). Ohio told to provide details on plan to improve Central State. *Chronicle of Higher Education*, p. A22.

Hearn, J. C. (1993). The paradox of growth in federal aid for college students: 1965-1990. In J. C. Smart (Ed.), *Higher Education: Handbook of Theory and Research*, vol. 9. New York: Agathon.

Hearn, J. C. and Anderson, M. S. (1989). Integrating postsecondary education financing policies: The Minnesota model. In R.H. Fenske (Ed.), *New directions for institutional research, No. 62, Studying the impact of student aid on institutions*. San Fransisco: Jossey Bass.

Hines, E. R. (1993). *State Higher Education Appropriations 1992-93*. Denver, CO: SHEEO.

Hossler, D. (1997). Historically black public colleges and universities: Scholarly inquiry and personal reflections. *Journal for a Just and Caring Education*, 3(1).

Jackson, G. A. (1977). *Financial Aid and Student Enrollment.* Prepared for the U.S. Office of Education. Cambridge, MA: Harvard Graduate School of Education.

Jackson, G. A. (1978). Financial aid and student enrollment. *Journal of Higher Education*, 49(6), 15-27.

Jackson, G.A. (1982). Public efficiency and private choice in higher education. *Educational Evaluation and Policy Analysis, 4*(2), 237-247.

Jacobs, F. and Tingley, T. (1977). *The Evolution of Eligibility Criteria for Title III of the Higher Education Act of 1965.* Prepared for the U.S. Office of Education. Cambridge, MA: Harvard Graduate School of Education.

Janschik, S. (1994a). Minority scholarships in a new light: Colleges study programs after federal court's ruling on the U. of Maryland's, *The Chronicle of Higher Education*, November 9, 1994, p. 130-131.

Janschik, S. (1994b). Student who sued over black scholarships keeps low profile, *The Chronicle of Higher Education*, November 9, 1994, p. A30.

Johnson, E. L. (1989). Misconceptions about the early land grant colleges. In L.F. Goodchild and H.S. Wechsler (Eds.) *ASHE Reader on the history of higher education* (pp. 211-225). Needham, MA: Ginn Press. (From *Journal of Higher Education*, 1981, 52(4)).

Johnson, J. R. (1996). *Leland University in New Orleans 1870-1915*, Ph.D.Dissertation, unpublished. University of New Orleans: New Orleans, LA.

Kramer, M. (1993). Changing roles in higher education finance. In *Background Papers and Reports.* Washington, D.C.: National Commission on Financial Responsibilities for Postsecondary Education.

Leslie, L. L. and Brinkman, P. T. (1988). *The economic value of higher education.* New York: ACE/Macmillan.

McPherson, M. S. and Schapiro, M. O. (1991) *Keeping college affordable.* Washington, D.C.: Brookings.

Manski, C. F. and Wise, D. A. (1983). *College choice in America.* Cambridge, MA: Harvard University Press. Marcus. L. R. (1981). The Adams case: A hollow victory? Peabody Journal of Education, 59(1), 37-42.

National Commission of the Financing of Postsecondary Education.(1973). *Financing postsecondary education in the*

United States. Washington, D.C.: Government Printing Office.

Pascarella, E. T. and Terenzini, P. T. (1991). *How college affects students.* San Francisco: Jossey-Bass.

Paulsen, M. B. (1990). *College choice: Understanding student enrollment behavior.* ASHE-ERIC Higher Education Report No. 6. Washington, D.C.: The George Washington University, School of Education and Human Development.

St. John, E. P. (1981). *Public policy on college management: Title III of the HEA.* New York: Praeger.

St. John, E. P. (1994). *Prices, productivity, and investment: Assessing financial strategies in higher education.* ASHE-ERIC. Higher Education Study No. 3b. Washington, D. C.: George Washington University Press.

St. John, E. P. (1997). Desegregation at a crossroads: Critical reflection on possible new directions. *Journal for a Just and Caring Education, 3*(1), 114-126.

St. John, E. P. and Byce, C. (1982). The changing federal role in student financial aid. In M. Kramer (ed.) *Meeting Student Aid Needs in a Period of Retrenchment.* New Directions for Higher Education.

Sawyer, R. M. (1987). The Gaines Case : The Human Side. *The Negro Education Review*, 38(1), 4-14.

Slaughter, S. (1991). The official 'ideology' of higher education: Ironies and inconsistencies. In Tierney, W.G. (Ed.) *Culture and ideology in higher education.* New York: Praeger.

Spikes, D. R. and Meza, J. (1996). The impact of the Brown decision on the Southern University System. In C. Teddlie and K. Lomotey, *Readings on equal education, Volume 13, Forty years after the Brown decision: implications of school desegregation for for U.S. education* (pp. 183-200). New York: AMS Press.

Stetar, J. M. (1989). In search of a direction: Southern higher education after the Civil War. In *ASHE Reader on the history of higher education* (pp. 237-312). Needham, MA: Ginn Press. (From *Higher Education Quarterly*, 29 (Fall,1985), 285-312.)

Stuart, R. (1974). We didn't have an approach before. *Compact*, 8(5), 2-4.

Teddlie, C. and Freeman, S. C. (1996). With all deliberate speed: An historical overview of the relationship between the *Brown* decision and higher education. In C. Teddlie and K. Lomotey, *Readings on equal education, Volume 13, Forty years after the Brown decision: implications of school desegregation for for U.S. education* (pp. 7-51). New York: AMS Press.

Wagoner, J.L. (1989) The American compromise: Charles Eliot, Black education, and the new south. In L.C. Goodchild and H.S. Wechsler (Eds.) *ASHE Reader on the history of higher education* (pp. 444-454). Needham, MA: Ginn Press. (From *Education and the Rise of the New South*. R.K. Goodenow and A.O. White, and G.K. Hall (Eds.), 1981, 26-46.)

Weathersby, G. B., Jackson, G. A., Jacobs, F., St. John, E.P. and Tingley, T. (1977). The development of institutions of higher education: Theory and assessment of four possible areas of federal intervention. In M. Gutentage (Ed.) *Evaluation Studies Review Annual*. Beverly Hills, CA: Sage.

Wechsler, H. S. (1989) An academic Grisham's law: Group repulsion as a theme in American higher education. In L.F.Goodchild and H.S. Wechsler (Eds.) *ASHE Reader on the history of higher education* (pp. 389-400). Needham, MA: Ginn Press (From *Teachers College Record*. 1981 (Summer), 567-588).

Wharton, J. H. (1995) Testimony. *Knight v. Alabama*. March 14, (CV-83-M-1676-5).

Williams, J. B. (1988). Title VI regulation of higher education. In J. B. Williams (Eds.) *Desegregating America's colleges and universities: Title VI regulation of higher education*. NY: Teachers' College Press.

Williams, J.B. (1991). System wide title VI regulations of higher education, 1968-88: Implications for minority participation. In C.V. Willie and A.M. Garibaldi. *The education of African Americans* (pp. 110-122). Boston: William Monroe Trotter Institute, University of Massachusetts, Boston,

Williams, J.B., Convener, System wide Desegregation Research collaborative, (1997). System wide desegregation of public higher education. *Journal for a Just and Caring Education..* *3*(1).

Willie, C. V. (1979). Black colleges redefined. *Change, 11*(7), 46-49.

Willie, C. V. (1994). Black colleges are not just for blacks anymore. *The Journal of Negro Education, 63*(2), 153-64.

Table of Legal Cases

Adams v. Califano, 430 F. Supp. 118 (D.D.C. 1977).

Adams v.Richardson, 356 F. Supp. 92 (D.D.C. 1973).

Adams v. Weinberger, 391 F. Supp. 296 (D.D.C. 1975).

Ayers v. Allian, 914 F ed 676 (CA 5 1990).

Ayers v. Fordice. 79 F. Supp. 1419 (1995).

Brown v. The Board of Education of Topeka, Kansas. 347 U.S. 483, (1954).

Knight v. Alabama. 900 F. Supp. 272 (1995).

Knight v. Alabama. CV 8-M1676-s, (Filed August, 1995).

Missouri ex rel Gaines v. Canada. 305 U.S. 377 (1938).

Plessy v. Ferguson, 163 U.S. 537 (1986)

United States v. Fordice. 112 S. Ct. 2727 (1992).

United States v. Louisiana. 718 F. Supp. 499,514 (ED La. 1989).

CHAPTER 9

HIGHER EDUCATION DESEGREGATION IN THE POST-*FORDICE* LEGAL ENVIRONMENT: A CRITICAL-EMPIRICAL PERSPECTIVE

Edward P. St. John and Don Hossler

It is essential that advocates for system-wide desegregation and HBCU development move toward a critical and empirically based approach. By "critical" we mean that this new policy discourse needs to be approached with an awareness of the role ideology historically played — and indeed continues to play in an albeit different context — in the public policy and litigation processes. By "empirical" we mean there is a need to use evidence from analytic studies to test the claims made from the various ideological points of view. There are, however, a couple of important caveats that need to be considered.

First, a distinction (St. John, Chapter 8, this volume) has been made between HBCU development and system-wide desegregation. When we begin to use an empirical approach to assess alternative strategies, it soon becomes apparent that some remedies may promote system-wide desegregation, or HBCU development, but not both. It is possible that some remedies that promote system-wide desegregation could actually harm HBCU development, and vice versa. Consider the prospect that raising admission criteria in HBCUs in Mississippi — a position advocated by justice experts (e.g., Conrad, 1994b; Conrad and Leslie, 1994) — might decrease access for some students while encouraging numeric desegregation. This illustrates that the new standards of evidence complicate the policy discourse. In the pre-*Fordice* environment, the dual emphasis on system-wide desegregation and HBCU development, coupled with a lack of emphasis on directly measurable outcomes, made it relatively easy to hold together a coalition in support of change, a broad array of plaintiffs that included HBCUs and the Justice Department. In the new environment, given the need for more empirically driven reasoning, these coalitions may be more difficult to hold together.

Second, adopting a critical-empirical approach means critically examining assumptions about what types of strategies are likely to influence desegregation in both HBCUs and historically white campuses. Perhaps the best way to contend with the new ideologies is to treat ideology as a set of claims that merits scrutiny (St. John, 1994; St. John and Elliott, 1994). When we subject claims from *both* leftist and rightist ideologies to empirical scrutiny, we sometimes find new solutions. For example, a recent study of voucher strategies for the Arizona Joint Legislative Budget Committee found that all of the proposals being floated by the new conservatives would have been too costly. An alternative approach was constructed, however, that enabled advocates of private colleges to build a coalition with two-year colleges in support of a new target-grant program with a high probability of success (St. John and Asker, 1997). This example illustrates the need to subject ideological claims about the effects of remedies to critical, empirical scrutiny.

In this chapter we propose a critical-empirical framework for dealing with crucial policy issues: HBCU development and systemwide desegregation. First, we suggest the framework, then we use the framework to examine these two important issues which have become less central to the post-*Fordice* policy discourse. Finally, we reflect briefly on the potential uses of this framework.

A Critical-Empirical Framework

In this section we present a framework we developed for assessing the effects of alternative desegregation remedies on student choice (St. John and Hossler, 1995a). We developed this framework as expert witnesses for the University of Alabama in *Knight v. Alabama.* We attempted to develop a framework that linked consideration of issues of concern to African Americans, such as access to higher education and expanded opportunity to graduate and professional education, with the narrower set of issues related to college choice by European American students. Given that this broader definition of student choice was accepted by Judge Murphy in the *Knight* case, it can potentially be used to further the discourse. However, since our research on the case (Hossler, et al., 1995; St. John and Hossler, 1995b) focused on desegregation of historically black colleges, we did not have the opportunity to address adequately issues related to system-wide desegregation.[1] Nevertheless, we think the framework can and should be expanded to address these dual concerns. Below we take a step in that direction in this chapter.

A Framework For Assessing Desegregation Remedies
The assessment of possible remedies to the segregated system of higher education represented a complex and potentially perplexing problem. After being introduced to the specific issues in the case, it became apparent to us that
- Student choice had become a central issue in the case, since the courts have increasingly focused on student choice since the *Fordice* decision.
- Multiple definitions of student choice were being used by the various experts in the case.
- The definitions of student choice being used by the various experts in the case seemed related to the ideologies of the experts and their clients.[2]
- A comprehensive and workable definition of student choice had not been previously developed by any of the experts.
- The remedies proposed by many experts seemed unrelated to college-choice processes as developed in the mainstream literature on student choice.[3]

Given these complexities, we decided it was necessary to start our efforts with a comprehensive and critical review of the literature on student choice. The review developed a perspective, or framework, that could be used to assess the range of possible remedies proposed by various experts in *Knight v. Alabama* (St.

John and Hossler, 1995a). The framework had four important features:

- First, we developed a comprehensive definition of student choice, starting with the formation of aspirations to attend postsecondary education, through choices to enroll in and persist in graduate education. A comprehensive definition of student choice[4] was necessary to develop a process that could be used to assess possible remedies.
- Second, we considered the applicability of three theoretical perspectives (sociological attainment, economic human capital theory, and higher education "student choice" theory) to construct a logical basis for assessing remedies.[5]
- Third, we considered research and opinions expressed in both the mainstream literature and in the African American literature. These provided us with an opportunity to consider more seriously and purposefully the perspective in both literatures than would have been possible had not this effort been made.
- Fourth, based on this work, we considered the possible linkages between desegregation remedies and student-choice processes. This final step provided a basis for identifying linkages between remedies and student-choice outcomes, although we were not given the opportunity to propose remedies to the court.

Based on this comprehensive and critical review of the literature on "student-choice processes,"[6] we developed a preliminary set of propositions about how possible remedies would influence the student-choice processes, which are identified in Table 1 (p. 130), along with our conclusions from the second study. Our initial propositions focused broadly on issues related to systemwide desegregation. We considered issues related to access as well as college choice, and enrollment by African Americans in historically white institutions, as well as by European Americans in HBCUs.[7]

Studies of HBCUs

The second phase of this project involved conducting a set of three studies that enabled us to make judgments about the "validity" of these propositions — i.e., whether they held when available empirical evidence was examined. However, given that our mandate was to examine desegregation in HBCUs, our research focused primarily on European American enrollment in HBCUs. Specifically, we examined whether there was evidence that our propositions were true and whether these propositions could be used to assess a range of possible remedies.

Toward these ends we conducted a set of studies that examined specific hypotheses pertaining to the desegregation of historically black colleges and universities (Hossler, et al., 1995). First, we examined current practices at a set of HBCUs with high percentages of European American enrollment and a set of HBCUs with low percentages of European American enrollment. This study supported most of our propositions, but we could not critically examine all of the propositions using this method. Second, we analyzed data collected on European American high school students in Huntsville and European American college students enrolled at the University of Alabama - Huntsville. These analyses provided further information used to assess the validity of our propositions (and this research supported several of those pertaining to European American enrollment in HBCUs[8]). The findings from this phase of the studies (Hossler, et al., 1995) are summarized below.

First, from our survey work, we found that most of the European American students living in and near Huntsville, Alabama were not considering attending Alabama A&M University. The small number who were considering A&M were doing so because they perceived it to be a more academically supportive environment. Students who were considering A&M were more likely to have attended racially diverse high schools and they were more likely to have lower grades. We also found that a large percentage of the students who did not plan to attend A&M reported that they would consider attending if the university were to offer special scholarships to attract them.

Second, from our case-study work, we found that competition from local predominantly white institutions (PWIs) appeared to have a small impact on the ability of an HBCU to attract other-race students. This finding, which surprised us, was evident when we compared the HBCUs with high and low percentages of white enrollment.

Third, from our case-study work, we also found that nearly all of the other-race students who were enrolled in HBCUs were part-time students. On many of the campuses, the other-race students were in graduate programs and typically came to the campuses in the evenings. The most popular programs of study were applied career-oriented majors such as business, education, criminal justice, social work, nursing, and counseling. This led us to conclude that enrollment-management approaches and program-delivery mechanisms may be among the most important factors in the ability of an HBCU to attract other-race students.

Fourth, we found that HBCUs located in states with higher proportions of African American citizens tend to have lower other-race enrollments than institutions in states with smaller proportions of African American citizens. This led us to speculate that those public HBCUs with more other-race students enrolled may have done so out of necessity, in order to sustain adequate enrollment levels. It also led us to hypothesize that some HBCUs, Mississippi Valley State University, for example, which is in a part of the state heavily populated by African Americans, may never be able to attract large numbers of other-race students. On the other hand, HBCUs located in metropolitan areas can probably more easily increase their proportion of other-race students.

Fifth, we found that most of the HBCUs with more other-race students had used, or were currently using, financial aid programs not unlike the programs that PWIs have used to attract more African American students. Similar findings were also reported by other experts.

Sixth, not surprisingly, we found that the faculty, administration, and students on some campuses actively opposed efforts to desegregate. Some presidents found themselves in extremely difficult situations in which they were being held accountable by the courts if they did not desegregate, but were also under tremendous pressure from all constituent groups, including alumni and trustees, not to desegregate.

Seventh, although we had limited data on this issue, it appears that even when other-race enrollments exceed 20%, integration might be best described as numerical integration and not real integration. Interviewees on most campuses said that there were few or no other-race students who live in the residence halls and that few other-race students participate in student activities, student government, athletics, Greek life, etc. One administrator described his campus as black by day and white by night, referring to the white part-time students who come to campus only in the evenings.

Perhaps the most compelling and vexing of our findings — and the most disquieting parts of our research — were the insights gained from conversations with administrators on campuses with higher other-race enrollments. At Lincoln University in Missouri, interviews were conducted with several senior administrators and faculty, many of whom were graduates of Lincoln. Prior to desegregation, Lincoln had often been referred to as the "Black Harvard of the Midwest." Within fifteen years after desegregation, however, their top faculty had either retired or were hired away by predominantly white institutions. Many of their best students were also recruited by predominantly white institutions. Campus admissions standards are now rated as noncompetitive in admissions guidebooks.

Over the last twenty-five years, Lincoln has actively recruited other-race students. European American students now comprise 57% of Lincoln's enrollments, but almost all of these students are part-time and entirely nonresidential. Even though the campus actually enrolls more African American students than it ever did when it was segregated, many African Americans no longer view Lincoln as an HBCU despite the fact that the residence halls, the athletic programs, student government, and Greek life programs are exclusively the domain of African American students.

One president, who had served in this position at two different historically black universities, talked openly about how strongly he had been criticized by constituent groups for his efforts to integrate. At one institution, students and faculty publicly criticized him. At the other, he had been verbally abused at a meeting of the alumni, and in another instance wound up in a heated argument that almost ended in a physical confrontation with members of the state legislative black caucus. In both instances, the policies he was pursuing were mandated by the state.[9] Another former president stated, "You are damned if you do and dammed if you don't." Our research and these candid conversations with faculty and administrators at HBCUs underscore the difficulty and complexity of these issues. For some HBCUs, financial pressures may leave them no choice but to try to attract more other-race students. For other institutions, court rulings may be the primary impetus for desegregation. It is an emotional issue, and just like their predominantly white counterparts, it remains an open question as to whether real integration takes place even when other-race students enroll in substantial numbers.

Additionally, we examined enrollment trends in HBCUs in relation to patterns of program transfer. The most striking finding from this investigation was that when programs were transferred, total enrollment by both African Americans and European Americans declined in the programs involved in the transfer (St. John and Hossler, 1995b). We suspect that the transfer of programs involves both institutional and program loyalties and, therefore, the local development of programs is a more viable way to attract and retain students than is the transfer of programs, at least in the short term. Indeed, we suspect it could take 50 to 100 years to change local attitudes sufficiently to overcome local backlash when program transfers are used. While new programs create a "fresh start," program transfers and institutional mergers seem to confuse all the mental images that people hold about institutions — the widely held beliefs that fostered creation of the dual system in the first place and that have sustained it for the past century.

The Post-Fordice Environment Reconsidered

From these studies we were able to develop an improved understanding of the factors that influenced European Americans to choose HBCUs, as indicated by the findings summarized in Table 1 (in brackets); however, we were not able to look at a broader set of questions related to system-wide desegregation in higher education. More importantly, broader questions related to system-wide desegregation were systematically overlooked by the courts, in spite of concerns raised about access issues by some experts in the case (Allen, 1994; Blake, 1991; St. John, 1995; St. John and Hossler, 1995a, 1995b). Given the changing legal context, two issues emerge as central to the ongoing debates about desegregation in higher education.

First, it is increasingly apparent that market conditions need to be considered when program development is being debated in HBCUs. The *Knight v. Alabama* decisions (i.e., 1991 and 1995) gave HBCUs priority in the development of new programs, which may give HBCUs a market advantage in the development of new programs of study. However, even when the courts do not give HBCUs this market advantage, HBCUs are still confronted by market forces when they develop new programs. For example, the Southern University system in Louisiana ran into some difficulties with their new programs because they failed to attract enough students to perpetuate the programs — to keep them economically viable (Wharton, 1995). Thus, a better understanding of student-choice processes may be vital in the future development of HBCUs in the post-*Fordice* environment.

Second, a broader set of issues related to system-wide desegregation have gone systematically unexamined by the courts. In Mississippi, arguments were made that the new admission criteria could limit opportunity for African Americans to attend four-year institutions (Blake, 1991). In the Louisiana court settlement, the state system of two-year colleges was bargained away in favor of a new community college in Baton Rouge where there was already extensive postsecondary opportunity. This suggests that the statewide access issue was not a priority to the parties in the Louisiana settlement. And in Alabama, reports and testimony that desegregation could result from a lack of coordination (e.g., Allen, 1994; St. John, 1995) did not receive serious consideration by the court.

In combination, these developments indicate a systematic pattern of ignoring the system-wide desegregation issues, including the question of access, in favor of a narrower issue of opportunity to choose by qualified students. Thus, the broader student-choice framework[10] could conceivably be used to develop refined arguments about system-wide desegregation. This focus would emphasize the linkages between state policies and:

- *access* (i.e., the number of African Americans enrolling);
- *choice of school* (the types of institutions in which they enroll); and
- *persistence* (whether they have the opportunity to persist in institutions of choice).

Tracking these linkages could give visibility to issues like: Are new conservative state finance policies and court-mandated admissions policies influencing a decline in access? Are the new conservative finance policies causing a pattern of resegregation (i.e., are more African Americans induced to enroll in community colleges or HBCUs due to financial policies or admissions standards[11])? These issues merit systematic analyses in the new context.

In our view, more critical-empirical research is needed to examine how state policies in finance and program approval, along with other ideas in the domain of state action, influence desegregation and resegregation with predominantly white institutions. If this new standard is being used to guide policy decisions about HBCUs, it should also be used in policy decisions about diversity in predominantly white institutions. Unless such steps are taken, the new wave of policies is simply increasing the unequal burdens.

Table 1. Propositions About the Linkages Between Possible Remedies and Student-Choice Processes (With Conclusions from our Analyses)

1. Postsecondary encouragement efforts can have a positive impact upon:
   (a) the enrollment rates of European American students at public HBCUs (strongly supported), and
   (b) access for African Americans in state systems of higher education (evidence not yet collected or examined).
2. Linking postsecondary encouragement efforts to school-reform efforts could increase the enrollment rates of European American students at public HBCUs. (modest support)
3. Coordinated efforts to strategically link tuition and aid policies could have a positive influence upon:
   (a) the enrollment rates of European American students at public HBCUs (support for other-race scholarships; no examples of coordination from our investigations of HBCUs),
   (b) access and persistence by both European Americans and African Americans in state systems (evidence related to this claim has not yet been collected or analyzed).
4. The transfer of academic programs from PWIs to HBCUs could have a positive effect on the enrollments of European American students at public HBCUs. (Not supported, based on a review of program transfers and enrollment trends[12])
5. The development of locally-situated and educationally-sound, high-demand programs at HBCUs can have a positive impact upon the enrollments of European American students at HBCUs. (Our results suggest that locally-situated, high-demand programs can be a very effective way to attract European American students.)
6. The nontraditional delivery of undergraduate programs (offering courses in evenings, weekends, and at off-campus locations) could have a positive influence upon the enrollment rates of undergraduate European American students at public HBCUs, as well as for access by African Americans. (Modestly supported. See points 3 and 5 above.)
7. Raising admissions standards at HBCUs may have a positive impact on their ability to enroll more European American students at public HBCUs, but could have a detrimental influence on access for African Americans. (There is modest support for this assertion.)
8. The nontraditional delivery of graduate programs (offering courses in evenings, weekends, and at off-campus locations) could have a positive

influence upon the enrollment rates of graduate white students at public HBCUs. (Our case study research and analysis of IPEDS data suggest that this proposition is true.)

9. Locally-situated competition from public or private institutions could negatively affect the enrollment rates of white students at HBCUs. (Modestly supported)

10. HBCUs situated in states and regions with higher percentages of African American residents will usually enroll fewer white students. (Strongly supported)

11. Campus leadership and support from alumni, trustees and other constituent groups can have influence on the ability of HBCUs to attract white students. (Supported)

Sources: Propositions restated from St. John and Hossler (1995a); findings, indicated in brackets (), from Hossler, et al. (1995) and St. John and Hossler (1995b).

Rethinking Desegregation In the Post-*Fordice* Environment

From the analyses above, it has become apparent that the courts have redefined the legal context for desegregation in public systems of higher education. In the past, before the *Fordice* decision, the *Adams* guidelines placed seemingly equal value on system-wide desegregation and black college development. In the post-*Fordice* environment, in contrast, the emphasis is placed on the removal of the vestiges of de jure segregation by promoting student choice. In this environment, HBCUs need to begin thinking about program development, and other forms of institutional development, as means of promoting enrollment by European Americans as well as African Americans. In addition, there is a set of deeper issues related to system-wide desegregation that has gone unconsidered in this new legal environment (St. John, this volume, chapter 8). In this section we consider how the new student-choice framework can inform the ongoing policy discourse about these issues. Both issues are examined, first focusing on some of the underlying issues, then on the types of strategies that are suggested by the new framework.

Rethinking HBCU Development

The focus of most remedial strategies adopted in the post-*Fordice* desegregation cases has been on which strategies will influence student choice. Some experts have focused exclusively on choice by European American students (e.g., Conrad, 1994a; Leslie, 1994), while others have also considered choice by African Americans (Allen, 1994). Our reviews and analyses above have focused on untangling the linking structures between possible remedies and student-choice processes by European and African Americans. However, in the process of conducting these analyses, we have encountered intervening factors that merit consideration in the crafting of institutional development strategies in public HBCUs. We briefly consider one of these intermediate issues — demography as destiny — before considering strategies for promoting HBCU development.

Overcoming Demography as Destiny. In our analysis of HBCUs with high and low percentages of European American students, we observed that demographics had a large influence on enrollment patterns. The HBCUs with high percentages of European American enrollments were located in local areas with high percentages of European Americans in the population, while the HBCUs with low percentages of European American enrollments were located in areas with low percentages of European Americans in the population. Based on our initial analysis of these forces, we examined regression analyses that measured the direct effects of population characteristics on the percentage of European American enrollments in HBCUs, which seemed to confirm this proposition (Hossler, et al., 1995).

These findings can be variously interpreted. From one vantage we could conclude that there is nothing we can do to change the pattern. On the other hand, this relationship can be viewed as a force that needs to be contended with, as remedy strategies (and other public and institutional policies) are crafted. While the extent of change in the percentage of enrollment may be constrained because of local demand by African Americans for an opportunity at HBCUs, these universities may also have opportunities to promote choice by European Americans that do not impair this historic function. We have taken this latter position. Our decision to take this approach is influenced by developments in higher education enrollment during the past two decades.

Fifteen to twenty years ago, many experts predicted that college enrollments would decline in the 1980s and early 1990s (e.g., Frankel and Gerald, 1980) and that these developments would cause the closure of many private colleges. Demographics were the basis for this projection — the size of the traditional college-age cohort was expected to decline. The "demographics as destiny"[13] did not eventuate. Rather, institutions adopted strategic-planning and enrollment-management techniques that helped them to attract new clientele — nontraditional-age adults and commuter students. Indeed, increased enrollment by part-time students and adults appears to explain why total enrollments did not decline as had been predicted (Gerald and Hussar, 1990).

The condition of HBCUs in the midsouth, states in which there are substantial numbers (and percentages) of African Americans, have an opportunity to maintain their core mission, which historically has been to provide opportunity to African American students. However, they are also faced with a challenge to achieve greater integration. In our view this additional mission, which is placed on HBCUs as a result of the integration process, can be best achieved by making changes in the delivery system to attract part-time students, the types of strategies that have been used in HBCUs with large percentages of white enrollments. These colleges provide a model because they have maintained their core mission of serving African American students while reaching out to new populations. However, these colleges (Langston State, Kentucky State, Lincoln University and so forth) discovered that they could attract whites when there was no longer sufficient demand by African Americans. In other words, they reached out to this new clientele as a means of surviving.

The HBCUs in the midsouth do not appear to be confronted by this basic challenge to their survival.[14] After all, there is a large African American population to be served in this region, which suggests a substantial demand for their historic mission. However, just as PWIs have opened their doors to resident African American populations, through special recruitment efforts, scholarships and special developmental programs, HBCUs must reach out to take on this additional mission (Willie, 1994). This distinction in mission, or rather the presence of a dual mission, was evident in the HBCUs with high percentages of white enrollments included in our study (Hossler, et al., 1995). They provide a model for how this dual mission can be achieved.[15]

For example, in Alabama, both models of conceiving of the missions of HBCUs are already evident. At Alabama A&M University, whites already comprise a moderate percentage of the student population (near the mid-range of HBCUs nationally), while at Alabama State University (ASU) the percentage of whites remains low (in the low range of HBCUs nationally).[16] Our review of past, current, and proposed practices at these universities (Hossler, et al., 1995) indicates that there is a difference in their offerings. In particular, there are more evening graduate offerings by A&M and most of the white students enrolled are graduate students. This seems to indicate that a dual mission has been developing at A&M. The historical focus on African American undergraduate education has been maintained, while more integrated graduate courses are offered through an alternate delivery of graduate courses. A similar pattern has not developed at ASU.

We suspect that development of this dual-mission strategy will be the most viable approach to the further integration at both institutions. Such a model may provide the greatest opportunity, at least in the short term, to overcome the demographics as destiny implicit in the current situation. However, caution is needed about the strict application of numeric standards.

Indeed, there are individual cases where racial isolation may make integration of a campus exceedingly difficult. For example, Mississippi Valley may be too isolated, but Jackson State is not, although both campuses are part of the state system. Therefore, it may be appropriate to take these variations into account and to focus more explicitly on desegregation of collective HBCUs and collective PWIs within the state system, rather than holding each campus to any particular numeric standard. In other words, there can be valid reasons for diverse patterns of desegregation, a situation that merits consideration as states "implement" their desegregation plans.

HBCU Development Reconsidered. The courts in Alabama, Mississippi, and Louisiana considered a large range of possible remedial strategies, from mergers of institutions, to the transfer of programs, to the development of new programs. For example, Department of Justice experts consistently recommended the transfer of large numbers of programs from predominantly white institutions to HBCUs (Conrad, 1994b, 1994c; Conrad and Leslie, 1994). The courts generally recommended a conservative approach: mandating limited sets of new programs in the Mississippi decision and the Louisiana settlement; and providing a funding mechanism and giving the HBCUs priority for new programs in Alabama. From our perspective, the most crucial issue facing the institutions now is to develop a workable approach to phased development of new programs[17] and which programs are put in place.

During the past few years public higher education in the United States has been undergoing a major readjustment, a restructuring in public systems of higher education (Gumport, 1993; Slaughter, 1993a, 1993b; St. John, 1994). Indeed, in 1993, most states faced a reduction in funding for public higher education (Hines, 1993). This restructuring has come about from a combination of unanticipated factors: demand for higher education was higher than expected in the past decade, due to changes in the labor market and more aggressive enrollment-management strategies; the country has been recovering from a period of economic stress; and the taxpayer revolt, the widespread objection to ever-expanding taxation, has hit higher education especially hard. These conditions mean that the present is not the best time to invest in new programs, especially in programs that will be a drain on revenues.

Now, when there is no pending litigation over desegregation, HBCUs can concentrate their new investments in locally-situated, high-demand programs that may have potentially high returns, i.e., a high yield of both European and African American students. Further, we would suggest linking these new programs to efforts to attract nontraditional students by altering the times of delivery of some courses. We make this suggestion because of the need to develop a dual mission: to retain and enhance the historic mission of providing an environment that supports the development of first-time college attenders.

Given the settlement of the cases, there is a clear opportunity for HBCUs to develop a two-phase strategy moving toward doctoral-granting status in midsouth HBCUs, an aim implicit in their proposals to the court in the midsouth cases. However, given that doctoral programs do not attract large numbers of students and are costly to operate, it is essential that HBCUs have productive undergraduate programs that create an infrastructure to support doctoral education over the long term. Therefore, it is important that the strategies used for introducing new undergraduate programs and alternative forms of program delivery be linked to plans to develop new doctoral programs.

Further, assuming the midsouth states, like most other states, face an uncertain future regarding the funding of public higher education (Hines, 1993), then it is important that HBCUs take steps to ensure their long-term financial health, as well as integration. Fortunately, these two aims can be linked because the types of programs that will attract European Americans are also the programs that will help colleges build a viable revenue base. Therefore the smaller HBCUs should concentrate on identifying two sets of programs, as part of a two-phase strategy:

- *Phase I.* In the first phase a set of locally-situated, high-demand programs should be started. When these programs are successfully operating and have attracted a sufficient number of students — European and African Americans — then there should be a better resource base to start more costly professional and doctoral programs.
- *Phase II.* During the second phase, high prestige doctoral programs should be developed, once there is a sufficient base to support the new infrastructure. These high prestige programs may not have the same potential to attract high numbers of students, but they are nonetheless important to the institutional-development process (e.g., attaining doctoral university status).

For large HBCUs in the midsouth (e.g., Southern A&M and Grambling State in Louisiana; Jackson State in Mississippi), there may be a sufficient enrollment base to begin a more concerted effort to build doctoral and professional programs in the short term. For example, there seems to have been a successful plan developed and implemented for development of doctoral programs at North Carolina A & T University, one of the larger public HBCUs. Thus, while the development of high-prestige programs needs to be carefully evaluated, to avoid starting programs that cannot be sustained after the initial start-up period, there is evidence that a careful, deliberate approach can be successfully implemented.

Such a strategy could easily be accomplished by HBCUs within the framework provided by the *Knight* decision in Alabama. In both Mississippi and Louisiana, however, action on such a strategy is a little more complicated, given that the decision in Mississippi and settlement agreement in Louisiana specified programs without adequate consideration of student demand. Nevertheless, it makes sense to conceive of program development as an integral part of a comprehensive institutional development process.

Alternative Delivery Systems. In all three states, the courts did not give sufficient consideration to alternative modes of delivery, in spite of the fact that alternative program delivery systems have become vital to the financial health of most public universities in recent decades, as well as to the desegregation process in many HBCUs in other regions (i.e., Lincoln in Missouri, Kentucky State, and Langston in Oklahoma). Two alternative modes of delivery also merit consideration by HBCUs in the midsouth and other states: delivery of courses for nontraditional students and the increased use of educational technology. Both approaches merit serious consideration by the states and the institutions involved.

First, the use of evening and off-campus courses, the alternative modes of delivery to attract nontraditional clientele, has proven to be a viable method for HBCUs to attract large numbers of European American students (Hossler, et al., 1995). This approach has been used at Alabama A&M University, which has attracted a significant percentage of white students. However, this alternative is not as well developed at ASU, where the percentage of European Americans enrolled remains small. Thus, focusing on alternative modes of program delivery represents an initial and necessary step in a genuine effort to move toward an integration model that maintains and enhances the historic missions of HBCUs.

Second, after decades of speculation about its potential, the electronic age apparently has arrived. The recent development of multimedia technologies — computers with voice capabilities, telecommunications linkages, and multi-image capabilities (stor-age of films, pictures, and even linkages to live remote filming), along with the mergers on the electronic superhighway — creates a new and rare opportunity for education and training. A number of universities across the country have begun to explore ways to bring university courses to this medium. However, an investment in people who have the skills and vision to develop a new age of interactive course ware, as well as an investment in technology, is required.

It makes sense for states to consider making this type of initial investment in one institution. For example, Arizona has made this investment in Northern Arizona University. An educational program that uses telecommunications and computer technologies holds the potential of expanding quality postsecondary opportunities and at lower costs than more conventional approaches (St. John, 1994). The fact is that selecting an HBCU for targeted investment in using the new technologies could help build an image, as well as diverse programs, that foster a more ethnically diverse and larger enrollment, but an enrollment that would make it possible to sustain its historic mission. Such an approach is analogous to the State of Kentucky's decision to provide subsidies to state employees attending Kentucky State, an approach that not only made this HBCU a model for others to follow (Burse, 1988), but also created a unique niche for the university. Concentrating new forms of alternative program delivery in HBCUs would create such a unique niche.

While these options did not receive much attention in the litigation in the midsouth, they merit consideration by HBCUs as they reconsider the system-wide desegregation goal. The capacity of HBCUs to embrace alternative modes of delivery seems crucial to the development of a dual mission — maintaining and enhancing the historic emphasis on providing quality education to traditional college-age African Americans, while responding to the new mandate for integration. The development of alternative programs within the university setting provides a means of maintaining the historic mission, while developing a new range of programs that not only responds to this new mandate, but also enhances the central function. More specifically, the additional resources and capabilities developed in the process of serving nontraditional clientele through alternative means of delivery can be used as a basis for building new elite programs that open new doors for African Americans.

Our discussion of HBCU development has been predicated on an assumption that desegregation of HBCUs has been mandated by the federal courts. While we question this goal because of the ongoing importance of HBCUs (St. John, 1997; Hossler, 1997), we recognize that resistance of this goal is not necessarily in the interest of HBCUs. Rather, we assumed the post-*Fordice* environment presents new challenges and opportunities for the HBCUs. We recognize that not all advocates of HBCU development agree with this pragmatic position. Further, as European Americans, we also recognize there are issues here that are difficult for us to fully appreciate. Therefore, we offer the comments above as an alternative perspective for HBCU advocates in their efforts to promote the development of these vital institutions.

System-wide Desegregation Reconsidered

Leadership within state systems is one of the most crucial forces for change in the integration process, in spite of the fact that it has received virtually no attention in the remedy plans approved by the courts in the midsouth. Before suggesting how state systems might attempt to address system-wide issues in the post-*Fordice* environment, we need to consider the reasons why the midsouth states lacked state-level leadership in taking an affirmative approach to desegregation.

Understanding the Problem. The systemic nature of the desegregation problem can be illustrated by contrasting a midsouth state to another southern state that has taken a more aggressive approach. Below we briefly compare developments in Alabama, a midsouth state that has resisted taking an affirmative approach to desegregation, to developments in North Carolina, a southern state that has taken a more affirmative approach.

The State of Alabama can be, and indeed has been, criticized for not providing leadership (Clark, 1993) on the resolution of the desegregation problems that existed in Alabama for more than a century. In the past, the early statewide planning documents for the state (e.g., Alabama Commission on Higher Education, 1975) simply endorsed the extant structure of higher education, which carried forward a set of historical precedents, embedded in historic mission statements and institutional classifications. This approach, which the court tried to remedy (i.e., the mission issue settled in "favor" of the plaintiffs), perpetuated the status quo, rather than putting forward a new vision for the future of higher education, as did many of the coordinating agencies created after the passage of the Education Amendments of 1972.[18]

In Alabama, as in most other states, the new planners who took charge of the "1202 Commission" in the early 1970s were faced with a leadership dilemma. On the one hand there was a history of institutional autonomy, which made meaningful coordination difficult; on the other, there was a need for effective coordination, which is why the federal government funded these commissions. To the extent that institutions had political influence in state legislatures and state houses, the 1202 Commissions found it difficult to forge a new vision and to develop new strategies in higher education. In a number of states that had desegregation plans accepted during the *Adams* period, a strong state role had emerged. The coordinating agencies and state boards in these states developed a capacity to plan and gave state systems new directions, which meant that issues, such as the mandate to desegregate higher education, could be addressed. In Alabama, as in the rest of the midsouth, these developments did not eventuate. Unfortunately, in Alabama, in *Knight v. Alabama*, the court failed to take a comprehensive look at system-wide coordination.

Fortunately, there are examples where state coordination has played a positive role in desegregation, as well as in the development of state systems of higher education. Indeed, many viable remedies seem to involve strong state coordination. For example, in North Carolina, a statewide governing board was created as part of the remedy planning process. North Carolina has one of the most successful integration records in the south, as measured by integration in HBCUs and PWIs. In the course of our study, for example, we learned that when other-race grants had been successful at Elizabeth City State, the system responded by implementing grants across the system. The capacity to make this type of adaptive response helps keep the court, and indeed the federal government, out of the change process in North Carolina. Thus, there is a need for new forms of leadership in public higher education in Alabama, as there is in other states in the midsouth.

Now that the legal debates are over for a period, those who are engaged in the policy and planning processes in the midsouth have an opportunity to reflect on past practices and to envision alternative approaches. While Mississippi still has an embattled environment, the other two states have made a fresh start. All three states have a chance to make the new decisions work in the interest of all the citizens. Indeed, they have an opportunity to take an affirmative approach toward system-wide desegregation. At the same time, advocates of system-wide desegregation (e.g., Southern Education Foundation, 1995; Williams, 1997) also have an opportunity to monitor the effects of these new strategies and to develop more systematic approaches to linking student outcomes to changes in state policy.

System-wide Strategies.   Our discussion of system-wide strategies examines issues overlooked by the courts in the midsouth. Our focus here is on maximizing choice within the economic constraints currently being faced by states. Given the lack of mandated statewide remedies, it seems there is an opportunity in the midsouth, as there is in other states, to take steps that insure broad access to higher education and that actually promote system-wide desegregation.

First, states have had a potentially important role to play in providing postsecondary encouragement. Recent experience in Indiana has shown that statewide efforts to provide information on postsecondary opportunities can improve postsecondary participation (Hossler and Schmit, 1995). For example, given that Alabama has low high school graduation rates (Halstead, 1994), statewide efforts to provide information could not only supplement institutional efforts to attract other-race students, but also encourage more students to complete high school and attend college.[19] We conclude that all three states need to develop a leadership role in the area of postsecondary encouragement — that is, providing a clear message to junior and senior high school students that postsecondary attendance is possible. They may even want to provide financial guaranties for students who seek the opportunity.

Second, while the other-race student aid included in court-approved remedies is probably a viable means of creating incentives for students to attend other-race institutions, there are broader questions about access that can only be addressed through coordination of state finance strategies, an issue virtually ignored by the courts. The underlying problem is that historically the funding issue was litigated on the sole criterion of funding (e.g., Leslie and Heubert, 1988) and when this criterion was used, funding seemed equitable.

However, the broader issues were not considered. Nevertheless, there is a substantial body of research that shows student access (Jackson, 1978, 1982; St. John, 1991b; St. John and Noell, 1989), college choice (Hossler, Bean and Associates, 1990; and Paulsen, 1990), and persistence decisions (Astin, 1975; St. John, 1989) are sensitive to both tuition and student aid. Subsidies to institutions, expenditure levels, and state student grants all influence these outcomes (St. John, 1994). Therefore, coordination of these strategies is desirable. Given the facts that the midsouth states lack substantial grant programs for students attending public higher education and that the erosion in Pell grants over the past decade has eroded minority access nationally (St. John, 1993, 1994), there is reason to be concerned about access in the midsouth. The midsouth states, like most other states, need to give more serious consideration to the coordination of financing strategies (i.e., Hearn and Anderson, 1989; St. John 1991a).

In the long term, it is important advocates for system-wide desegregation (e.g., Southern Educational Foundation, 1995;

Williams, 1997) develop ways of monitoring system-wide desegregation that consider both: (1) trends in access (as measured by the number of students enrolled in different types of institutions); and (2) other-race enrollment in both historically white and historically black colleges and universities. The first issue is important precisely because evidence of decline in African American participation in the late 1970s and early 1980s (e.g., Teddlie and Freeman, 1996) has not been systematically considered in the policy process in most states or at the federal level. The second issue is important because of the prospect that the new conservative finance policy will influence resegregation of public systems. Such analysis may provide a bias for more informed state action. Or alternatively, if states fail to take the initiatives necessary to ensure access, then perhaps a better research base can be used to inform a new wave of litigation.

It is also important that these efforts consider the effects of federal policies on the success of state desegregation plans. Untangling the complex desegregation and resegregation effects on state funding policies is a complex process. The potential resegregative effects of new conservative finance strategies only became visible when the interactions between state and federal student aid policies were considered (St. John, 1994). For example, a recent study of the effects of increased funding on the state grant program in Washington found that increases in state grants in the early 1990s had improved retention of minority students in public four-year institutions (St. John, and Starkey, 1996), thus mitigating the effects federal loans have had on redistributing lower-income students to community colleges. Thus, evaluations of state desegregation policies need to consider the mitigating effects of federal postsecondary policies. This approach would lead states toward a greater emphasis on state grants, an approach that has been devalued and de-emphasized historically in the midsouth.

This systematic approach would both: (1) provide visibility into the effects of recently mandated remedies in the midsouth; and (2) provide evidence on the ways state policies influence patterns of desegregation and resegregation. It is vitally important that desegregation advocates develop ways of assessing whether the new conservative policies in desegregation and higher education finance actually reverse progress, or whether they promote new forms of de facto segregation. Armed with such evidence, desegregation advocates could probably reverse some of the destructive policies promoted by the new conservatives.[20]

Concluding Reflections

In this chapter we have: (1) proposed a critical-empirical framework for emerging desegregation remedies; (2) considered how the proposed framework can potentially be used to develop an understanding of how this new round of remedies influences student outcomes; and (3) suggested practical strategies for promoting HBCU development and system-wide desegregation in this environment. As a conclusion, we summarize our findings in these three areas.

First, we suggested a critical-empirical framework when we reconsidered the Supreme Court's *Fordice* decision, along with the subsequent Circuit Court decisions (*Ayers* and *Knight*) and settlement (Louisiana) in the midsouth states. We concluded there had been a substantive change in the legal and policy context for desegregation of higher education (St. John, this volume, chapter 8). Under the *Adams* guidelines, which had been used as a basis for approving state plans, both system-wide desegregation and HBCU-development were treated as strategies for desegregation. These structural solutions were not treated in the same way in the post-*Fordice* legal environment. Instead of emphasizing these structural remedies per se, the courts decided the issue based on a new criterion: whether historically white and historically black institutions had removed vestiges of de jure segregation that impeded the freedom of students to choose an institution. We characterized this approach as being overly concerned about numeric desegregation in HBCUs. Our position has been that a broader construct of student choice is needed to begin to refocus attention on system-wide desegregation and HBCU development. In fact, in *Knight v. Alabama*, a broad definition of student choice was adopted that included explicit consideration of factors that influence choice (opportunity to attend, choice of college, persistence, major choice, and graduate education) for both African Americans and European Americans. While the recent *Knight* decision focused exclusively on desegregation in HBCUs, the framework developed for this case can also be used to more systematically address a broader set of issues related to HBCU development and system-wide desegregation.

Second, it is crucial that advocates for desegregation use a critical-empirical lens for the policy debates in the post-*Fordice* environment. The old liberal ideology that the dual goals of system-wide desegregation and HBCU development can be achieved through improved state planning and increased public investment has not only been challenged, but has been refuted by the courts in the post-*Fordice* legal environment. However, this should not be viewed as a defeat by those who value social equity and promote desegregation. The ground has shifted, but the goal has not been refuted. Indeed, the fact that empirical evidence has been used successfully in the courts to make arguments about desegregation remedies, arguments that broke with liberal conventions, mean that empirical evidence can also be used to examine critically the current neoconservative policies. It is possible to pursue desegregation in the new environment, especially if a critical, empirical approach is used by desegregation advocates.

One of the most crucial issues facing desegregation advocates is the role HBCUs play in providing opportunities for first-generation college student in need of special developmental attention during their college years. Research on HBCU choice by African Americans (McDonough, et al., 1997), an issue that was essentially ignored by the court in *Knight*, can help build a better understanding of this issue. In fact, as HBCUs in the midsouth begin to make efforts to build programs that attract more European Americans, they also need to focus on meeting the needs of the first-generation students they have historically served. Indeed, HBCUs that have successfully desegregated seem to have preserved their emphasis on providing opportunity for African Americans while building new programs for a more diverse population (Hossler, et al., 1995). This dual-mission focus merits more serious consideration in the future debates about HBCU development.

Another crucial issue facing advocates of desegregation is the leadership role of states in expanding opportunity for those who have been historically excluded, a crucial part of the historic emphasis on system-wide desegregation. In the wake of cuts in federal student grant programs in the past two decades, few states have sufficiently expanded student aid to ensure opportunity (St. John, 1997 & 1994). As a result, student choice (especially access, college choice, and persistence) is being artificially constrained for low-income students (St. John, 1994). Thus there could be a real decline in opportunity at the same time the new, court-approved desegregation plans are being implemented. Systematic analysis of these issues should be integrated into attempts to evaluate the most recent round of court decisions about college desegregation. Assessing "implementation" simply is not sufficient. Indeed, it is essential to evaluate how a range of state policies (financial policies as well as desegregation policies) influence opportunities for African Americans as well as European Americans.

In this new conservative era of public policy in higher education, discussion related to desegregation of (or increased diversity in) historically white colleges seems to have fallen off the policy table. Given the increased emphasis on empirical indicators of desegregation in HBCUs by the federal courts, we think it now is time to turn this new critical-empirical lens onto predominantly white institutions, possibly linking increases in funding to their success in attracting and retaining more diverse clientele.[21]   In particular, state need-based grants may have a central role to play in promoting desegregation. While at first glance this may seem extreme, it is, on second glance, no more extreme than the new standards that had been used to make decisions about *Knight* and *Ayers*.

Indeed, given the recent *Hopwood v. Texas* (1996) decision and the recent vote in California to overturn affirmative action, there is a need for a new social critical lens for viewing equity in higher education. Consideration of how financing strategies, and especially the availability of sufficient need-based aid to promote equal opportunity, as measured by student choice (i.e., college choice and persistence), may be the best way to hold states accountable in this new environment. In *Hopwood,* the court decided that race-based aid was illegal. Therefore, the alternative — that is, need-based aid — should be emphasized. Also, merit-based aid programs deserves serious scrutiny in this new context.

There may be times when these historic goals — HBCU development and system-wide desegregation — appear in conflict. However, it is also possible to find ways to reframe the policy discourse, especially if we use empirical evidence to discern new, previously unconsidered solutions. Indeed, it is possible that by reframing the questions , and critically examining diverse ideological claims (i.e., both old liberal and new conservative claims), we will discover new ways of moving toward these goals. In particular, we think that now is an opportune time for administrators in predominantly white institutions, as well as for administrators of HBCUs, to turn their attention to designing and perfecting institutional development strategies that promote and maintain diversity.

Notes

1. We tried to incorporate these issues in our framework and testimony, but the Court was clearly focused on HBCU desegregation (St. John and Hossler, 1995a & b). However, our research on the case was restricted to HBCU development (Hossler, et al., 1995).

2. Walter Allen's (1991) discussion of ideology was especially helpful in clarifying this dilemma. His thoughts on this issue essentially identified the need to explicitly consider ideology — and especially the points of view expressed by authors in the mainstream and African American literature on student choice and higher education desegregation.

3. We treated research on student choice published in major higher education journals (e.g., *Research in Higher Education, Journal of Higher Education, Review of Higher Education,* and *Journal of Student Financial Aid*) and major journals in sociology and economics as mainstream. We have also made an extensive effort to consider the more diverse viewpoints expressed in more diverse literature (e.g., *Black Issues in Higher Education, Integrated Education,* and *The Journal of Negro Education*).

4. Specifically we included the following components of student choice: (1) formation of the aspiration to attend; (2) formation of career aspirations (and initial major choice); (3) opportunity to attend; (4) choice of college (from a choice set); (5) changes of major in college; (6) persistence in college; and (7) choice to enroll and persist in graduate and professional programs.

5. We considered these foundations for each component of student choice.

6. Hereafter, we will hold our comprehensive definition of student-choice processes, as defined in note 4 (and developed by St. John and Hossler, 1995a), as the particular meaning of this term in the remainder of this text.

7. In our view, a more systematic approach to examining how various policies influence desegregation and resegregation of historically white campuses is also needed (St. John and Hossler, 1995a).

8. In particular, this research supports the position that moving major programs would have a negative influence on college-choice processes by whites.

9. In our view it is troubling that the HBCU administrators are under this pressure to "desegregate," while administrators in white institutions are being encouraged by states (i.e., the recent vote on affirmative action in California) and the courts (i.e., *Hopwood v. Texas*, 1996) to ignore the call to desegregate.

10. The broader construct was adopted by the court in *Knight*, which means there is legal precedence for using the framework.

11. There is evidence in Louisiana, for example, that increasing admission standards at the University of New Orleans has reduced enrollments (Trammell, 1995), while enrollment at the nearby HBCU and community college improved. This suggests a de facto pattern of resegregation.

12. We conducted supplemental analyses on this topic using information from desegregation cases and enrollment trends. The analyses do not support this claim. After programs were transferred, total European American and African American enrollment dropped (St. John, 1995; St. John and Hossler, 1995b).

13. We adopted this term from Norris and Poulton (1987).

14. The possible exception to this claim is Mississippi Valley State which faced a formidable challenge given its mandate to raise admissions standards, coupled with the fact that it is located in an area with low percentages of European Americans in the local population.

15. The concept of having multiple missions is consistent with the tradition of most universities. As they developed from being primarily undergraduate institutions into research universities, the land grant colleges, for example, became multi-purpose institutions (Kerr, 1963).

16. The fact that Alabama A & M had attracted more European Americans, largely through evening programs, should not go unacknowledged. In fact, such developments should merit increased state investment, if the state had an affirmative desegregation policy. This is also noteworthy because A & M had in no sense lost its identity as an HBCU, indicating it is possible to find a path toward desegregation that does not impair the historic missions of HBCUs.

17. The theory implicit in arguments by Conrad (1994 a & b) and other Justice Department experts was that if new "high demand"

programs were developed at HBCUs, then more whites would come. The comparative analyses indicates this claim did not hold and, as a result, the courts took a more conservative approach. However, as we have argued (St. John, this volume, chapter 8; and, Hossler, 1997), black college developments remain an important issue.   Therefore, tight linkage between program development and seeking more (and more diverse) enrollment is needed.

18. The Education Amendments of 1972, which reauthorized the Higher Education Act, created planning monies for state commissions in Section 1202, part of Title XII.

19. Indeed, there may be a need for better coordination between higher education and the strategies being used in education reform. The basis for this claim is developed in St. John and Hossler (1995a).

20. We choose the word "destructive" because the new conservative policies — including those that link funding to student achievement, shift aid from grants to loans, and increase public sector tuition without increasing need-based grants — have the potential of fostering resegregation in public higher education (St. John, 1993, 1994, in press).

21.   Indeed states that are serious about maintaining equal opportunity may need to examine seriously and empirically the funding of need-based grants as an alternative to direct institutional subsidies.

References

Allen, W. R. (1991). Introduction. In W. R. Allen, E. G. Epps, and N. Z. Haniff (Eds.) *College in black and white: African American students in predominantly white and in historically black public universities* (pp. 1-14). Albany, NY: State University of New York Press.

Allen, W. R. (1994). The determinants of student choice and access in the Alabama state system of higher education, 22 December, 1994, memo. (Updated 1995).

Astin, A. W. (1975). *Preventing students from dropping out.* San Francisco: Jossey-Bass.

Blake, E. (1991). Is higher education desegregation a remedy for segregation but not educational inequality?: A study of the *Ayers v. Mabus* desegregation case. *Journal of Negro education*, 60(4), 538-65.

Burse, R. M. (1988). *Adams* litigation: One state's unique response for the enhancement of its historically black university. In Williams, J. B. (Ed.), *Desegregating America's colleges and universities: Title VI regulation of higher education* (pp. 77- 90). New York: Teachers College Press,

Clark, E. C. (1993). *The schoolhouse door: Segregation's last stand at the University of Alabama.* New York: Oxford University Press.

Conrad, C. F. (1994a). *Factors contributing to the matriculation of White students in public PBIs: A foundation for identifying policies and practices to advance desegregation in predominantly black institutions,* November 8, 1994.

Conrad, C. F. (1994b) *Proposed desegregation plan for Mississippi,* June 28, 1994, memo.

Conrad, C. F. (1994c). *Study of program duplication in Alabama's colleges and universities: A report to the U.S. Department of Justice.* November 17, 1994, memo.

Conrad, C. F. and Leslie, L. L. *Plan for remedy: State of Alabama.* November 23, 1994, memo.

Frankel, M. J., and Gerald, D. E. (1980). *Projections of education statistics to 1988-89.* Washington, D.C.: National Center for Education Statistics.

Gerald, D. E. and Hussar, W. J. (1990). *Projections of education statistics to 2001.* National Center for Educational Statistics. Washington, D.C.: GPO.

Gumport, P. (1993). The contested terrain of academic program reduction. *Journal of Higher Education,* 64(3), 283-311.

Halstead, K. (1994). *Three R's of race retention rates by states.* Washington, D.C.: Research Associates of Washington.

Hearn, J. C. and Anderson, M. S. (1989). Integrating postsecondary education financing policies: The Minnesota model in R. H. Fenske (Ed.) *Studying the impact of student aid on institutions, new directions for higher education,* No. 62, pp. 55-73. San Francisco: Jossey Bass.

Hines, E. R. (1993). *State higher education appropriations 1992-93.* Denver, CO: SHEEO.

Hossler, D. (1997). Historically black public colleges and universities: Scholarly inquiry and personal reflections. *Journal for a Just and Caring Education.* 3(1).

Hossler, D., Bean, J., and Associates (1990). *The strategic management of college enrollments.* San Francisco: Jossey-Bass.

Hossler, D., St. John, E. P., Foley, J., Ramin-Gyurnek, J., and Smail, B. (1995). *An analysis of the factors that influence student choice at HBCUs: Three studies of external and internal factors affecting white enrollment.*

Hossler, D. and Schmit, J. (1995). The Indiana postsecondary encouragement experiment. In E. P. St. John (Ed.), *Rethinking tuition and student aid strategies, New Directions for Higher Education, no. 89.* San Francisco: Jossey-Bass.

Jackson, G. A. (1978). Financial aid and student enrollment. *Journal of Higher Education,* 49(6), 15-27.

Jackson, G. A. (1982). Public efficiency and private choice in higher education. *Educational Evaluation and Policy Analysis,* 4(2), 237-247.

Kerr, C. (1963). *The uses of the university.* Boston: Harper Touchbooks.

Leslie, L. L. (1994). *A report on field studies of historically black universities.* November 1994, memo.

Leslie, L. L. and Heubert, J. (1988). Determining financial inequities in previously segregated public systems of higher education. In Williams, J.B. (Ed.), *Desegregating America's colleges and universities: Title VI regulation of higher education* (pp. 179-204). New York: Teachers College Press.

McDonough, P. M., Antonio, A. L., and Trent, J. W. (1997). Black students, black colleges: An African American, college choice model. *Journal for a Just and Caring Education* 3(1).

Norris, D. M. and Poulton, N. L. (1987). *A guide for new planners.* Ann Arbor, MI: Society for colleges and University Planners.

Paulsen, M. B. (1990). *College choice: Understanding student enrollment behavior.* ASHE-ERIC higher education report no. 6. Washington, D.C.: The George Washington University, School of Education and Human Development.

St. John, E. P. (1989). The influence of student aid on persistence. *Journal of Student Financial Aid,* 19(3): 52-68.

St. John, E. P. (1991a) A framework for reexamining state resource-management strategies in higher education. *Journal of Higher Education, 62*(3), 263-287.

St. John, E. P. (1991b). What really influences minority student attendance? An analysis of the high school and beyond sophomore cohort. *Research in Higher Education, 32*(2), 141-158.

St. John, E. P. (1993). Untangling the web: Using price-response measures in enrollment projections. *Journal of Higher Education, 64*(6), 676-695.

St. John, E. P. (1994). *Prices, productivity, and investment: Assessing financing strategies in higher education.* An ASHE/ERIC Higher Education Study. Washington, D.C.: George Washington University.

St. John, E. P. (1995). Testimony, March 16, 1995. *Knight v. Alabama.*

St. John E. P. (1997) Higher education desegregation in the post-*Fordice* legal environment: An historical perspective. In R. Fossey (Ed.) *Readings on equal education, volume 15, Race, the courts, and equal education: the limits of the law.* New York: AMS Press.

St. John, E. P. (1997). The historic value of price impact studies: a case study of the Arizona higher education voucher study. Working Paper. Dayton, Ohio: Center for Public Policy Research, University of Dayton.

St. John, E. P. and Elliott, R. J. (1994). Reframing policy research: A critical examination of research on federal student aid programs. In J.C. Smart (ed.) *Higher education: Handbook of theory and research, Vol 10,* (pp. 126-180). New York: Agathon Press.

St. John, E. P. and Hossler, D. (1995a). *Assessing the effects of desegregation remedies on student choice: Analytic framework and study plan.* Prepared for the University of Alabama, Office of Counsel.

St. John, E. P., and Hossler, D. (1995b). *Assessment of possible desegregation remedies in Alabama public higher education: Assessment of possible remedies and optimal strategies,* Prepared for the University of Alabama, Office of Counsel.

St. John, E. P., and Noell, J. (1989). The effects of student financial aid on access to higher education: An analysis of progress with special consideration of minority enrollment. *Research in Higher Education, 30(*6), 563-581.

St. John, E. P., and Starkey, J. B. (1996). *The impact of financial aid on persistence: Logistic analysis of 1991, 1992, and 1993 cohorts.* Prepared for the Higher Education Coordinating Board. State of Washington. Bethesda, MD: JBL Associates.

Slaughter, S. (1993a). Introduction. *Journal of Higher Education, 64*(3), 247-249.

Slaughter, S. (1993b). Retrenchment in the 1980s: The politics of prestige and gender. *Journal of Higher Education, 64*(3), 250-282.

Southern Education Foundation. (1995). *Redeeming the American promise.* Atlanta: Southern Education Foundation.

Teddlie, C. and Freeman, J. (1996). With all deliberate speed: An historical overview of the relationship between the *Brown* decision. In K. Lomotey and C. Teddlie. *Readings on equal education, Volume 13, Forty years after the Brown decision: Implications of school desegregation for U.S. education* (pp. 7-51). New York: AMS Press.

Trammell, M.L. (1995). Estimating the enrollment effects of a midyear surcharge. In E.P. St. John (ed) *New directions for higher education, No. 89, Rethinking tuition and student aid strategies* (pp. 65-74). San Francisco: Jossey Bass.

Wharton, J. M. (1995) Testimony. *Knight v. Alabama.* CV-83-M-1676-S., March 14, 1995.

Williams, J.B., Convener, system-wide desegregation research collaborative, (1997). System-wide desegregation of public higher education. *Journal for a Just and Caring Education.* 3(1).

Willie, C.V. (1994). Black colleges are not just for blacks anymore. *The Journal of Negro Education, 63*(2), 153-64.

Table of Legal Cases

Adams v. Califano, 430 F.Supp. 118 (D.D.C. 1977).
Adams v. Richardson, 356 F.Supp. 92 (D.D.C. 1973).
Adams v. Weinberger, 391 F.Supp. 296 (D.D.C. 1975).
Ayers v. Allian, 914 F ed 676 (CA 5 1990).

Ayers v. Fordice, 79 F. Supp. 1419 (995).

Brown v. The Board of Education of Topeka, Kansas. 347 U.S. 483, (1954).

Hopwood v. Texas 78 F. 3rd 932 (5th circ. 1996). *Cert. denied* 116 s. ct. 2581 (1996).

Knight v. Alabama. 787 F. Supp. (D.D.C. 1991).

Knight v. Alabama. CV 8-M1676-s, (Filed August, 1995).

Missouri ex rel Gaines v. Canada. 305 U.S. 377 (1938).

United States v. Fordice. 112 S. Ct. 2727 (1992).

United States v. Louisiana. 718 F. Supp. 499,514 (ED La. 1989).

CHAPTER 10

THE *PODBERESKY* CASE AND RACE-BASED FINANCIAL AID

Anne Wells and John L. Strope, Jr.

The United States Supreme Court's decision of May 23, 1995 not to review a federal court of appeals decision in *Podberesky v. Kirwan* (1994) made headlines across the nation. By declining to grant certiorari the Supreme Court let stand a lower court's findings that a race-exclusive scholarship, awarded only to African Americans at the University of Maryland, violates the 14th Amendment to the U.S. Constitution and Title VI of the Civil Rights Act of 1964.[1] While the decision is legally binding only in the jurisdiction of the Court of Appeals for the Fourth Circuit (the states of Maryland, North Carolina, South Carolina, Virginia, and West Virginia), it does establish a significant legal precedent.

On the other hand, Department of Education guidelines, issued in February 1994, advise that race exclusive scholarships are legal if they are designed to remedy past discrimination or to promote diversity (Non-discrimination in federal programs, 1994).

This chapter was originally published in the *Journal of Student Financial Aid* (26)1, 1996, pp. 33-43.

Yet, recent legal decisions have made it increasingly difficult to prove the existence of *present* effects of *past* discrimination, thereby justifying remedies, such as race-based financial aid.

Financial aid officers now wonder how to administer institutional aid programs. Colleges and universities are being advised by the American Council on Education "don't do anything different from what you are doing." (Jaschik, June 2, 1995, p. A25). But Richard Samp of the Washington Legal Foundation (and Daniel Podberesky's attorney) stated, "it would be virtually impossible for colleges to meet the legal standard set by the Fourth Circuit to justify minority scholarships," and "it will take only a few multi-million dollar [damage] awards for schools to start thinking differently" (Jaschik, June 2, 1995, p. A25).

The purpose of this article is to review the *Podberesky* decision and to discuss the implications of that decision on race-based financial aid awards.

The *Podberesky* Case

In 1991, Daniel Podberesky, a Hispanic American, filed suit against William E. Kirwan, president of the University of Maryland at College Park (UMCP) and the University because he was denied a Banneker Scholarship. Although Mr. Podberesky possessed the academic qualifications, Banneker Scholarships were awarded only to African American students. Therefore, he was not an eligible candidate for the scholarship award.

The Banneker scholarship program came into existence as part of a desegregation plan submitted by the State of Maryland in an effort to comply with the Civil Rights Act of 1964. Enforcement of title VI of the Civil Rights Act, which prohibits racial discrimination in any organization receiving federal funds, was placed with the Office of Civil Rights (OCR) in the U.S. Department of Health, Education, and Welfare.[2] States determined to be operating segregated systems of higher education were required to submit comprehensive plans to desegregate.

The State of Maryland submitted, modified, and re-submitted a series of desegregation plans throughout the 1970s and 1980s that ultimately were approved by OCR. Included in the plans were efforts by UMCP to recruit and retain more African American students. The Banneker Scholarship, funded with both state and private funds, was implemented in 1979. Although these scholarships were not mentioned by name in the desegregation plan, offering financial aid on a race-exclusive basis was approved as a method of attracting and retaining more minority students.

District Court I and Appeals Court I

Podberesky's lawsuit contended that the awarding of Banneker Scholarships only to African American students violated the equal protection clause of the 14th Amendment to the U.S. Constitution, as well as Title VI of the Civil Rights Act of 1964. The courts have emphasized the need to examine with strict scrutiny situations where people are treated differently because of their race. In the 1978 *Bakke* decision, the Supreme Court stated, "all legal restrictions which curtail the civil rights of a single group are immediately suspect. That is not to say that all such regulations are unconstitutional. It is to say that courts must subject them to the most rigid scrutiny" (*Regents of the University of California v. Bakke*, [*Bakke*], 1978, p. 2748). Therefore, to meet the strict scrutiny of the courts, UMCP had to show how the Banneker Scholarship Program served a compelling state interest, and was a narrowly tailored solution.

The equal protection argument presented in *Podberesky* involved the determination of: (1) intent to discriminate against certain people in offering the Banneker Scholarships, and (2) a suspect class, in this case, all races other than African Americans. The government then had to present evidence of compelling interest to continue the discriminatory practice — in this case, continuing to award the Banneker Scholarship — and demonstrate that doing so was a means narrowly tailored to remedy current effects of past discrimination.

Neither side in *Podberesky* disputed the fact that the scholarship was intentionally discriminatory. The Banneker Scholarship was awarded only to members of one race, African Americans. Podberesky argued that "no federal agency has ever found that Maryland operated a racially segregated system of higher education in violation of Federal law." He contended that OCR's findings were "insufficient to demonstrate a history of discrimination;" that OCR "misapprehended ... the necessity of affirmative remedies for past constitutional violations;" that the Banneker Scholarship Program, per se, was never approved by federal officials; and, even if the Banneker could have been justified in the past, UMCP was now free from discrimination (*Podberesky v. Kirwan* [*Podberesky I*], 1991, p. 373).

The university argued its compelling interest was the "goal of remedying the effects of past discrimination at UMCP" (*Podberesky I*, p. 372). The defendants pointed to attempts by the State and the University to become certified in final compliance with the OCR. University officials asserted that the Banneker Scholarship Program was narrowly tailored to recruit and retain African American students. They claimed that race-neutral alternatives had been considered, and in fact co-existed with the Banneker Scholarship (particularly the Francis Scott Key Scholarship), but were ineffective in increasing minority enrollment.

In its analysis the district court raised an "unsettled legal question: the Supreme Court's affirmative action cases do not directly address the question of when past discrimination ceases to justify present remedies" (*Podberesky I*, p. 374). To justify race-conscious remedies, the court said that the state had to prove that past discrimination has continuing effects on the present. Podberesky argued that UMCP had exceeded its goal for recruiting African American freshmen, citing President Kirwan's deposition that the university had not discriminated against African Americans in many years (*Podberesky I*, pp. 374-5).

However, the district court was not swayed by Podberesky's arguments, stating that is was "premature to find that there are no present effects of past discrimination at the institution" (*Podberesky I*, p. 375) and while a scholarship is a "desirable benefit" it is not one that prohibits him from attending the university (*Podberesky I*. p. 376). A judgment in favor of the University of Maryland was entered.

Podberesky immediately appealed to the Court of Appeals for the Fourth Circuit. In a January 31, 1992 decision, the court declared that the district court wavered in not specifically identifying the *present* effect of *past* discrimination (*Podberesky v. Kirwan* [*Podberesky II*], 1992, p. 56). The case was remanded to the district court to determine "whether present effects of past discrimination exist and whether the remedy is a narrowly tailored response to such effects" (*Podberesky II*, p. 57).

District Court II

After remand, the district court asked the university to engage "in an administrative fact finding process to decide whether to continue the Banneker Program" (*Podberesky v. Kirwan* [*Podberesky III*], 1993, p. 1076. The product of that investigation was *Decision and Report*, a position paper recommending the continuation of the scholarship. University officials engaged in additional fact finding to demonstrate the present effects of past discrimination, the result of which was the compilation of an extensive history of discriminatory acts by UMCP.

Prior to the 1954 landmark decision, *Brown v. Board of Education*, Maryland, like other southern states, operated separate institutions of higher education for African Americans that were "segregated, vastly under funded and consistently neglected" (*Podberesky III*, p. 1077). After *Brown*, UMCP accepted African Americans, but the "state did little to promote integration" (*Podberesky III*, p 1078). A historical recounting of university inattentiveness to African American student concerns was cited.

In the 1960s the university refused to permit the Congress for Racial Equality to organize a campus chapter. Martin Luther King, Jr. was discouraged from speaking at the campus, while George Wallace was permitted to speak. The Ku Klux Klan was allowed to march on campus when dormitories were desegregated. Furthermore, university chaplains were prohibited from taking part in civil rights activities; and African American student enrollment was less that 1% of the undergraduate student population (*Podberesky III*, pp. 1078-9).

In the 1970s, the university cited numerous problems in seeking compliance with the OCR desegregation order. There was also resistance to integrating campus housing and lack of university financial support for building African American sorority and fraternity houses. In addition, facilities for African American student programs were generally substandard. In the area of admissions, new admissions standards were imposed without consideration to their impact on minorities, and the admissions office resisted recruiting minorities. UMCP's failure to develop cooperative and feeder programs with historically black Maryland colleges and universities was another significant problem during this period (*Podberesky III*, pp. 1078-81).

In the 1980s, the university noted that with the submission of yet another desegregation plan to the OCR, UMCP had revised its minority admission goals downward, using the term "other race," rather than focusing specifically on African Americans. The university had only concentrated recruitment efforts on first-time, full-time freshmen (*Podberesky III*, pp. 1081-82). UMCP officials presented four arguments of the present effects of past discrimination:

- The poor reputation of UMCP in the African American community.
- The under representation of African Americans in the UMCP student body.
- The high attrition rates of African Americans at UMCP.
- The perception that the university is a hostile climate for African Americans (*Podberesky III*, pp. 1082-94).

Podberesky challenged all four arguments.

Poor reputation. University officials had commissioned an evaluation of the reputation of the university community by an outside consultant. He interviewed high school counselors and conducted four student focus groups, concluding that UMCP has "done a poor job of serving the black community" (*Podberesky III*, p. 1084). He noted that many African Americans, because of the history of segregation at UMCP, were referred to historically African American institutions by counselors and by family.

Podberesky challenged the findings of the surveys conducted. He stated that the questionnaires were flawed and the statements were made to elicit negative responses. Furthermore, he claimed the results did not show any link between past discrimination and the present racial climate.

Under representation. The UMCP did not have rigid admission standards, and extensive debate resulted concerning the identification of an appropriate reference pool for measuring the percentages of African Americans who entered UMCP. The reference pool debate ranged from all graduating high school seniors in Maryland, to takers of the SAT, to those high school seniors successfully completing a core curriculum to be eligible for college, to students scoring above particular levels on the SAT- all compared to the total number of African Americans entering the freshman class at UMCP. UMCP officials made the case that despite all their efforts, and no matter which reference pool was used, African American students were still under represented at UMCP.

Podberesky argued that African Americans were no longer under represented at UMCP, suggesting that university officials manipulated the statistics to state their case. He stated that the percentage of African American undergraduates at UMCP was proportionate to that at many northern institutions which did not have segregated pasts.

High attrition. UMCP officials contended that the proportionally higher attrition rates of African Americans was directly attributable to the university's segregated past. They showed how African Americans had the lowest retention and graduation rates of any other group at UMCP. In 1986, a total of 42.5% of African American freshmen graduated within six years, compared to 66.5% of white freshman (*Podberesky III*, p. 1091). Podberesky countered with statistics showing that comparable northern institutions had similar African American attrition rates.

Hostile climate. Citing a 1989 study at UMCP, officials noted the chilly climate for African Americans on campus (*Podberesky III*, p. 1092). They cited incidents of racist comments, the lack of African American leaders, the failure of campus media to cover the accomplishments of African American faculty, staff, and students, condescending attitudes, racial epithets, and the segregated atmosphere that continued to permeate the campus. Podberesky concurred that a hostile climate did exist toward African Americans at UMCP. However, he disputed whether this was due to the effects of past discrimination or was merely the effect of present societal discrimination.

To consider whether the remedies offered by UMCP were narrowly tailored to justify such actions, the court applied a framework derived from the 1987 Supreme Court decision in *U.S. v. Paradise*. UMCP was required to demonstrate: "1) the necessity for relief and the efficacy of alternative remedies; 2) the flexibility and duration of the relief; 3) the propriety of the program's numerical goals; and 4) the impact of the program on the rights of third parties" *(U.S. v. Paradise*, pp. 1094-97).

Relief and alternative remedies

UMCP officials argued that offering Banneker Scholarships had increased the number of African Americans admitted and expected to graduate, and had helped establish a base of supportive African American alumni who would potentially serve as role models and mentors. Officials argued that race-neutral and need-based scholarship programs were not nearly as effective in attracting African American students.

Flexibility. University officials conceded that the Banneker scholarship was not flexible in that it was offered to African Americans only, but noted that the existence of the Banneker Program was "not a perennial feature" (*Podberesky III*, p. 1096), and was to be reviewed at least every three years.

Propriety of goals. UMCP argued that the Banneker Program satisfied this requirement because it compared the number of scholarship recipients to the incoming freshman class. Although the notion of an accurate reference pool was cloudy, the court accepted UMCP's argument that the number of scholarships offered represented less than 1% of the entering freshman class, and that "[t]he percentage is small compared to any of the possible goals that the parties have bandied about ..." (*Podberesky 3*, p. 1096).

Impact on the rights of third parties. One of the greatest benefits of the Banneker Program, officials argued, was that it did not conflict with the rights of others. The program comprised only 1% of the UMCP financial aid budget and did not impinge on non-African Americans' rights to attend UMCP.

On remand, the district court upheld its previous decision, insisting that the program satisfied the requirements for addressing the present effects of past discrimination. Judge Frederick Motz said that the appeals court had constructed too rigid a framework for considering this case, noting that most affirmative action cases relate to employment disputes, rather than educational considerations. He concluded:

> ... [T]he Supreme Court has consistently recognized that discrimination in schooling is the most odious form of discrimination ... Accordingly, it seems entirely proper that in order to cure these effects, legislatures and educational administrators be given more leeway in fashioning remedies that take into account the vast extent of the damage that has been done by our shameful legacy of involuntary segregated education (Podberesky III, p. 1097).

Appeals Court II

Podberesky appealed the case again. A decision of the Fourth Circuit Court of Appeals was handed down October 27, 1994, overturning the district court's findings. The court rejected all four of UMCP's compelling reasons. It stated that the lower court had failed to show how Maryland's segregated past justified the existence of the current Banneker Scholarship Program, stating that "mere knowledge of historical fact is not the kind of present effect that can justify a race-exclusive remedy" (*Podberesky v. Kirwan* [*Podberesky IV*], 1994, p. 154). The court rejected arguments about the under representation of African Americans as well as attrition rates because of concerns with the accuracy of the statistics. It insisted that the lower court had not established an accurate reference pool nor had it established precisely the minimum admission criteria for UMCP, both factual issues that were "not inconsequential and could have been resolved at trial" (*Podberesky IV*, p. 157). The court also rejected the "hostile climate" argument, suggesting that was due more to present societal discrimination, rather than the university's segregated past.

Next, the court turned to the narrowly tailored aspects of the remedy, rejecting the university's arguments, concluding that the district court had failed to show how a scholarship program that attracts high achieving African Americans, who are probably college bound already, will remedy low retention rates and under-representation of African American students at UMCP. Moreover, in the appellate court's view, offering awards to non-residents makes it "... apparent that the Banneker Program considers all African American students for merit scholarships at the expense of non-African American Maryland students" (*Podberesky IV*, p. 158). The court pointed out that the reference pool used by UMCP was arbitrarily defined and flawed in myriad ways, resulting in a "series of inconclusive and possibly inflated figures ..." (*Podberesky IV*, p. 159), and implied that the figures consti-tuted a quota (*Podberesky IV*, p. 160); also "the university has not made any attempt to show that it has tried, without success, any race-neutral solutions to the retention problem" (*Podberesky IV*, p. 161). Finally, the court rejected UMCP's "role model" and "societal discrimination" theories (*Podberesky IV*, p. 161).

In January 1995, the University of Maryland appealed to the United States Supreme Court. The Department of Justice, 19 colleges and universities, 8 law schools, and numerous higher education and civil rights groups filed brief, urging the Court to consider the case and to uphold the legality of race exclusive scholarships (Jaschik, May 12, 1995). However, on May 23, 1995, the Supreme Court announced, without comment, its refusal to review the case.

Future Considerations
By refusing to consider *Podberesky* the Supreme Court allowed the appeals court decision to stand. Though it is legally binding only in the states of the Fourth Circuit, it serves as a precedent for future lawsuits throughout the country. The door has been opened to future challenges, with some perhaps having the potential for punitive damages awards. When placed in the context of affirmative action cases over the past decade, the *Podberesky* result is unsurprising. The Supreme Court has continued to define more narrowly the scope of allowable affirmative action remedies.

The first legal challenge to affirmative action in higher education was the *Bakke* case in 1978, which struck down the principle of "set-asides" or quotas in the admissions process, but which validated the concept of striving to achieve a diverse student body as an acceptable compelling interest of a university (*Bakke*, 1978). (One can only speculate whether diversity would stand up as a compelling interest under the 1995 Court's scrutiny. Diversity was not an argument in *Podberesky*.)

In the 1980s, the Supreme Court continued to refine the concepts of "compelling interest" and "narrowly tailored" in subsequent employment related decisions.[3] The two most recent affirmative action cases decided by the Supreme Court on June 12, 1995, *Adarand v. Pena* and *Missouri v. Jenkins*, reflect an increasingly tightly constructed framework for establishing a compelling state interest and a narrowly tailored remedy. After *Podberesky*, it is unclear if *any* university will be able, under these parameters, to justify legally the awarding of race exclusive financial aid.

Podberesky is making many colleges and universities re-examine their policies regarding the recruitment and retention of minority students, as well as the awarding of race-based financial aid. A 1994 Government Accounting Office (GAO) report determined that while small numbers of students are served by race-based financial aid (7% of undergraduates, 4% of graduate students, and 15% of professional students), nearly two-thirds of all colleges and universities offer at least one race-based scholarship. After *Podberesky*, some institutions may decide to abandon race-based scholarships, although some colleges and universities outside the fourth Circuit may take a "wait and see" approach before eliminating minority scholarships likely to become the object of the next *Podberesky*-like lawsuit.

Department of Education guidelines vis-a-vis Podberesky. Current DOE guidelines (1994) expressly state that financial aid to remedy past discrimination is justifiable "without waiting for a finding to be made by the Office of Civil Rights, a court or legislative body, if the college has a strong basis in evidence of discrimination ..." (*Non-discrimination*, p. 8756). DOE also permits the awarding of race-based financial aid when it is used to create diversity and is "narrowly tailored ... to have a diverse student body that will enrich its academic environment" (*Non-discrimination*, p. 8756). The guidelines use a framework to define narrowly tailored as when: (1) race-neutral means of achieving diversity would be ineffective; (2) less extensive or intrusive use of race in awarding financial aid for diversity would be ineffective; (3) the use of race is of "limited extent" and "applied in a flexible manner;" (4) the institution regularly re-examines its use of race in financial aid awards; and, (5) the race-based criteria are used sparingly "so as not to create an undue burden on [non-minority students] to receive financial aid." In general, the less severe and more diffuse the impact on non-minority students, the more likely a classification based on race will meet the DOE guidelines (*Missouri v. Jenkins*, pp. 8760-2). The University of Maryland presented the facts of its case within these very guidelines and failed to convince the court.

Meeting institutional mandates to increase minority participation. As a corollary, colleges and universities must re-evaluate their internal mandates and evaluate their efforts to increase minority enrollment. When the *Bakke* decision was handed down in 1978, colleges and universities throughout the nation re-evaluated their admissions processes and made necessary changes to meet the letter of the law. It is clear, when examining subsequent cases, that the universities were successful in amending admissions policies to comply with new standards. All cases upheld university admissions standards and considered special programs to better prepare at-risk students to be legal.[4] Will colleges and universities be able to catch on to the newest standards set forth by the courts?

Moreover, UMCP, in making its case in *Podberesky,* publicly admitted an extensive record of previous discrimination. By documenting its discriminatory past, has it laid itself open to future discrimination lawsuits? Anyone wanting to prove that the university has a history of discrimination now has ready-made evidence.

Government funded v. privately funded scholarships. The Banneker Scholarship Program was only partially funded with state monies. It is unclear how the recent court decisions will affect privately funded scholarships. Current DOE regulations expressly state that privately funded scholarships are permissible (*Nondiscrimination,* p. 8762-3). When the institution administers the scholarship program, does the funding source matter?

Historically black colleges and universities. Another possible impact of the recent legal decisions is on the historically black colleges and universities (HBCUs). Justice Clarence Thomas, the only African American member of the Supreme Court, expressed support for HBCUs in a June 1995 opinion: "Because of their 'distinctive histories and traditions,' black schools can function as the center and symbol of black communities and provide examples of independent black leadership, success, and achievement" (*Nondiscrimination,* p. 4500). DOE regulations further confirm that special consideration must be given by the federal government (by both the legislative and executive branches) because HBCUs have a special mission in serving as "key link to the chain of expanding college opportunity for African American youth ..." (*Non-discrimination,* p. 8763). However, recent court rulings call for the re-evaluation of desegregation and affirmative action efforts. Do these rulings pose a danger to the continued existence of HBCUs? Can either publicly or privately funded financial aid be given special consideration in the HBCU environment?

Conclusion

Since the historic *Brown v. Board of Education* decision in 1954 and the enactment of the Civil Rights Act of 1964, government has sought far reaching remedies to eliminate racial discrimination. Justice Thomas, in his concurring opinion in *Missouri v. Jenkins* (1995) reflects on the most recent trend to reign in the power of government:

Our impatience with the pace of desegregation and with the lack of a good-faith effort on the part of school boards, led us to approve ... extraordinary remedial measures. But such powers should have been temporary and used only to overcome the wide-spread resistance to the dictates of the Constitution. The judicial overreaching we see before us today perhaps is the price we now pay for our approval of such extraordinary remedies in the past. ... Our willingness to unleash the federal equatable power has reached areas beyond school desegregation. ... The point of the Equal Protection Clause is not to enforce strict race-mixing, but to ensure that black and whites are treated equally by the State without regard to their skin color (pp. 125).

We are in the midst of a changing political and legal climate. Colleges and universities are faced with re-examining their values, policies, and procedures. This is but a microcosm of what our entire society now faces.

Notes

1. Equal protection as stated in the 14th Amendment applies only to public institutions. However, Title VI (Civil Rights Act of 1964, 42 U.S.C. § 2000d, *et seq.*) applies to both public and private institutions. The framework used to analyze equal protection claims is also used for Title VI. Therefore, the *Podberesky* decision may impact all higher education decisions, public or private.

2. Enforcement of Title VI was turned over to the Department of Education after its inception in 1978.

3. *Wygant v. Jackson Board of Education* (1986) and *City of Richmond v. J.A. Corson Company* (1989) struck down racially determined set-asides for employment lay-offs and the awarding of city contracts. *U.S. v. Paradise* (1987), while upholding the constitutionality of a plan to integrate the Alabama Highway Patrol, produced a more limiting framework for defining narrowly tailored remedies that has been applied in *Podberesky* and subsequent cases.

4. Several post-*Bakke* lawsuits challenged the constitutionality of admissions policies that considered race as one of many factors in admissions decisions (*DeRonde v. Regents of the University of California*, 1981; *Doherty v. Rutgers School of Law*

- *Newark*, 1980 and 1981; *Davis v. Halpern,* 1991). Several other cases challenged the constitutionality of at-risk programs from which less well qualified minority and disadvantaged students were considered for admission *(McDonald v. Hogness,* 1978; *DiLeo v. Board of Regents of the University of Colorado*, 1978; *McAdams v. Regents of the University of Minnesota,* 1981). All of these cases were decided in favor of the universities. The courts upheld the constitutionality of all admissions' decisions cases (none used quotas), as well as the special programs designed for at-risk students because a student's participation did not guarantee admission.

References

General Accounting Office (1994). *Higher education - Information on minority targeted scholarships* (GAO Publication No. GAO/HEHS-94-77). Washington D.C.: U.S. General Accounting Office.

Jaschik. S. (1994, February 23). Education department upholds most minority scholarships. *The Chronicle of Higher Education.* p. A36.

Jaschik. S. (1995, February 3). U of Maryland suspends scholarship programs for blacks, pending review of controversial case by Supreme Court. *The Chronicle of Higher Education.* p. A26.

Jaschik. S. (1995, May 12). Supreme Court is urged to overturn ban on minority scholarships. *The Chronicle of Higher Education.* p. A34.

Jaschik. S. (1995, June 2). "No" on black scholarships. Supreme Court won't second-guess ruling against race-exclusive awards. *The Chronicle of Higher Education.* p. A25, A29.

Williams III, J.B. (1988). Title VI regulation in education. In J. Williams, III (Ed.), *Desegregating America's colleges and universities* (pp. 3-53). New York: Teachers College Press.

Table of Legal References

Adarand v. Pena, 515 U.S. 200 (1995).
Brown v. Board of Education, 347 U.S. 483 (1954).
City of Richmond v. J.A. Croson Company, 488 U.S. 469 (1989).
Civil Rights Act of 1964, 42 U.S.C. § 2000d.
Davis v. Halpern, 768 F. Supp. 968 (D. N.Y. 1991).

DeRonde v. Regents of the University of California, 172 Cal.Rptr. 677 (1981).

DiLeo v. Board of Regents of the University of Colorado, 590 P.2d 486 (Colo. 1978).

Doherty v. Rutgers School of Law - Newark, 487 F. Supp. 1291 (D. N.J. 1980).

Doherty v. Rutgers School of Law - Newark, 651 F.2d 893 (3d Cir. 1981).

McAdams v. Regents of the University of Minnesota, 508 F. Supp. 354 (D. Minn. 1981).

McDonald v. Hogness, 598 P.2d 707 (Wash., 1979).

Missouri v. Jenkins, 515 U.S. 70 (1995).

Non-discrimination in federally assisted programs; Title VI of the civil rights act of 1964; notice. *59 Federal Register*, p. 8756 (1994).

Podberesky v. Kirwan, 767 F. Supp. 364. (D. Md. 1991).

Podberesky v. Kirwan, 956 F.2d 52 (4th Cir. 1992).

Podberesky v. Kirwan, 838 F. Supp. 1075 (D. Md. 1993).

Podberesky v. Kirwan, 38 F.3d 147 (4th Cir. 1994).

Regents of the University of California v. Bakke, 98 U.S. 2733 (1978).

U.S. v. Paradise, 480 U.S. 149 (1987).

Wygant v. Jackson Board of Education, 478 U.S. 1014 (1986).

CHAPTER 11

"AFFIRMATIVE ACTION": PAST, PRESENT, AND FUTURE

Lino A. Graglia

"Affirmative action" insofar as it is controversial, is a euphemism for racial discrimination. As knowledge of it grows, however, it tends to become more a pejorative than a euphemism, and so is increasingly replaced with a new buzz word, "diversity." How did it happen that American institutions of government and other institutions should in the late twentieth century adopt an official policy of dealing with people on the basis of race? How can such a policy be justified, how can it continue in the face of the intense opposition it necessarily generates, and what are its prospects?

The Origins of Affirmative Action

The modern law of race discrimination began with the Supreme Court's 1954 decision in *Brown v. Board of Education* and its companion case *Bolling v. Sharpe* (1954). The Court held

This chapter was originally published in *Ohio Northern University Law Review* (22), 4, 1996, pp 1207-29.

that school racial segregation and, it soon appeared (*Mayor of Baltimore v. Dawson*, 1955; *Holmes v. Atlanta*, 1955), all racial discrimination by government, state or federal, was prohibited by the Constitution. With the "all deliberate speed" formula of the following year (*Brown v. Board of Education*, 1955), however, the Court withdrew, except for the Little Rock case (*Cooper v. Aaron*, 1958), from attempting to enforce *Brown* for ten years. It became effective and enforceable only by reason of the 1964 Civil Rights Act, the most important piece of civil rights legislation in our history. In the 1964 Act, Congress in effect ratified and endorsed what it and everyone else understood to be the *Brown* principle: all racial discrimination by government is constitutionally prohibited. Congress not only endorsed this principle in education, mandating the end of segregation (Civil Rights Act of 1964, 42 U.S.C. §§ 2000c-9), but extended it to all institutions that receive federal funds (42 U.S.C. § 2000d) and even to private institutions in regard to public accommodations (42 U.S.C. §§ 2000b-3) and employment (42 U.S.C. §§ 2000e-17). The 1965 Voting Rights Act effectively ended racial discrimination in voting, and the 1968 Civil Rights Act prohibited racial discrimination in connection with housing. Virtually all official and public racial discrimination had finally been prohibited in America; we could look forward to a time, it seemed, in which people would no longer be advantaged or disadvantaged on the basis of race.

The history of the law of race discrimination since the 1964 Civil Rights Act has been a history, however, of judicial misbehavior without parallel in law. In a series of extraordinary decisions, the Supreme Court turned both *Brown* and the various titles of the Act on their heads, converting them from prohibitions of racial discrimination to their opposite, requirements of or permission for racial discrimination. The reason for this incredible judicial feat is that although segregation and racial discrimination were now effectively prohibited, the results were soon considered disappointing in relation to the unreasonable expectations that had been aroused. School segregation, for example, quickly ended as a result of the 1964 Act; children were no longer assigned to schools on the basis of race. This great achievement turned out to have only a limited effect, however, on the racial composition of the schools (Bickel, 1964).

Although racial assignment ended in the schools of the South, non-racial assignment to neighborhood schools meant, because of residential racial concentration, that racial separation would continue to exist, just as it had always existed in the schools of the North and West. Specifically, most African American students, then and now, in the South as elsewhere, continued to attend predominantly African American schools. There is no reason to believe that such schools are necessarily inferior to predominantly white schools, but the civil rights establishment that had grown up and prospered in the fight to end racial discrimination was not about to declare itself out of business simply because its objective had been achieved. Total victory is less likely to produce contentment than a search for new worlds to conquer.

Although segregation had ended and all official and public racial discrimination had been prohibited, an achievement hardly imaginable a few years before, the cry went up that "nothing had happened." The frightening thought arose that ending segregation and racial discrimination might actually make little difference in terms of the social position of African Americans. Instead of taking this as showing that racial discrimination was not nearly as important as they had thought, civil rights professionals took it as showing that further legal action was necessary. If ending segregation would not produce a high degree of school racial integration, for example, integration would have to be produced by legal fiat. That, however, was obviously a formidable task. One seemingly insuperable obstacle was that it would mean abandoning the prohibition of racial discrimination that had just been securely established and returning to a requirement of racial discrimination in school assignments, despite *Brown* and the 1964 Act. The Supreme Court, however, riding a wave of acclamation as the nation's moral leader as a result of the success of *Brown*, was up to the task, even though it would not be possible to make the move openly.

Justice William J. Brennan, Jr., the Court's super-activist, was clearly the man for the task, and he led the Court to its historical reversal of direction with his opinion for the Court in *Green v. County School Board of New Kent County,* in 1968. Although it was conceded that the district's formerly segregated schools were being operated without racial discrimination, the district was held not to be in compliance with *Brown* because only a limited amount of integration resulted. The requirement, it was therefore obvious, was no longer the elimination of racial discrimination as in *Brown*, but the practice of racial discrimination to increase integration.

Brennan explicitly denied this, however, insisting that the requirement was not integration, but something very different, "desegregation," which was merely the requirement of *Brown* (*Green v. County School Board of New Kent County*, 1968, pp. 437-38). If you have some difficulty following this, don't be discouraged; it was necessary to watch the pea closely when Justice Brennan was operating the shells.

Racial discrimination to increase integration would be required, we were apparently to understand, not because integration was required as such, but only to undo or "remedy" the effects of the prior unconstitutional segregation (*Green v. County School Board of New Kent County,* 1968, p. 437). This rationale was necessary for several reasons. First, it made the Court appear to be merely enforcing *Brown*, despite requiring rather than prohibiting racial discrimination, saving it from the impossible task of openly repudiating or qualifying *Brown*. Second, it seemed obvious that a requirement of "desegregation" would apply only to the South, which in the opinion of the North at the time undoubtedly deserved whatever the Court was doing to it, leaving the North with nothing to worry about. Third, it saved the Court from the further impossible task of explaining why it was requiring integration, something it has never done. Thus was born the remedy rationale for racial discrimination—the justification of racial discrimination as a means of combating earlier racial discrimination—that was later extended to other fields.

One problem with the *Green* definition of "desegregation" is that it is exactly the opposite of the definition in the 1964 Civil Rights Act. Title IV of the Act defines "desegregation" as the "assignment of students to public schools . . . without regard to their race," adding, redundantly, just to be sure that even federal judges would understand, that it "shall not mean the assignment of students to public schools in order to overcome racial imbalance" (42 U.S.C. § 2000c (b)).

In *Swann v. Charlotte-Mecklenburg* in 1971, however, the Court held that "desegregation" meant the exclusion of children from their neighborhood schools because of their race and their transportation across a giant urban-suburban school district in order to achieve a near-perfect racial balance, precisely what the 1964 Act was meant to preclude. This was nonetheless consistent with the Act, Chief Justice Burger explained, incredibly, because Congress did not mean its definition of "desegregation" to apply to the South (*Swann v. Charlotte-Mecklenburg*, 1971, pp. 16-18; Graglia, 1976, pp. 118-19). How is such a thing possible? the incredulous layman asks when I tell this story. I can only explain that the Court is not supreme in name alone, that anything is possible to those with uncontrolled power and the willingness to abuse it.

What the Court did to Title IV of the 1964 Act in *Green* and *Swann* it did to Title VII, which prohibits racial discrimination in employment, in *Griggs v. Duke Power Company* in 1971. The Court held that an employer's use of ordinary and appropriate employment criteria, such as literacy, level of education completed, or performance on an aptitude test, constituted racial discrimination prohibited by the Act when its effect, as is almost always the case, is to disqualify a disproportionate number of African Americans. The employer can then avoid liability only by undertaking the nearly impossible task of showing to the satisfaction of officials of the Equal Employment Opportunity Commission that its use of such employment criteria is a "business necessity." The only practical response for most employers is simply to hire a sufficient number of African Americans in preference to better qualified whites. The effect of the decision, probably the most litigation-spawning in our history, was to convert Title VII from a provision requiring that employment decisions be made without regard to race to a requirement that they not be made without taking race into account. In *United Steelworkers v. Weber* in 1979, the Court made explicit that Title VII's prohibition of racial discrimination in employment did not apply to whites.

Finally, what the Court did to Title IV in *Green* and *Swann* and Title VII in *Griggs* and *Weber*, it did to Title VI, which prohibits racial discrimination by any institution that receives federal funds, in *Regents of the University of California v. Bakke* in 1978. Alan Bakke, a rejected applicant, challenged the use of racial preferences in granting admission to the Medical School of the University of California at Davis, an institution that, like nearly all institutions of higher education, receives federal funds. With the other Justices splitting four to four on the applicability of Title VI to whites, Justice Powell wrote the deciding opinion, choosing, typically for him, to have it both ways. Title VI applies every bit as much to whites as to blacks, he said (*Regents of the University of California v. Bakke*, 1978, pp. 284-87), except that just a little bit of discrimination against whites would be okay. Race could be considered in making admissions decisions, but only as a "plus factor" to "tip the balance" in close cases, and all applicants would have to compete for each seat (*Regents of the University of California v. Bakke,* 1978, p. 322).

This completed the Court's work of perverting the 1964 Civil Rights Act and establishing, despite *Brown*, that racial discrimination to increase integration or advantage African Americans—that is, "affirmative action"—was required or permissible in grade school education, employment, and admission to institutions of higher education. In 1980, *Fullilove v. Klutznik* upheld discrimination against whites in federal contracting, although that holding, as we shall see, is in some doubt as a result of the Court's decision last year in *Adarand v. Pena* (1995).

The central question presented by "affirmative action" is, of course, whether government and government supported institutions should grant advantages to some individuals, thereby necessarily disadvantaging others, on the basis of race. For most people, ordinary American citizens, the answer could not be more clear. Such discrimination is plainly in violation of the basic American ideal that all persons are equal before the law and must be treated as individuals, not given a preferred or disfavored status by reason of being assigned membership—itself often a difficult and controversial issue—in a particular racial group. The *Brown* decision made this ideal a matter of constitutional principle, and the 1964 Civil Rights Act made it a statutory requirement. We have seen how racial preferences have, nonetheless, come to be. But disregarding their wrongful origin, how, if at all, can they be justified, and despite opposition by a large majority of the American people, continue?

Justifications Offered for Affirmative Action

What justifications can be offered for the use of racial preferences in admission to and award of benefits by, specifically, institutions of higher education? The basic argument for "affirmative action" in admission to colleges and universities when it began some thirty years ago was that the ordinary admission criteria—performance on scholastic aptitude or achievement tests and high school or college grade point averages—were racially or culturally biased, specifically and most importantly, against African Americans. If this were true, the application of lower objective standards to African American applicants would not be a matter of racial discrimination at all, but of simply making the criteria more accurate predictors of likely academic success. It is now settled beyond doubt, however, that the ordinary criteria are not biased against African Americans, that is, they do not under- predict African American academic performance (Klitgaard, 1985). In fact, as if to make the problem even more intractable, they tend to over predict as to African Americans (Klitgaard, 1985). The alleged cultural bias of the ordinary admission criteria, it may also be noted, apparently has not impeded the extraordinary academic success of members of some Asian groups, including some recently arrived on these shores.

The argument most frequently heard today for "affirmative action" in higher education is simply that without it African Americans would be "underrepresented" or, more typically, "grossly underrepresented" in such institutions. The fallacies of this argument are many. First, it is not really an argument at all, but merely assertion of the tautology that African Americans should be specially admitted to institutions of higher education in order that there be more African Americans in such institutions. It does not offer a reason why an additional African American entrant should be considered more desirable than an additional equally or even better qualified white entrant. Second, the argument assumes, contrary to the principle of political equality, that racial groups rather than individuals are the relevant entities. Individualism means that each of us as individuals represents only ourself, which is burden enough without having to represent other members of our racial or other group.

Third, institutions of higher education are not, in any event, meant to be representative institutions, but institutions that select entrants on the basis of ability and interest regarding the course of instruction. It never happens in the world, and there is no reason to expect, that members of all racial or ethnic groups will appear proportionately in all occupations or activities (Sowell, 1990). Finally, African Americans are not in fact "under represented" but "over represented" — that is, their numbers are disproportionately high — in institutions of higher education once IQ scores are taken into account (Herrnstein & Murray, 1994). In general, more than half of the students in the bottom 10 percent of a school's IQ range will be African American; with an IQ in this range a African American's chances of getting into an institution of higher education are many times better than a white's (Herrnstein & Murray, 1994, pp. 450, 472).

The most common substantive argument for "affirmative action" in higher education, as in other areas, is the argument, based on *Green*, that it provides a "remedy" for past racial discrimination, discrimination that has, in the case of education, resulted in educational or cultural disadvantage. The argument is obviously fallacious in that if remedying disadvantage were the concern, disadvantage, not race, would be the criterion. Race cannot be used as a proxy for disadvantage because not all and not only African Americans have suffered disadvantage. Indeed, African Americans who apply to institutions of higher education are typically among the most advantaged of African Americans. Preferential admission to such institutions would be a most peculiar and misdirected way of helping those African Americans who are truly in need of help, the unfortunate members of the so-called underclass. As Glenn Loury (1988) has pointed out, "The suffering of the poorest blacks creates, if you will, a fund of political capital upon which all members of the group can draw when pressing racially-based claims" (p. 20).

"Affirmative action" in higher education does not typically stop with admission, but extends to the granting, often automatic, of financial benefits. At the University of Texas Law School, for example, students who would be automatically rejected if they were white are not only admitted, but offered and given scholarships regardless of need (Graglia, 1995). The specially-admitted children of well-off African American professionals, judges, lawyers, doctors, businessmen, are automatically awarded unneeded financial aid that better qualified white students in real need are denied. My colleagues frequently point out to me that, as a believer in free markets, I am in no position to object to this. The African Americans are simply selling what we want, African American faces — they make the school immune from the devastating charge that it is "lily white" or that African Americans are "grossly underrepresented" — and in a market economy, you must expect to pay for your wants.

At Penn State, African American students, and African American students alone, are paid $580 for every year in which they achieve an average of C and $1,160 for any average above C+ (D'Souza, 1991). This is in addition to any financial aid, and is not related to need. At Florida Atlantic University, all African

Americans admitted are offered free tuition regardless of need (D'Souza, 1991). Even Harvard University has recently discovered that simply admitting African American students may not be sufficient to induce them to enroll. It lost one African American admittee, it discovered, to another school that gave him a straight grant of $85,000.00 plus $10,000.00 for summer travel expenses (Herrnstein & Murray, 1994). The market in skin color, it appears, is working well.

As the remedy rationale for "affirmative action" has become more obviously untenable, its proponents have increasingly relied on the argument that it provides a needed educational "diversity." Selection of students by race, however, provides "diversity" in nothing but race. If diversity of views or experiences were the concern, they, not race, would be the basis of selection. Race can no more used as a proxy for any characteristic relevant to higher education than it can be used as a proxy for economic or cultural disadvantage. The typical African American applicant to institutions of higher education comes from a middle or upper middle class background not readily distinguishable from that of the typical white applicant. Further, to specially admit African Americans on the ground of a presumed difference in views from those of whites is to create an expectation and perhaps even an obligation that they demonstrate these differences in their behavior, that is, that they "act black." Fulfilling this expectation usually means, unfortunately, displaying an exceptional ability to discern and protest supposed racial slights.

The irrelevance of the remedy and diversity arguments to "affirmative action" in higher education in practice is shown by the fact that no African American has ever been denied preferential admission to the University of Texas Law School, for example, on the ground that he was not economically or culturally advantaged (or, indeed, was exceptionally advantaged) or that his background and views seemed indistinguishable from those of the average white. It is only necessary, and it is entirely sufficient, that he be African American.

The effects of "affirmative action," the use of racial preferences by government, is obviously objectionable in principle. Even putting principle aside, however, it must be opposed on the purely practical ground that the size of the preferences typically involved is so large that their use cannot operate to increase racial equality or respect. It is generally understood today that "affirmative action" means racial preferences, but it is not generally understood, even by college and graduate students, just how large the preferences are. As Richard Herrnstein and Charles Murray put it in *The Bell Curve* (1994), "data about the core mechanism of affirmative action—the magnitude of the values assigned to group membership—are not part of the public debate" (pp. 449-50). "Affirmative action" is still often misunderstood as involving the use of race as something of a tie breaker in making selections among roughly equal applicants or candidates; its proponents invariably insist that although the programs are "race conscious," as they delicately put it, only "fully qualified" people are selected. In practice, however, "affirmative action" means not the bending or shading of the usual standards but the virtual abandonment of standards and the awarding of positions or other benefits to persons of preferred races who would not be considered for a moment if they were white.

The facts as to the difference between whites and African Americans in performance on standard tests of academic ability or achievement are exceedingly discouraging. It is easy to understand why most people are extremely reluctant to discuss or even to consider these facts. Indeed, one of the greatest values and benefits of a policy of race neutrality, of treating people as individuals rather than as members of racial groups, is that it makes all issues of racial group differences irrelevant. Discussion of such issues is then made not only unnecessary, but perhaps even objectionable. "Affirmative action," however, by making racial group membership paramount, makes the facts as to racial group differences crucial and discussion of them unavoidable.

The central fact of racial group differences relevant to higher education is that since the beginning of testing for intelligence or academic ability more than sixty years ago, there has been a consistent and apparently intractable difference of about fifteen points between the mean score of African Americans and the higher mean score of whites on standard tests (Graglia, 1993). It is an artifact of distributional curves that a small difference in the mean results in very large differences at the extremes, and a difference of fifteen points, about one standard deviation, is not small. This difference means that only about 11 percent of African Americans have an I.Q. above 100, as compared with about 50 percent, by definition, of the population as a whole, that 30.9 percent of whites but only 2.32 percent of African Americans have an I.Q. above 110, and that 13.4 percent of whites but only .32 percent African Americans have scores above 120 (Graglia, 1993, pp. 131-32).

There is, of course, a close correlation between I.Q. scores and scores on the SAT and similar tests of academic readiness. In 1993, for example, only 129 African Americans in the country scored 700 or better on the SAT verbal test, as compared with 7,114 whites (Herrnstein & Murray, 1994). Such facts mean that obtaining large numbers of African Americans at selective colleges requires admitting them with scores much lower than those required of whites. The result is that the premium for black skin in application to selective colleges today is about 180 combined SAT points. In 1988 the difference between the SAT score of the average white and the average African American admitted to the University of California at Berkeley, the flagship institution of California public higher education, was 288 points (Herrnstein & Murray, 1994). Less than 15 percent of the African American admittees overlapped with white admittees, and the gap between African Americans and Asians was even larger (Herrnstein & Murray, 1994). In 1976, 13,151 whites had a LSAT test score above 600 and a college GPA of 3.25 or better; the number of African Americans with these qualifications was 39 (Klitgaard, 1985). In 1992, only 7 percent of incoming African American law students had scores above the white mean (Herrnstein & Murray, 1994). A 1977 study of ten selective law schools showed that the average African American law student was in the bottom 1 percent of the white distribution (Powers, 1977). At the University of Texas Law School, recent litigation revealed, the score required for the automatic admission of African Americans was *lower* than the score applied for the automatic rejection of whites (*Hopwood v. Texas*, 1996).

One of the perverse affects of "affirmative action" is virtually to guarantee that most African American students, even among the highest scoring, will be placed in schools above the level at which they can fully compete. A student meeting or nearly meeting the ordinary admission qualifications to the University of Texas Law School, for example, would likely be bid away from Texas by Harvard or Yale, just as Texas takes students away from the many less selective schools where they would be fully competitive. Again, all questions of principle aside, it is difficult to imagine a racial policy better calculated to maximize dissatisfaction and dissension. Paul Fussell (1988) wrote that "there are some ideas so preposterous that only an educated person could believe them." Only a very highly educated person could insist that admissions, scholarships, and hiring be allocated on the basis of race, despite the enormous differences in qualifications involved, and then purport to be dumbfounded as to the source of racial tensions on campus. "Affirmative action" is a prescription for racial conflict and animosity, and the prescription is being filled.

"Affirmative action" students are almost always convinced, reasonably enough, that they are qualified to compete and expected to succeed at the institutions that have made such great efforts to induce them to enroll. When they discover, as most soon must, that they cannot compete with their classmates, no matter how hard they try, their perception that they have not been helped but used and deceived is well founded. Finding themselves unable to play the game being played, they will insist, as self-respect requires, that the game be changed. Thus are born demands for African American studies and multiculturalism. These innovations perform the twin functions of reducing the need for ordinary academic work while also providing support for the view that the academic difficulties of the African American students are the result, not of their substantially lower qualifications, but of racial antipathy. If racial preferences engender white resentment, as they must, it will be taken to indicate only that whites require additional specialized instruction in the deplorable history and moral shortcomings of their race. Thus are born racism seminars and compulsory sensitivity training.

Forces powerful enough to institute so radical and misguided a program will necessarily be powerful enough to respond to its disastrous consequences with something other than an admission that they have made a terrible mistake. When there is no credible response to criticism of a policy that will not be changed, the response will be an attempt to suppress the criticism. Thus is born the insistence on political correctness and its enforcement with "hate speech" and "anti-harassment" codes. The very epitome of political incorrectness is to point out that a school's "affirmative action" policy is actually a policy of racially preferential admissions. The only thing worse is to specify the actual disparity in the admissions standards being applied to persons from different racial groups. Proponents of "hate speech" codes are certainly correct that it is extremely humiliating to racially preferred students to have a public discussion of the standards by which they were admitted. Instead of concluding that the policy must, for that reason alone, be rejected, they conclude that such discussions must be banned.

The only surprise about "affirmative action" in higher education is not that it produces protest and turmoil, but that the protest has not come sooner and been much greater. Who would have thought that American citizens would submit so quietly and so long to discrimination against themselves and, especially, their children because of their race? This apparent acquiescence has been due in part to the fact that "affirmative action" programs have from the beginning been characterized by misrepresentation and deceit. They were introduced and are still defended as programs for the "culturally or economically disadvantaged" although in fact they were and are based solely on race (Graglia, 1993; Graglia, 1970). Their proponents face the dilemma that we have "affirmative action" programs in higher education only because African Americans can not compete academically with whites, but to admit that fact would largely defeat the point of the programs which is to create the appearance that African Americans can successfully compete (Mansfield, 1991). Concealment and evasion are therefore essential and pervasive. For example, when Georgetown University law student Timothy Maguire made public that African Americans were admitted to the school with lower scores than whites, Law School Dean Judith Areen flatly and falsely denied that racial discrimination was involved (Maguire, 1992).

Another and probably even more important reason for the apparent acquiescence by white Americans in "affirmative action" is not that they have acquiesced — they have not — but that they have been intimidated into silence. To question preferential treatment for African Americans has been to open oneself to the devastating charge of "racism," even though it is the proponents of "affirmative action" who insist on the centrality of race. In academia, there has been something of a contest among professors as to who could show that he is the most "anti-racist." To voice the slightest question about "affirmative action" would be to disqualify oneself from this contest, and that is a burden that few academics have been willing to bear. The function of the insistence on "political correctness" that pervades our campuses is to make it as costly and threatening as possible to object to racial discrimination.

The Future of Affirmative Action

This brings us, finally, to the question of the future of "affirmative action." There are many indications that its prospects are not good. As the extent and seriousness of racial preferences has become more clear, as the number of victims has increased, and as the false facade of providing a remedy for the disadvantaged has dropped away, more and more people have found the courage to openly oppose it. "Affirmative action" has finally been put up for public debate by the open opposition of several candidates for the Republican presidential nomination. Governor Pete Wilson of California has succeeded in inducing the Regents of the University of California System to order the termination of all "affirmative action" programs in the system (Olsen, 1996). Illustrative of the intense resistance that can be expected from academics and the educational bureaucracy, however, the Governor and the Board of Regents have encountered the recalcitrance, not to say insubordination, of the President of the University System who is seeking to delay implementation of the decision as long as possible (Honan, 1995).

Perhaps most important is the California Civil Rights Initiative, which took the question of "affirmative action" out of the hands of judges, political leaders, and bureaucrats and put it directly in the hands of the people. The Initiative, a resounding victory for popular self-government, amended the California Constitution by referendum to prohibit race and sex preferences in public education, employment, and contracting. If California, one tenth of the nation, can successfully end "affirmative action," its proponents will find it difficult to resist popular movements to end it elsewhere.

"Affirmative action" may also be losing support and encountering opposition in the federal courts, the very institutions that wrongfully gave it birth. Three decisions handed down in the past year are highly significant in this regard. *Kirwan v. Podberesky* (1995) involved a challenge to a lush financial aid scholarship program for which only African Americans were eligible. A federal district judge, finding that African Americans were "underrepresented" at the university, upheld the program as a remedy for past discrimination by the formerly segregated university (*Podberesky v. Kirwan*, 1993). The program, he found, would help the university overcome the "poor reputation" it allegedly had among

African Americans and the alleged perception by some African Americans of a "hostile racial atmosphere on campus," both traceable to the university's history of discrimination (*Podberesky v. Kirwan*, 1993, pp. 1084-85, 1092-94).

A unanimous panel of the Court of Appeals for the Fourth Circuit reversed (*Podberesky v. Kirwan*, 1994). The court held that the university came before it with a presumption that its race-based program could not be sustained. It rejected the "poor reputation" and "hostile racial attitude" claims as insufficient to support racial preferences, and rejected the district court's finding of "underrepresentation" as based on an improper comparison. The scholarship program failed to meet either requirement of the "strict scrutiny" test that the court found to be applicable: it was not shown to serve any "compelling need" or shown to be "narrowly tailored" in terms of such need. For example, the program, like nearly all "affirmative action" programs in higher education, gave preference even to out-of-state African Americans, which is difficult to justify as a remedy for the university's past discrimination against residents. The Fourth Circuit ordered that the scholarship program be made available to all applicants without regard to race. The Supreme Court denied certiorari, allowing the decision to stand (*Kirwan v. Podberesky*, 1995). This result is certainly a bad omen for the racially discriminatory scholarship programs that are now pervasive in higher education. If the court's skeptical and realistic approach is adopted by other courts, it would be a very bad omen for racial preferences in higher education in general.

Hopwood v. Texas (1996) could be the *Bakke* case of the present day, the decision that determines the fate of "affirmative action" in admission to institutions of higher education. Plaintiffs were rejected white applicants to the University of Texas Law School who would have been automatically admitted had they been African American or Mexican-American. Justice Powell's decisive opinion in *Bakke*, as noted above, permits racial discrimination against whites in university admissions, despite *Brown* and the 1964 Civil Rights Act, but only, supposedly, if race is used only as a "plus factor" to "tip the balance" in close cases. In fact, however, *Bakke* is treated by colleges and universities across the country as carte blanche for discrimination against whites. The University of Texas Law School did not make even a pretense of complying with *Bakke*'s supposed limitations. Instead of requiring that all applicants compete for admission, as required by *Bakke*, the law school simply set up a separate "minority" admissions committee to pass on applications from African Americans and Mexican-Americans and grant them admission until the desired numbers were reached (*Hopwood v. Texas*, 1996). The school practiced "race norming," according to which African Americans competed only with African Americans, Mexican-Americans only with Mexican-Americans and whites (and Asians) only with whites (*Hopwood v. Texas*, 1996). The school established number scores for the automatic admission of African Americans and Mexican-Americans that were lower than the scores established for the automatic rejection of whites (*Hopwood v. Texas*, 1996).

A federal district judge found, as he could hardly have avoided, that the law school violated the plaintiff's constitutional and statutory rights (*Hopwood v. Texas,* 1994). He refused, however, to order their admission to the school or to grant them damages, attorneys fees, or any other substantial relief. In fact, he explicitly and enthusiastically endorsed the law school's objective of making each entering class at least 10 percent Mexican-American and 5 percent African American. This cannot be done, however, if African American and Mexican-American applicants are made to compete with whites, as he purported to require, unless race is used not merely as a plus factor but as the determining factor. In effect, the judge required only that the law school pursue its racially discriminatory practices less openly.

On appeal by plaintiffs, the Fifth Circuit handed down a thoroughgoing condemnation of almost all use of racial preferences in higher education (*Hopwood v. Texas*, 1996). The state sought to bring the case to the Supreme Court, but the Court declined to hear it, permitting the decision of the Fifth Circuit to stand (*Thurgood Marshall Legal Society v. Hopwood*, 1996).

In a previous discussion of the *Hopwood* case, I wrote that "the Fifth Circuit, unfortunately, cannot overrule *Bakke*." (Graglia, 1995a). The Fifth Circuit did effectively overrule *Bakke*, however, or at least what most people thought *Bakke* meant. Justice Powell's decisive opinion in *Bakke* stated that the use of race as a "plus factor" in making admissions decisions could be justified by a school's interest in "diversity" in the student body, an interest that he found "compelling" because protected, he said, by the First Amendment (*Regents of the University of California v. Bakke,* 1978*)*.

In *Hopwood* (1996), the court argued that "diversity" was never accepted as a compelling interest justifying racial discrimination by any justice except Powell and that later cases hold that the need to remedy past racial discrimination is the only compelling interest. The court therefore held that "diversity" is not a justification for racial preferences. The court also held that the remedy justification is not applicable to so-called societal discrimination, but only to discrimination by the particular institution using racial preferences (*Hopwood v. Texas*, 1996). Further, there must be a finding that the past discrimination has present effects and a determination of the magnitude of those effects, and the racial preference given must be limited to what is necessary to remedy those effects (*Hopwood v. Texas*, 1996, pp. 950-952). Under these standards, it is safe to say, racial preferences in admission to institutions of higher education will be justifiable very rarely.

Most academics and the academic bureaucracy are strongly committed to "affirmative action" for purely political reasons. In Texas, for example, the Black Caucus in the state legislature wants to know only why there are not more African Americans in the law school; the Mexican-American Caucus wants to know why there are not more Mexican-Americans. No one complains if highly qualified and deserving whites are denied admission. The result is that if academics can engage in racial discrimination at all, they will find ways of making race determinative. The only way this conduct can be deterred is by making it dangerous and expensive. In *Hopwood*, the Fifth Circuit affirmed the district court's denial of punitive damages to the plaintiffs. It explicitly stated, however, that "if the law school continues to operate a disguised or overt racial classification system in the future, its actors could be subject to actual and punitive damages" (*Hopwood v. Texas*, 1996, p. 959). One may assume that will catch the law school's attention.

The third recent decision important to the future of "affirmative action," though not directly related to higher education, is the Supreme Court's decision last year in *Adarand v. Pena* (1995). Exactly what the decision means is unclear. Supreme Court Justices, all being lawyers, are not, unfortunately, burdened with a passion for clarity and consistency, with the result that their pronouncements can resemble those of the Oracle at Delphi. Explicitly overruling *Metro Broadcasting v. FCC* (1990), Justice Brennan's last contribution to the nation's welfare, the Court held that the so-called strict scrutiny test must be applied to federal as well as state race-based programs. This certainly sounds like bad news for "affirmative action," but how bad is hard to say because of the ambivalence of the opinion, which was by the characteristically ambivalent Justice O'Connor. "Strict scrutiny" supposedly means that a challenged program is to be presumed unconstitutional, as the Fourth Circuit pointed out in *Podberesky*, and upheld only upon a showing of a "compelling interest" that cannot be served in a less objectionable way. As Powell's *Bakke* opinion shows, however, what is or is not a "compelling interest" is, even more than beauty, in the eye of the beholder—surely no one except him would have imagined that racial "diversity" is a "compelling interest" in higher education.

Justice O'Connor's *Adarand* opinion insists that the use of racial preferences must be viewed with "skepticism" and given "a most searching examination" (*Adarand v. Pena*, 1995, pp. 2100, 2111). Skepticism is the last thing, as *Podberesky* illustrates, that racial preference programs can survive. The basic justification for such programs, that they are used to remedy cultural or educational disadvantage, is, as I have tried to show, simply false. At the same time, however, the *Adarand* Court refused to explicitly overrule *Fullilove v. Klutznik*, which upheld a racial set-aside program in federal contracting that could not survive the least degree of skepticism or searching examination. The Court also refused to enter judgment for the discriminated-against plaintiff-contractor in *Adarand*. Instead, it merely remanded the case for reconsideration by the district court in accordance with the newly established correct standard, although it is hard to see how the challenged program can possibly survive a realistic application of that standard. Finally, as if to throw cold water on any enthusiasm for the decision, the Court insisted that strict scrutiny does not mean "strict in theory, but fatal in fact" (*Adarand v. Pena*, 1995, pp. 2101, 2117-2118). It also stated that there is still plenty of racial discrimination to be "remedied" (*Adarand v. Pena*, 1995, p. 2109), keeping up the pretense that racial preferences have something to do with remedying discrimination.

The result of all this ambivalence was that Justice Souter—the latest living testimonial to the incompetence of Republican presidents in selecting judges—was able to argue that essentially nothing had happened. He saw no reason why the lower courts could not comply with the Supreme Court's decision by simply reaffirming their earlier decisions upholding the program with just a little change of language (*Adarand v. Pena*, 1995). It would be a mistake, therefore, for opponents of racial preferences to get their hopes too high on the basis of *Adarand*, especially considering that it was a five to four decision and that the dissenting justices, Stevens, Souter, Ginsburg and Breyer, can be relied on to stick to their support of "affirmative action," while not all members of the majority can be trusted to consistently oppose it.

Finally, there is the question of the proper role of the courts, if any, in ending "affirmative action" rather than leaving it to the decision of elected legislators, as is more appropriate in a system of representative self-government, or to the people themselves as through the California referendum process. Even putting the Fifth Circuit's *Hopwood* decision aside, if the lower federal courts and state courts would apply the *Bakke* limitations on the use of the race in good faith, permitting its use only as a plus factor, not the decisive factor, the result would be largely to eliminate race-based admission programs in higher education. The Supreme Court, for its part, should take the first opportunity to overrule *Bakke* as based on a gross perversion of Title VI of the 1964 Civil Rights Act. Title VI prohibits all racial discrimination at institutions that receive federal funds, as nearly all colleges and universities do, and that should settle the question of the illegality of race-based programs unless and until Title VI is repealed. This is only to say, again, that the function of judges is to enforce the law in good faith; the *Bakke* decision was not an instance of judicial good faith.

It is also arguable, of course, that racial discrimination by state institutions of higher education is not only illegal under the 1964 Act but unconstitutional under *Brown*. In my view, however, this is a much more difficult question. I very much doubt that the Equal Protection Clause of the Fourteenth Amendment was meant to preclude state efforts to help African Americans as African Americans. I equally doubt, however, that it was meant to prohibit school racial segregation either. One may distinguish logically between racial discrimination meant to advantage members of minority groups from racial discrimination that disadvantages them, even if it is not always easy to tell the two apart. The strength and success of *Brown* rests, however, on the understanding—the understanding that gave us the 1964 Civil Rights Act—that it established a principle of moral-like certainty, the principle that all racial discrimination by government is impermissible. An argument can be made that the Court should stand by that principle, that it cannot be qualified without being severely and dangerously weakened.

Another argument for judicial disallowance of "affirmative action" programs in the name of the Constitution is that such programs are largely products of judicial misbehavior. It is essentially the Supreme Court that invented "affirmative action," quite wrongly and deviously, in a series of decisions beginning with *Green*. If the Court should now disallow "affirmative action" programs as unconstitutional, it would be to a large extent simply correcting its own mistake and acting to undo some of the incalculable injury to the nation it has caused.

There can be no doubt, nonetheless, that it would be better if "affirmative action" were ended through the ordinary political process. It would be healthy for American democracy to develop the habit of making major policy decisions without the Supreme Court's help. I do not expect to see "affirmative action" eliminated from American life, and perhaps it should not be as far as private institutions are concerned. It appears, however, that the days are numbered for the use of racial preferences by government institutions. The California Board of Regents has barred the use of racial preferences in the state's system of higher education. The people of California have adopted the California Civil Rights Initiative, barring the use of race and sex preferences by state agencies in employment, contracting, and higher education. These developments in California, traditionally the bellwether of the nation, give us reason to expect to see the proponents of "affirmative action" programs in full retreat.

References

Bickel, A. (1964). The decade of school desegregation: Progress and prospects. *Columbia Law Review*, 193-203.

Civil Rights Act of 1964, Pub. L. No. 88-352, 78 State. 24 (codified as amended at 42 U.S.C. §2000a-2000h-6 (1994)).

Civil Rights Act of 1968, Pub. L. No. 90-284, 82 Stat. 73 (codified as amended at 42 U.S.C. § 3601-3619 (1994)).

D'Souza, D. (1991). *Illiberal education: The politics of race and sex on campus.* New York: The Free Press.

Fussell, P. (1988). *Thank god for the atom bomb and other essays.* New York: Summit Books.

Graglia, L. A. (1970). Special admission of the "culturally deprived" to law school. *University of Pennsylvania Law Review, 119,* 351-352.

Graglia, L. A. (1976). *Disaster by decree: the supreme court decisions on race and the schools.* Ithaca: Cornell University Press.

Graglia, L. A. (1993). Racial preferences in admission to institution of higher education. In H. Dickman (ed.), *The imperiled academy* (pp. 127-151). New Brunswick: Transction.

Graglia, L. A. (1995). Hopwood v. Texas: Racial preferences in higher education upheld and endorsed. *Journal of Legal Education, 45,* 83.

Graglia, L. A. (1995a). Affirmative action: *Podberesky, Hopwood,* and *Adarand*: Twilight for race-based programs. *Texas Lawyer, Sept 25, 1995,* 26.

Herrnstein, R. J., & Murray, C. (1994). *The bell curve.* New York: The Free Press.

Honan, W. H. (1995, July 19). Regents prepare for storm on affirmative action. *The New York Times,* p. B7.

Klitgaard, R. (1985). *Choosing elites.* New York: Basic Books.

Loury, G. C. (1988). The moral quandary of the black community. *The public I nterest, 79,* 9-22.

Maguire, T. (1992). My bout with affirmative action. *Commentary, 93(4),* 50-52.

Mansfield, H. C., Jr. (191). *America's constitutional soul.* Baltimore: Johns Hopkins.

Olsen, F. (1996). Symposium on the trends in legal citation and scholarship: Affirmative action: Necessary but not sufficient. *Chicago-Kent Law Review, 71,* 937-945.

Powers, D. E. (1977). Comparing predictions of law school performance for black, Chicano, and white law students. *Reports of LSAC Sponsored Research, 3,* 721-775.

Sowell, T. (1990). *Preferential policies: An international perspective.* New York: William Morrow.

Table of Legal References

Adarand Constructors, Inc. v. Pena, 115 S. Ct. 2097 (1995).
Bolling v. Sharpe, 347 U.S. 497 (1954).
Brown v. Board of Education, 347 U.S. 483 (1954).
Brown v. Board of Education, 349 U.S. 294 (1955).
Cooper v. Aaron, 358 U.S. 1 (1958).

Fullilove v. Klutznik, 448 U.S. 448 (1980).

Green v. County School Board of New Kent County, 391 U.S. 430 (1968).

Griggs v. Duke Power Co., 515 F.2d 86 (4th Cir. 1975).

Hopwood v. Texas, 861 F. Supp. 551 (W.D. Tex. 1994), *rev'd,* 78 F.3d 932 (5th Cir. 1996), *cert. denied,* 116 S.Ct. 2581 (1996).

Hopwood v. Texas, 78 F.3d 932 (5th Cir. 1996), *cert. denied,* 116 S. Ct. 2581 (1996).

Kirwan v. Podberesky, 115 S.Ct. 2001 (1995).

Mayor of Baltimore v. Dawson, 350 U.S. 877 (1955) (public beaches).

Podberesky v. Kirwan, 838 F. Supp. 1075 (D. Md. 1993), *rev'd,* 38 F.3d 147 (4th cir. 1994), *cert. denied,* 115 S. Ct. 2001 (1995).

Podberesky v. Kirwan, 38 F.3d 147 (4th Cir. 1994), *cert. denied,* 115 S. Ct. 2001 (1995).

Regents of the University of California v. Bakke, 438 U.S. 265 (1978).

Swann v. Charlotte-Mecklenburg Board of Education, 402 U.S. 1 (1971).

Thurgood Marshall Legal Society v. Hopwood, 116 S.Ct. 2581 (1996).

United Steelworkers v. Weber, 444 U.S. 889 (1979).

Voting Rights Act of 1965, Pub. L. No. 89-110, 79 Stat. 437 (codified as amended at 42 U.S.C. § 1973 (1194)).

CHAPTER 12

FACULTY "REMNANTS" OF JIM CROW AND MINORITY-TARGETED SCHOLARSHIP PROGRAMS

Monique Weston Clague

> *Ghosts of the past, which potentially have segregative effects by stimulating a climate nonconducive to diversity on the historically white campuses, include the lack of minority faculty as well as their absence in significant numbers in top positions within Mississippi's academia.*
> *U.S. & Ayers v. Fordice*, 1995, p. 1471

In 1954, the United States Supreme Court outlawed government mandated apartheid in the nation's public K-12 schools in its monumental decision in *Brown v. Board of Education*. In 1955, in *Brown v. Board of Education - II*, the Court held that segregated schools must be abolished. In 1968, thirteen years of "massive resistance" later, the Supreme Court ruled in *Green v. New Kent County School Board* that *Brown I* and *Brown II* meant school boards were charged with an "affirmative duty" to convert to "unitary" school systems. It was not until 1992, twenty-four years after *Green,* that the Supreme Court ruled for the first time,

in *U.S. & Ayers v. Fordice*, that public university systems also have
an affirmative obligation to dismantle prior de jure segregated
colleges and universities. The "race neutral and free choice"
standard for which the state of Mississippi argued in *Fordice*, and
which was endorsed by the lower federal courts, no more satisfies
the affirmative duty in a public university context than it did in the
context of public elementary and secondary education.

Although agreeing with the Court of Appeals that "a state
university system is quite different in very relevant respects from
primary and secondary schools", (p. 278) and that the remedies for
contemporary "remnants" of de jure segregation would differ, the
Supreme Court nevertheless invoked its landmark 1968 decision in
Green. Fordice, then, is, to an extent as yet uncertain, higher
education's *Green*. But just how far the Supreme Court is willing
to carry the judiciary into institutional reform litigation is still far
from clear.

This chapter focuses on some of the unanswered questions
and unresolved contradictions that mark two particular facets of
higher education desegregation litigation since the Supreme Court's
1992 *Fordice* decision: faculty "remnants" of Jim Crow on the one
hand, and minority targeted scholarship support programs on the
other. Such programs will be referred to generically as MTS
programs, following the term used by the U.S. General Accounting
Office (GAO) in its January 1994 study (conducted at the request
of Democratic Senators and Congresspersons). Strongly
supportive of MTS programs as tools to recruit and retain minority
students, the GAO report undergirded the U.S. Department of
Education's May 1994 Final Policy Guidance on the lawfulness of
race-exclusive scholarships under Title VI of the Civil Rights Act
of 1964, the statute that prohibits race discrimination in federally
funded programs. It is a central point of this chapter that MTS
programs should be considered not only in terms of student
recruitment, but also as race-specific affirmative action that can
address, in the long run, the supply side of the problem of small
numbers, in most cases token presence, of minority American
faculty at predominantly white colleges and universities. But the
connection between supply side MTS programs and greater faculty
integration in higher education in the long run is one the federal
courts have (as of the date this chapter goes to publication)
completely missed.

Affirmative Duty: Affirmative Action?

Does the fact that the Supreme Court rejected the equation in *Fordice* of a state's affirmative constitutional duty to integrate with a law of race neutrality imply that some kind of race-specific, and preferential affirmative action may be constitutional? The opinion was notably enigmatic on this matter. The Court remanded *Fordice*, then in its seventeenth year of litigation, back to the District Court for Northern Mississippi to figure that out, to be guided by this newly formulated, question-begging, and confusion-generating standard:

> If the state perpetuates policies and practices traceable to its prior system that continue to have segregative effects. ... [Part I] and such policies are without sound educational justification [Part II] and can be practicably eliminated, [Part III] the state has not satisfied its burden of proving that it has dismantled its prior system (pp. 730-731).

What if plaintiffs successfully show the traceability (a term that has generated inconsistent tests of causation) of present policies and practices that continue to have segregative effects? Can a court order race-specific remedies? The negating verbs "eliminate" and "dismantle", employed in the sentence just quoted, as well as others also used by the Justices — "disestablish", "reform", "negate", "undo", "minimize", "counteract" — did not clarify just how race-specific remedies may be. Indeed, the phrase "affirmative action" appears only in a footnote in *Fordice*, and not once in the main body of the majority opinion.

Could and would the Supreme Court's 1992 *Fordice* decision be read by the District and Appeals courts on remand to countenance the creation of minority targeted scholarship programs — one example of race-specific affirmative action — as one means of satisfying Mississippi's affirmative duty to dismantle its prior de jure system of higher education? Would the district court mandate that Mississippi initiate and expand minority scholarship programs in order to recruit and retain African American students at Mississippi's historically white institutions (HWI)? Would the district court for northern Mississippi mandate participation in minority doctoral support programs as part of a long term strategy for increasing the size of the pool from which future African American faculty might be drawn? The answer to these questions to date (November 1996) is no. The March 1995 opinion on remand of the District Court   did not include the remedy of minority scholarships in its decree.

What does *Fordice* mean for other formerly de jure segregated state colleges and universities that either did not follow or belatedly departed from Mississippi's model of steadfast resistance to the desegregation challenge with its invocation of the defense of race neutrality? May state colleges and universities voluntarily undertake race-specific remedial initiatives for what they determine to be the continuing segregative effects of policies and practices traceable to their Jim Crow pasts?

And what of "induced voluntary" MTS programs such as the Benjamin Banneker Fellowship Program for high-achieving African Americans at the University of Maryland at College Park (UMCP)? This MTS program was developed in partial response to pressures from the U.S. Office for Civil Rights (OCR) stemming from the 20 year old "*Adams*" litigation. Originally titled *Adams v. Richardson* (1973), this unusual case was initiated in 1969 by the NAACP/Legal Defense Fund as part of a wholesale strategy against the OCR for its "conscious policy of non-enforcement" of Title VI against ten state systems of higher education. *Adams* ended in 1990, when the Court of Appeals for the District of Columbia dismissed the case, rejecting the very premise of the *Adams* model. Congress had not authorized actions by private parties under federal civil rights statutes, the Court held, to challenge the "tardigrade enforcement of antidiscrimination statutes by their federal enforcement agencies" (*Weal v. Cavasos*, p. 747).

The year before closure of the *Adams* litigation, *Podberesky v. Kirwan* began. Daniel Podberesky, a non-African American UMCP student who was denied a Banneker scholarship, challenged UMCP's Banneker program as unlawful "reverse discrimination." In 1993, the Fourth Circuit rejected the District Court's reliance on OCR determinations of UMCP's past discrimination and continuing non-compliance with Title VI.

In May 1994, on his second appeal to the Fourth Circuit, Podberesky won. The Appeals Court gave the Supreme Court's *Fordice* decision scant attention. Instead it relied heavily on its understanding of the Supreme Court's earlier decision in *City of Richmond v. Croson* (1989) — a case that had nothing to do with the desegregation of educational institutions. The Fourth Circuit's application of *Croson* to *Podberesky* meant that to demonstrate a "compelling governmental interest" justifying affirmative action, the burden was on the defendant University of Maryland to show the present effects of its past de jure segregation, whereas *Fordice* put the burden on defendant Mississippi to show there are no present effects.

In June 1995, the Supreme Court declined review of *Podberesky's* stunning blow to an MTS program. A year later, the high court also declined review of the Fifth Circuit's decision in *Hopwood v. Texas* (1996) holding that the University of Texas Law School "may not use race as a factor in law school admissions." The Fifth Circuit's opinion in *Hopwood* relied on *Croson*, and in good measure on *Podberesky.*

Because the Supreme Court declined to review both *Podberesky* and *Hopwood*, these particular cases are closed. But the issues they addressed remain alive. The refusal to review did not mean affirmation; it postponed showdowns. As this manuscript goes to press, however, *Fordice* remains at least partially open. On March 7, 1995, the federal District Court for Northern Mississippi issued its remand decision in *Fordice.* Parts of that decision are now on appeal to the Fifth Circuit Court of Appeals, the court that decided *Hopwood.*

Throughout the twenty-one years of the continuing *Fordice* litigation, which began in 1975, the most visible and politically charged questions have centered on the continued existence of Mississippi's historically black colleges and universities (HBCUs — referred to as historically black institutions, HBIs, in *Fordice*). But *Fordice* also deals with many other challenged "remnants" of Jim Crow, among them the faculty "remnants" of Mississippi's state system of higher education and its facially neutral scholarships that go disproportionately to whites. In this chapter, the treatment of *Fordice* is limited primarily to these latter two issues.

Fordice and Faculty "Remnants"?

At both the 1987 trial, which took place four years before the Supreme Court's decision in *Fordice*, and at the second trial on remand in 1994, faculty integration at HBCUs was *not* at issue, for the District Court acknowledged that "[t]he statistical presence of other-race (i.e., non-black) faculty at the historically black institutions is substantial and unchallenged" (*Ayers*, p. 1537). The faculties of the HBCUs were, therefore, in the eyes of the law, racially integrated, even if the gross disparity in the proportion of

African American faculty at the HWIs compared to the HBCUs was treated as an indicator of racially identifiable institutions. Thus, testimony focused primarily on the racial composition of the faculties at Mississippi's HWIs.

The Defense Frames the Issues
    "We Can't Find Any Defense." At the 1987 trial and again at the 1994 trial on remand, Mississippi's defense strategy was to conceptualize the faculty issue strictly as a recruitment and hiring problem, as if *Fordice* were an employment discrimination case, which of course it is not. The defense argument ran as follows: The five HWIs, which claimed to recruit on a nationwide basis, faced keen competition in attempting to hire from the low and declining pool of African Americans earning doctorates; they faced competition for "the same limited supply" of black PhD.s not only from colleges and universities nationwide, but also from business and industry as consumers of PhD.s as well. Poor Mississippi, the state with the lowest per capita income in the nation, a state which had cut funding for higher education, a state which offered the lowest average salaries of all the Southern Regional Education Board institutions, couldn't find many African American faculty. Moreover, the defense's expert witness (Feisel, 1987) argued, it was difficult to attract African American faculty to the University of Mississippi because Oxford, its home town, lacked a cadre of African American professionals, and because Mississippi had an "image problem" - the image, referred to repeatedly at the 1994 trial, of "Mississippi Burning."
    As considered more fully below, framing the faculty piece of the integration mosaic in terms of meeting affirmative action hiring goals by race neutral means, in light of the small existing pool of eligible African Americans with doctorates, was, of course, as the defense wanted it, a way of protecting the status quo. Given the very tiny number of African American faculty in positions of power and influence in Mississippi's HWIs — discussed in more detail below — an employment, *qua* hiring framework ignores the history that helps explain the very limited contemporary African American presence of faculty and staff. It ignores the psychologically stressful performance pressures which tokenism imposes on minorities (Kanter, 1977a, 1977b; Bell, 1987; Ely, 1995). It avoids consideration of the role of Mississippi's doctoral granting HWIs, which have a virtual monopoly on doctoral production in

Mississippi, in contributing to the size of the pool of African American doctorates from which they seek to hire. And *a fortiorari,* it protects the defense from even considering the possibility that MTS programs might offer long-term, "educationally sound" production-side strategies for expanding the pool of African American doctorates.

If Mississippi's "we can't find any" argument had a certain plausibility within the confines of an employment discrimination framework, two other arguments the defense offered in 1987 to explain the small number of African American faculty at HWIs now read more like concessions, in advance of the Supreme Court's 1990 decision in *Fordice,* that Mississippi's HWIs experience continuing effects of past discrimination.

Tenured-In. In 1987, Mississippi included an argument that implied that even if the HWIs could find some eligible African Americans, it couldn't hire them in tenure track positions because the HWIs were "tenured in" (Feisel, 1987). But surely being tenured in with non-African American faculty is a legacy of tenuring in white faculty when zero or few African American faculty were eligible — because of segregation and discrimination in employment and education, including exclusion from graduate education at the HWIs. Is this not a striking example of the way in which racial inequality perpetuates itself? In the early 1990s, the faculty profile at Mississippi's white institutions of higher education still exhibited serious traces of *Mississippi: The Closed Society,* a society described by University of Mississippi Professor James Silver in his riveting book, first published in 1963 - that consciously fostered insularity which both fed on and sustained the notion of white supremacy; a society that considered "non-white Mississippians and all others as outlanders" (p. 164).

A catalog count for 1992, conducted by the author of this chapter, revealed that over 400 white faculty, roughly one-third of the tenure track and tenured ranks at the five HWIs, had received their highest graduate degrees from one of Mississippi's three white doctoral granting institutions. Compared with the national norms, these figures bespeak a history of a very strong "grow-your-own" white faculty policy and practice. By comparison, only sixteen African American tenure track and tenured faculty teaching at the five HWIs (out of a total of 55-60) earned their highest degree from a Mississippi HWI, of whom only seven were tenured.

"Mississippi Burning." If the tenured-in argument seemed to make the case for traceability in advance of *Fordice*, so did a third defense argument that was used at both the 1994 and 1987 trials. Mississippi has an image problem with African American doctorates. Specifically, the defense argued, Mississippi's HWIs are handicapped in their ability to recruit and to hire African American faculty because of the image of "Mississippi Burning." This is a defense? Does not the image argument illustrate how the HWIs are haunted by the "ghosts" of their Jim Crow past? But that is not the way the defense saw it. In essence, Mississippi turned an admission of traceability into as an exonerating defense of the small number of African American faculty and administrators in positions of power and influence at its HWIs.

In the District Court's 1987 decision, the decision vacated by the Supreme Court in 1992, one was presented with a portrait of valiant Mississippi doing as best it could, given a PhD. supply-side problem that was nationwide in scope. Mississippi's "we can't find any" argument won the day.

> The evidence shows ... that the defendants have adopted racially neutral hiring policies with respect to faculty and staff at each of the institutions of higher education ...The Court is not aware of any additional minority faculty and staff recruitment procedures the defendants could implement which would assure greater minority faculty and staff representation at the predominately white institutions ... . (p. 1563)

Faculty Remnants: Plaintiffs Frame the Issues

In November 1992, following the Supreme Court's remand of *Fordice*, private plaintiffs and the United States submitted a "Unified List of Policies and/or Practices" - (i.e, remnants). They identified, *inter alia*, three faculty-related remnants: (1) the policy and practices of the system governing board of ratifying employment recommendations of individual universities which perpetuate the racial identifiability of those universities as well as the recommendations themselves; (2) the policies and practices of the individual universities that result on the whole in whites being hired at HWIs and African Americans at HBCUs. (3) the HWIs' practices of granting full professorships and tenure status to few African-American persons; and (4) the policy and practice of paying lower salaries to the faculty at the HBCUs than to the faculty at the HWIs. In 1993, private plaintiffs linked the small number of African American faculty at the HWIs to the fact that Mississippi offered few graduate programs at the HBCUs in the de jure period to the present (Private Plaintiffs, p. 10, U.S. Findings, 1993).   In the de jure era, no African Americans could earn doctoral degrees in the state; few earned them for many years after. Even so late in the segregated post-de jure era as the decade 1979-1989, when the HWIs had close to a monopoly on doctoral degree production in the state, only 8% of Mississippi's doctorates were awarded to African Americans — over two-thirds of them in education.

  Disaggregation and Desegregation. For the U.S. and private plaintiffs it would have accomplished little to engage Mississippi in an argument over its recruitment/hiring defense.   Even if successfully countered, given the small and declining pool of African American doctorates nationally, and evidence of a revolving door syndrome at the HWIs, remedies limited to hiring policies hold little promise for developing a "critical mass" of tenured African American faculty and administrators. Though plaintiffs were not so foolhardy as to compare the percentage of African American faculty to the percentage of African Americans in Mississippi's population — an argument doomed to fail because, in Title VII employment cases, the relevant comparison is to the number of minorities with the qualifications required for the particular employment at issue. However, they were not going to concede that Mississippi, a state with the largest percentage African American population in the United States, a state saturated with a racist history, could disclaim all responsibility for the "acute shortage" of "qualified" African Americans in the early 1990s. Plaintiffs' arguments concentrated instead on disparities in rank and status of faculty by race and on the contribution of Mississippi doctoral granting HWIs to the "acute shortage" of African American doctorates.

  Although African American faculty at Mississippi's HWIs are presumably "black citizens and taxpayers" — therefore the same as members of the plaintiff class — the author, as an expert witness for the United States, was not permitted to talk with or survey African American faculty or staff. Working perforce within the limits of what had been gained through discovery, data limited to names and job title, the essential first question was — who counts as African American faculty? In neither the District Court's 1987 decision nor the Supreme Court's *Fordice* opinion were any definitions offered. On the assumption that meaningful integration "in the world" means significant power-sharing, which requires in turn at least a critical mass of African American faculty with senior status and job security, it was essential to compare African American and non-African American faculty by rank and tenure status at the HWIs. The concept of faculty had to be disaggregated.

Reference to generic "faculty," whatever the Supreme Court and Mississippi meant by that term, as well as the defense's recruitment/hiring-only frame of reference, failed to address questions about social relations, influence, and power. Few academics in the United States would consider either non-tenure track faculty or non-tenured, tenure track faculty as secure players in academic governance of even the most shared of academic governance systems. Rank, tenure, and longevity comparisons between African Americans and non-African Americans are of great consequence. Generally speaking, non-tenured tenure track faculty, regardless of race, lack power and influence because they are probationers dealing with academe's ambiguous promotion and system. And non-tenure track personnel — e.g., instructors, adjuncts, part-time temporary instructors, teaching assistants, and 4-H Club teachers — have an even more tangential relationship to universities. They are poorly paid; they lack job security; they enjoy none of the prerogatives of academic citizenship; they have little or no opportunity for upward mobility in faculty ranks or to influential administrative positions. Thus, for the 1994 trial, the United States' witness included only tenure track and tenured African American faculty: i.e., Assistant, Associate and Full Professors.

Faculty By Race: HWIs and HBCUs
The first of the employment "remnants" upon which the private plaintiffs and the United States agreed in submitting their "Unified List" of November 1992 was "the policy and practice of the governing board of ratifying employment recommendations of individual universities which perpetuate the racial identifiability of those universities as well as the recommendations themselves" (Plaintiff's [sic] Response to 10-22-92 Order, p. 7). Even though, as noted above, the District Court agreed in 1987 that the presence of "other-race" (non-African American) faculty at Mississippi's HBCUs was "substantial and unchallenged" (*Ayers*, 1987, p.

1537), plaintiffs argued, however, that the disproportionate employment of African Americans at HBCUs and whites at HWIs, overall, perpetuates the segregated system.

What Mississippi's fiscal year 1992 data showed was that there were only sixty-three African American tenure track and tenured faculty — representing three percent of the faculty — at Mississippi HWIs, whereas there were 315 African American tenure track and tenured faculty — representing sixty-seven percent of the faculty - at Mississippi HBCUs (and this uses the data most favorable to the state.) Putting aside for now what, if any remedy for such a disparity there should be, the conclusion is inescapable that these patterns show the continuing effects of de jure segregation. Judging by responses to interrogatories that permitted the author to identify African American faculty by name, the absolute number of tenure track and tenured African American faculty at HWIs in Spring of 1993 was probably at most fifty-three or fifty-four, considerably less than the sixty-three identified by Mississippi's numbers for fiscal 1992.

Tenured Faculty. If one consider only tenured faculty, for which the ranks of associate and full professors served as a proxy, the racial disparities become greater. What Mississippi's data showed was that only twenty five, or two percent, of the 1,364 tenured faculty at the HWIs were African American (Answers to interrogatories #46 & #47). By comparison, African American faculty represented sixty-six percent and whites twenty-two percent of the 269 associate and full professors at Mississippi's HBCUs.

Full Professors. Not surprisingly, racial disparities are greatest as one moves up to the senior rank of full professors. What Mississippi's data showed was that only nine professors, a mere one percent of the full professors at HWIs, were African American (Responses to Interrogatories #46 & #47). (There were zero African American female full professors at the HWIs in fiscal 1992.) By comparison, African American faculty represented sixty-two and white faculty twenty-two percent of full professors at the HBCUs. One policy that severely limits the ability of Mississippi's HWIs to increase the number of senior African American faculty, the United States argued, is the governing board's prohibition on making tenure offers to faculty already tenured in other states. Given the image of "Mississippi Burning," why would African American faculty tenured elsewhere in the

United States give up tenure to take a position at a Mississippi institute of higher learning?

Noteworthy, although not accorded legal significance in *Fordice,* were the differences in the numbers of African American full professors among Mississippi's HWIs in FY 1992. Mississippi University for Women and the University of Mississippi — the institution that ceased being de jure all white in 1962 only by virtue of a court order protecting student James Meredith from rioting defenders of apartheid — had but one African American full professor each. And in fall of 1993, there were zero African American full professors at these two HWIs. At the three other HWIs, Delta State, University of Southern Mississippi and Mississippi State University, there were one, two and five African American full professors respectively — better than zero, but hardly a critical mass. In view of the fact that line administrators, especially those in the academic area, normally come from the ranks of tenured faculty, one would expect few African American administrators at the HWIs. And that, not surprisingly, is what Mississippi's data showed: at all five HWIs combined in fiscal 1992 there were only two or three line African American academic administrators (two percent maximum).

Faculty Remnants on Remand: The March 1995 Decision

Does the disaggregated faculty data identify traceable faculty "remnants" of Jim Crow? The District Court's March 1995 decision on remand seemed to agree that, yes, it does, but, staring this conclusion in the face, ended by concluding it does not. Yes, the District Court agreed, Mississippi's HWIs "remain racially identifiable [i.e. white] at the administrative and tenured faculty ranks" (p. 1162). And yes, the Court further agreed, this state of affairs is "to some extent attributable to *de jure* segregation."

What then of the disparities in faculty rank by race at the HWIs? The Court acknowledged the faculty data presented by the United States disaggregating faculty by rank, by full-time and part-time status, by non tenure track, tenure track, and tenured (pp. 1460-61, citing Clague). What is more - a lot more - the Court agreed with plaintiffs that "the desegregation of a university is advanced when blacks hold *visible* and *influential* positions within the university" [emphasis added], and that the "presence of blacks in influential positions sends a signal to other blacks in the community that the university is committed to sharing power" (p.

1160). Here then was recognition of the importance of African American visibility and influence to meaningful integration, a critical component of plaintiffs' arguments. The Court even agreed that "the racial makeup of university faculty and of the various levels of faculty affects student choice" (p. 1160). Furthermore, the Court also agreed, "[i]t is likewise true that *de jure* segregation has materially contributed to the shortage of minority faculty and administrators at the HWIs" (p. 1462). And yes, the judge agreed, noting the testimony of both plaintiffs' and defendants' experts, "diversity in faculty ranks of an institution creates diversity in all other facets of the university" (p. 1163). In support of one of plaintiffs' traceability arguments, the Court even agreed that Mississippi itself has "to some degree affected the qualified pool of black applicants for faculty positions" (p. 1462). The Court also found, in agreement with plaintiffs' disaggregation of African American doctorates by discipline, that "[t]he percentage of African Americans earning doctorates in education [by comparison with black doctorates in other disciplines] in Mississippi is extremely high ..." (p. 1461) by national comparison. A remarkable sixty-eight percent of all doctorates earned by African Americans at Mississippi's institutes of higher learning in the decade 1979-89 were in the field of education, compared with fifty-two percent nationally in the same decade (Wagner, 1991). Because the overwhelming majority of education doctorates are oriented toward employment outside of higher education, this data, the Court also attested, agreeing with plaintiffs, bespeaks the limited contribution of Mississippi's doctoral production to the production of African American academics. But the Court failed to make the connection between this contemporary phenomenon and the fact, noted by the Supreme Court in *Fordice* (p. 721, 738), that during the de jure era, two of Mississippi's HBCUs were created for the purpose of training African American teachers for African American students in segregated K-12 public schools.

To summarize and emphasize, the district court agreed with plaintiffs on all of the following issues:
- that the faculty of the HBCUs and HWIs are racially identifiable,
- that this state of affairs is "to some extent attributable to *de jure* segregation,"
- that "the acute shortage of qualified [black] faculty is to some extent - but by no means exclusively - a product of

the *de jure* segregation practiced throughout the South" (p. 1471),

- that the ghosts of de jure segregation have materially contributed to the shortage of minority faculty and administrators at the HWIs,
- that governing board policy, by preventing offers of tenure at the time of hiring to potential recruits with tenure at other universities handicaps Mississippi's ability to hire senior black faculty,
- that the desegregation of a university is advanced when blacks hold "visible and influential positions within the university" and yet few are present in the HWIs,
- that the presence of blacks in influential positions "sends a signal to other blacks in the community that the university is committed to sharing power,"
- that "the racial makeup of university faculty and of the various levels of faculty affects student choice,"
- that "diversity in faculty ranks of an institution creates diversity in all other facets of the university,"
- that "[a] more racially diverse faculty will be associated with a more positive racial climate" (p. 1467), and
- that Mississippi itself has, by virtue of limited black doctoral production "to some degree affected the qualified pool of black applicants for faculty positions."

So, it would seem then that plaintiffs successfully satisfied the first part of the *Fordice* standard and the existence of a faculty remnant traceable to the former system was established. However, in March 1995, the District Court concluded otherwise. Still wed to an employment *qua* recruitment/hiring model, it went on to ratify, in effect, once again, Mississippi's "we can't find any" defense. Relying, in the findings section of the opinion, on faculty data used by one of Mississippi's expert witness (Siskin), data the Court presented without differentiating by rank or by tenure, rank, full or part-time status, the Court resolved nevertheless that "[c]urrent employment policies and practices are not traceable to *de jure* segregation" (p. 1477).

It is as if plaintiffs had failed to prove intentional systemic discrimination under Title VII, a burden they are not required to shoulder. It was a burden that a class of all African Americans denied employment or promotion in Alabama's postsecondary education system (comprising the technical, junior, and community colleges) took on in *Shuford v. Alabama* (1994). Their challenge resulted in a consent decree providing, among other provisions, for reform of the standardless, discretionary hiring and promotion system, institutional and system hiring goals, and the appointment of recruitment and selections committees with at least forty percent African American membership (p. 1516, 1994). The District Court in Mississippi made no reference to this Alabama case, nor of course, suggested that Mississippi's African American faculty "follow suit."

Revealing of the district court's selective empathy was its treatment of testimony about a 1993 report of the Black Faculty and Staff Organization (BFSO) at the University of Mississippi. This report attested to the university's "hostile, intimidating environment," and suggested seeking a national public forum for their grievances or a "class action suit on behalf of African Americans and other minorities" on campus (p. 1467). Should the university fail to act on BFSO-recommended race relations/multi-cultural training workshops and development of a racial harassment policy, the report suggested that BFSO should "encourage African American students not to enroll at the University" (p. 1467). Rather than see this testimony as evidence of the plight of token African American faculty, the Court virtually scolded them for this "ironic stance" (pp. 1467-68) of discouraging potential African American student enrollment, thus belittling the importance of what African American faculty and staff say they experience. The Court then proceeded to laud the university for its diversity-oriented initiatives.

Because the District Court concluded that there are no current employment policies and practices traceable to *de jure* segregation and that therefore Mississippi's HWIs have, with regard to faculty and staff employment, satisfied their affirmative duty, it follows that the Court's remedial decree contains no reference to faculty. And because the Court accepted the defense's framing of faculty issues as a demand side recruitment and hiring problem, the Court did not mandate expansion of minority fellowship support programs as part of a long-term, supply side remedy. Nor did the Court suggest, much less mandate that Mississippi change its policy of not offering tenure to faculty already tenured elsewhere.

In another section of the opinion, however, one which examines and rejects plaintiffs' claims that campus climates at the HWIs are hostile to African American students, the District Court made a brief and approving reference to African American doctoral support programs. One of the reasons the Court offers in support of its conclusion that "there are no current policies and practices traceable to the *de jure* segregation that foster a racially inhospitable climate at the HWIs" (p. 1471), is the existence of the University of Mississippi's (UM) recently established minority graduate outreach program" with full tuition and stipends for "qualified African Americans" (p. 1468), UM's participation in "national, regional and state fellowship programs/consortia designed to increase minority participation" in graduate education (p. 1268), as well as the University of Southern Mississippi's recent participation with the Southern Regional Education Board (SREB) in support of African American doctoral students (p. 1469). This, presumably, is a reference to SREB's initiative, in collaboration with other regional boards, to develop a national compact on faculty diversity, a program modeled, in part, on Florida's McKnight Black Doctoral Fellows Program [BDF].

What the Court did not note, however, is that the express mission of the BDF and the SREB initiative is to increase the pool of doctorates from which participating states can hire larger numbers of minority faculty (Abraham, 1994; Clague, 1989; Stampp & Tribble, 1993). Nor did the Court point out that the BDF excludes doctorates in education (with the exception of math education) precisely because so few education doctorates lead to faculty careers in higher education.

So what is the District Court suggesting? It seems it is suggesting that all Mississippi has to do to prove that climates inhospitable to African American students at the HWIs are not traceable to the de jure era is to begin to take a few modest race conscious initiatives benefitting African American students. (As of 1994 there was but one African American Mississippi graduate student participating in the SREB program (A. Abraham, personal communication, April, 1994). Although there is a message that some evidence of belated affirmative action and diversity initiatives suffices to free the former de jure segregated state system of liability, it is important not to ignore the affirmative action implications of the District Court's opinion. Mississippi is permitted, at least, but not required, to participate in MTS programs, precisely the kind of program the Fourth Circuit ruled unconstitutional in *Podberesky*. Minority-specific scholarships were not, however, the only scholarships permitted by the District

Court's 1995 opinion. Plaintiffs had challenged the governing board policy of using a minimum ACT score as a cutoff for providing scholarships to children of out of state alumni and HWI policies that use an ACT cutoff — "set beyond the range of what most black students achieve" (p. 1433) — as the sole criteria for academic scholarships, ignoring "academically sound" consideration of overall academic performance. Not a traceable policy or practice, the District Court concluded, thereby permitting Mississippi to place far greater weight on standardized test scores than even the test's creators support.

After *Fordice*: *Podberesky - II*

In 1991, the federal District Court of Maryland held that OCR's repeated determinations that the State of Maryland had not desegregated its state system in compliance with Title VI (consequent to its *Adams* responsibilities) satisfied *Croson's* demand for "a strong basis in evidence" of the need for remedial affirmative action. But in 1992, six months before the Supreme Court's decision in *Fordice,* the Fourth Circuit rejected the university's reliance on OCR findings. Ignoring K-12 precedents requiring remedial measures for past de jure segregation in public schools, it chose instead an interpretation of *Croson* at odds with OCR's interpretation of Title VI, at odds with the U.S. Department of Justice as plaintiff in *Fordice*, at odds with the U.S. Department of Education as amicus curiae in support of the Banneker program in *Podberesky*. OCR's unquestioned, overwhelming evidence of past discrimination did not suffice to justify the Banneker Program. The burden was placed on UMCP on remand to document the "present effects" of its Jim Crow past.

Thus, unique among institutions of higher education, UMCP decided to meet the challenge by documenting its *mea culpa* for present effects of past discrimination, not, to be sure, for contemporary discrimination. In April 1993, the results of this unprecedented institutional self-examination were made public under the name of UMCP's President William Kirwan. The summary of the sixty-page *Decision and Report of the University of Maryland at College Park Regarding The Benjamin Banneker Scholarship Program* encapsulated the Report's findings and conclusions as follows:

The University of Maryland at College Park, through its President, William E. Kirwan, concludes that effects of past discrimination against African Americans in Maryland still exist in the form of an adverse reputation among members of the African American community; perceptions of a hostile campus climate; and in low enrollment, retention and graduation rates for African American students at the University (University of Maryland, *Decision and Report,* 1993, p. 1).

In October 1993, after the Supreme Court's decision in *Fordice,* the District Court, praising UMCP for its "moral courage", reaffirmed the lawfulness of UMCP's Banneker Scholarship Program. The outcome was clearly foretold in the opening sentence of the opinion:

> The question posed in this case is whether a public university, racially segregated by law for almost a century and actively resistant to integration for at least twenty years thereafter, may, after confronting the injustices of its past, voluntarily seek to remedy the resulting problems of its present, by spending one percent of its financial aid budget to provide scholarships to approximately thirty high-achieving African American students each year (1993, p. 1076).

Required by the Fourth Circuit to satisfy *Croson,* Judge Motz interpreted "strong evidentiary basis" to mean "strong" evidence of "some" present effects (p. 1083, citing *Croson,* p. 57). Thus, strong evidence of only one of the present effects would have sufficed. The Court concluded, however, based on the data reported in UMCP's *Decision and Report,* that "all four of UMCP's findings are supported by strong evidence" (p. 1083). The governmental interest was thus "compelling" enough to justify affirmative action. And the means, the Banneker Scholarship Program, was tailored narrowly enough to satisfy *Croson* guidelines for voluntary affirmative action as well: The number of Banneker Scholarships is small; their slice of the financial aid budget is tiny; their impact on non-African Americans is negligible; the impact on Podberesky in particular, who was admitted to Maryland and had the financial resources to attend, was "at bottom . . . the insult to his sensibilities caused by . . . a program which he believes to be wrong in principle" (p. 1096-1097).

Education is Different. Judge Motz' decision supporting the Banneker Program was the first post-*Croson* decision to validate "induced voluntary" affirmative action. But this is not what made Judge Motz's opinion extraordinary. He felt "compelled to add a few words (p. 1097)" and it was these added words — dicta — which made his opinion so extraordinary and so galling to the Fourth Circuit.

Application of this *Croson* standard to the education context created too rigid an analytic framework. Developed in cases involving challenges to affirmative action in employment, it "provides imperfect analogies for determining the constitutionality of an affirmative action program in an educational context":

> the various restrictions that the Court has applied to affirmative action programs in the employment context — particularly the prohibitions against remedying the effects of "societal discrimination," or discrimination that was done by another "governmental unit" — appears inappropriate in the education context where the effects of past discrimination are obviously societal in scope (pp. 1097-1098).

Rejection of the rigid dichotomy between state and society is grounded in the view that education is different. Educational institutions should not be treated, for example, like fire departments, whose employment practices have limited impact on the larger society. Educational institutions are society's matrix; their "ripple effect necessarily affects every aspect of our economy and society" (p. 1098). Public education plays "a vital role . . . in forming and transmitting values . . . ." Educational opportunities are the foundation that enable society's members to compete for employment opportunities. Judge Motz' rejection of the rigid dichotomy between state and society also evoked explicitly the spirit of *Brown-I* (if not the rigid de jure/de facto distinction of it remedial progeny). Of all forms of discrimination, discrimination in education is the "most odious" (p. 1097). And it is because education is central to our democratic society that the Supreme Court "has created aggressive affirmative duties in the area of primary and secondary school desegregation."

Adherence to the sharp distinction federal jurisprudence has drawn between state-imposed discrimination and societal discrimination prohibits public institutions of higher education from taking responsibility, through preferential affirmative action, for combating "the culture of bigotry inculcated over centuries ... ." (p. 1096). What is more, the artificial segmentation of the public educational system by the "governmental unit" limitation prohibits public institutions of higher education from taking responsibility, through race conscious affirmative policies, for countering "the damage. . . done by our shameful legacy of involuntary segregated education" (p. 1096) in pre-collegiate education, damage that inevitably carries over to post-secondary education, and upon which post-secondary education builds.

Additionally and finally, the District Court criticized the *Croson* standard for its focus solely on *past* discrimination inflicted by the defendant state educational agents or agencies.

> Let us assume for the purpose of argument that each generation is, in fact, born cloaked in innocence and pure of soul. If effects of racism nevertheless appear on our university campuses, would it not be a paradox, the height of irony, that our educational institutions could not attempt to cure them because it is we, not our parents or grandparents who are their source (p. 1098)?

This was not the reasoning of a court that expected to convince the Fourth Circuit Court of Appeals. And it did not. In October 1994, four and a half months before the District Court's remand ruling in *Fordice*, which seemed to sanction MTS programs in Mississippi, the Fourth Circuit ruled in *Podberesky* that UMCP's Banneker Fellowship was unconstitutional. *Fordice*, which OCR decided to apply to the review of the desegregation plans in Maryland and other states (59 Fed. Reg. 4271, 1994), received scant attention. In May 1996, the Fifth Circuit Court of Appeals ruled, in partial reliance on the Fourth Circuit's *Podberesky* decision and the burdens it placed on defenders of affirmative action, that the University of Texas minority admissions program was unconstitutional.

November 1996: Unresolved Contradictions and Ironies

The contradictions and ironies that strain federal jurisprudence dealing with the integration of higher education invite clarifying test cases of the numerous issues, among them the lawfulness of MTS and minority admissions programs, and the weight to be placed on standardized test scores. The Supreme Court's refusal to hear *Podberesky* and *Hopwood* has not closed the book on MTS programs. The Department of Education's Final Policy Guidance on MTS programs (1994), which supports their diversity and remedial uses, *Podberesky* notwithstanding, stands. But, as this manuscript goes to press, we are left with an unresolved and contradictory state of lower court case law.

As a result of the Fourth Circuit's opinion in *Podberesky*, UMCP terminated the African American-only Banneker Program in fall 1995. It had cost less than $600,000 in 1990-91, a mere 1% of UMCP's financial aid budget. Although the selection process for the new, highly competitive Banneker-Key Fellowship scholarship considers many non-cognitive variables, it nevertheless relies heavily on test scores and grades. The mean SAT score (1309) and the mean high school GPA (3.854) for fall 1995 combined Banneker-Key Scholars exceeded the mean GPA (GPA 3.690) and SAT score (1136) for Banneker recipients the previous year (UMCP, Admissions Office). The consequences: Compared with Banneker recipients of 1994, the representation of African American men among Banneker/Key recipients of 1995 dropped drastically — down 80% — from 15 to 3, while representation of African-American women fell 29%, from 21 to 15 (Clement, 1995).

In March 1995, as UMCP was proceeding to dismantle its MTS program, the lower court ruled in *Fordice* that Mississippi may, but is not required, to initiate or participate in MTS programs. Mississippi may participate in MTS programs, but Mississippi must create scholarships for white students to attract them to two HBCUs, Jackson and Alcorn State Universities (p. 1495). Mississippi may also continue alumni scholarships and other scholarships that are awarded disproportionately to whites because they are based on ACT test score cutoffs that few African Americans attain. Furthermore, Mississippi must implement the same admissions standards at all of the state's institutions of higher learning — African American and white — a mandate that includes, as Mississippi proposed, a uniform minimum ACT score. (Despite a predicted dramatic, negative effect on African American access to higher education the Supreme Court refused, in April 1996, to stay implementation of the new cut-off score of 16 (*U.S. & Ayers v Fordice*, 1996).

Compare *Podberesky* with the pre-*Fordice*, pre-*Croson* decision of the Sixth Circuit Court of Appeals in *Geier v. Alexander* (1986), Tennessee's higher education desegregation case. Endorsing the theory of an "affirmative duty" to integrate six

years before the Supreme Court's *Fordice* decision, the Sixth
Circuit approved of a consent decree designed to settle the then
eighteen- year-old case. Included in the court-approved agreement,
which the Reagan Justice department unsuccessfully opposed as a
violation of the law of race neutrality (Memorandum, 1984), was
a program to prepare African American college students for
graduate professional schools, and to enhance their chances of
graduate admission. The same year that *Geier* was decided, the
Supreme Court had equated consent decrees with voluntary action.
Thus, the Sixth Circuit supported Tennessee's voluntary combined
MTS/admission program, whereas the Fourth Circuit declared
UMCP's voluntary MTS program unconstitutional.

Compare the Maryland post-*Fordice* decision with the post-
Fordice decision of the District Court for the Northern District of
Alabama in *Knight v. Alabama* (1995), one of two Alabama higher
education desegregation cases. In August 1995, the Court decreed
that Alabama must provide up to $1,000,000 to the Trustees of the
two HBCUs to attract "other-race" (i.e., white) students, many of
whom might be characterized as low achieving. To qualify for full
ride fellowships the non-African American students must average
a 2.0 GPA, whereas African American students at Alabama State
must have a 3.25 GPA to be eligible for a full scholarships
(personal communication with Patrick Healy, March 1996).

Compare, finally, the outcome of *U.S. v. Louisiana*,
Louisiana's higher education desegregation case. Six months after
the Supreme Court's decision in *Fordice*, in the eighteenth year of
the Louisiana litigation, the District Court for Eastern Louisiana,
chastising the state defendants for their "relentless struggle to
maintain the status quo" (1992, p. 1159), confirmed its prior
rulings that Louisiana was still operating a racially segregated
college system. Included in its wide-ranging remedial order was a
mandate for an MTS program: Louisiana State University Law
Center must recruit African American and other minority students,
inter alia "through the enhancement of scholarships, tuition
waivers, and other forms of financial assistance specially designed
to attract minority students. . . ." (1992, p. 1165). Although the
Fifth Circuit vacated the District Court's 1992 remedial order and
remanded *U.S. v. Louisiana* for further litigation on newly disputed
Fordice factual issues, the parties brought closure to the case in
November 1994 by means of a settlement agreement that provides
for the appropriation of $900,000 annually for a period of ten

years, for the support of "other race recruitment of doctoral candidates at [Louisiana's] predominantly white institutions" (p. 21). Maryland's MTS program is dead, but not all MTS programs are dead.

MTS Programs: Educationally Sound and Practical

The Supreme Court only denied review of the Appeals Courts' rulings in *Podberesky* and *Hopwood*. It did not affirm them. The opportunity remains open for more searching attention to what can be learned from the substantial body of research on college student retention and from studies of successful minority targeted fellowship programs, successful as measured by sociological concepts of "social and academic integration (Tinto)": positive peer interactions with students of same and other races, intellectual engagement, participation in leadership roles, and high retention and graduation rates. In this sense, surely MTS programs satisfy the as-yet-to-be-defined notion of "educationally sound". Although MTS programs may be denounced as separatist by those who fear that race consciousness disunites, evidence to date suggests that on the contrary, MTS programs have on balance fostered greater integration in the sense of multi-racial involvement and status equality "in the world" of predominantly white institutions than has a legalistic concept of integration implied by an atomistic law of "race neutrality," UMCP's creation and support of the Banneker Program put out a "welcoming mat." The Banneker Program was manifestly not, as the District Court had pointed out, an exercise in racial spoils — a central concern of the Supreme Court's *Croson* decision. And the stereotypes it sought to combat were those that characterize African Americans as intellectually not up to the academic demands of UMCP. In many cases, MTS programs provide more than financial support. Some are fellowships that create bonds and support systems that counteract the isolation, loneliness, and alienation that is widely thought to contribute to minority student departure from predominately white institutions of higher education (Clague, 1989; Smith, 1990).

Not only are they "educationally sound," MTS programs might help even a conservative Supreme Court define the meaning of "practical alternatives." It is still possible that the Supreme Court might one day make the strategic connection, which was missed in both *Podberesky* and *Fordice,* between MTS programs and a long-term strategy for increasing the number of minority faculty. MTS programs work through the educational missions of institutions of higher education; they do not dismantle what is educationally worthy about even still tainted HWIs.

Conclusion

On April 23, 1997, the Fifth Circuit Court of Appeals issued its third substantive ruling in *U.S. & Ayers v. Fordice*. At issue was the trial court's 1995 remedial decree, which enjoined the state of Mississippi from maintaining specified remnants of a prior system of racially segregated public universities or engaging in practices that would impede the complete desegregation of Mississippi's higher education institutions.

In a forty-page decision, the Fifth Circuit ruled:

- The trial court had properly approved the adoption of a uniform admissions standard along with a special applicant-screening and remedial program designed to improve higher education opportunities for African Americans. However, the appeals court ordered the trial court to reconsider its decision to eliminate existing remedial courses.
- The trial court erred in finding that the use of ACT cutoff scores as a criterion for awarding scholarships at HWIs was not traceable to the state's former system of illegal desegregation. The trail court was directed to determine whether it was practical and educationally sound to reform this aspect of HWI scholarship policies.
- Awarding new academic programs to two HBIs was proper.
- The trial court had not erred by declining to alter the way research and extension services were provided at the state's historically white and the state's historically black land grant institutions.
- Mississippi's formula for funding public universities was not traceable to de jure segregation and did not need adjustment.
- The trial court's finding that library allocations did not need adjustment was approved, but the Fifth Circuit directed the trial court to make further factual findings concerning equipment disparities between HBIs and HWIs.

- Mississippi's higher education employment policies and practices, including policies on rank, salary, and tenure, were not traceable to illegal segregation and need not be modified.
- The racial composition of the Board of Trustees and its staff did not evidence vestiges of de jure segregation. No judicial intervention was required concerning this issue.

In its decision, the Fifth Circuit observed:

The very low percentages of blacks holding either full professor status or administrative rank at HWIs are indeed a sobering reflection of longstanding efforts to limit the educational opportunities of black citizens, not in Mississippi alone (p. 1227).

Nevertheless, the court concluded that this state of affairs was not the result of any current exclusionary practice. Mississippi had engaged in "continuous substantial affirmative efforts to correct this imbalance" (p. 1227) the court noted. Thus, in the Fifth Circuit's view, it would be inappropriate to impose liability based on the state's prior exclusionary admissions policies, even if those policies had reduced the pool of qualified African American academicians.

Given the Fifth Circuit's affirmation of the district court's ruling on faculty and administrator employment, no remedial order requires Mississippi to change faculty and staff employment practices. But, that still leaves the question as to whether Mississippi may do what the courts have not required it to do. May it take "affirmative action" in employment? The Fifth Circuit is not clear. The Fifth Circuit did not use the term "affirmative action" to describe Mississippi's recent efforts to attract and retain qualified black faculty.

What are the implications? If Mississippi's policies for hiring and retaining African American faculty and administrators do not entail affirmative action, then they are presumable race neutral. But if the state's employment policies have included some affirmative action strategies, then it seems that the Fifth Circuit has at least implicitly ratified those strategies. Moreover, the Fifth Circuit acknowledged that the under-representation of African American faculty is a present effect of past discrimination (p. 1227); although it did not use the "present effect" phrase. If that is the case, then presumably, Mississippi may, under the *Croson* standard, engage in voluntary affirmative action to hire and retain African American professors and administrators.

References

Bell, D. (1987). *And we are not saved: The elusive quest for racial justice.* New York: Basic Books.

Blackwell, J. E. (1987) *Mainstreaming outsiders: The production of black professionals* (2nd ed.). Dix Hills, N.Y.: General Hall.

Clague, M. (1989). *Minority doctoral support programs: Three case studies.* College Park, MD: National Center for Post-secondary Governance & Finance, University of Maryland.

Clague, M. (1989). Legal aspects of minority participation in higher education. *Education and Urban Society, 21* (3), 260-281.

Clement, L. (1995). Memorandum, August 30, 1995.

Ely, R. J. (1995). The power in demography: women's social constructions of gender identity at work. *Academy of Management Journal, 38*(3), 589-634.

Fries-Britt, S. (1994). *A test of Tinto's retention theory on the Meyerhoff Scholars, A case study analysis.* Unpublished doctoral dissertation, University of Maryland, College park, MD.

Kanter, R.M. (1977) Some Effects of Proportions on Group Life: Skewed Sex Ratios and Responses to Token Women. *American Journal of Sociology 82*( ),

Kanter, R. (1978). Access to Opportunity and Power: Measuring Racism/Sexism Inside Organizations. In Alvarez (ed.), *Social indicators of institutional discrimination: management and research tools.*

Pascarella, E.T. & Terenzini, P.T. (1991). *How college affects students.* San Francisco: Jossey-Bass.

Stamps, S. & Tribble, I (1993). *The McKnight black doctoral fellowship program: An evaluative study*

Silver, J. [1964]. *Mississippi: The closed society.* New York: Harcourt, Brace & World.

Smith, D. (1989), *The challenge of diversity: Involvement or alienation in the academy,* Washington: ASHE/ERIC.

Tinto, V. (1987). *Leaving college; Rethinking the causes and cures of student attrition.* Chicago: University of Chicago Press.

University of Maryland (1993). *Decision and report of the University of Maryland at College Park regarding the Benjamin Banneker Scholarship Program.* College Park, MD.

United States Department of Education, Final Policy Guidance on Non-Discrimination in Federally Assisted Programs. 45 Fed. Reg. 8756. United States General Accounting Office (1994). *Report to congressional requesters, higher education: Information on minority-targeted scholarships* (GAO/HEHS-94-77).

United States, *Finding of fact & conclusions of law,* Oct 1993 in *U.S. & Ayers v. Fordice.*

Wagner, U. (1991). *Environments of support: A report prepared for the American Council on Education.*

White, J. W. (1995). *Increasing the flow of black Ph.D's: A comparison of black doctoral fellows in a comprehensive support program with black doctoral students without a comprehensive support program* (1995), Unpublished doctoral dissertation, University of Maryland, College Park, MD.

Table of Legal References

Adams v. Richardson, 356 F. Supp. 92 (D.D.C. 1973).

Ayers v. Allain, 674 F. Supp. 1523 (N.D. Miss. 1987).

Brown v. Board of Education, 347 U.S. 483 (1954).

Brown v. Board of Education-II, 349 U.S. 294 (1955).

City of Richmond v. J.A. Croson, 488 U.S. 469 (1989).

Geier v. Alexander, 801 F. 2d 799 (6th Cir. 1986).

Green v. New Kent County School Board, 391 U.S. 430 (1968).

Hopwood v. Texas, 861 F. Supp. 551 (W.D. Texas, 1994); 78 F.3d 932 (5th Cir. 1996), cert. denied, 116 S.Ct. 2580 (July 1, 1996).

Knight v. Alabama, 787 F. Supp. 1030 (N.D. Ala. 1991)900 F. Supp. 272 (N.D. Ala. 1995), 14 F.3d 1534 (11th Cir. 1994).

Podberesky v. Kirwan-I 764 F. Supp. 364 (D. Md. 1991); 956 F. 2d 52 (4th Cir. 1992)

Podberesky v. Kirwan-II, 838 F. Supp.1075 (D. Md. 1993); 38 F. 3d 147 (4th Cir. 1994), *cert. denied,* 115 S. Ct. 2001 (1995).

Regents of the University of California v. Bakke, 438 U.S. 265 (1978).

Shuford v. Alabama, 846 F. Supp. 1511 (M.D. Ala. 1994).

Title VI of the Civil Rights Act of 1964, 42 U.S.C. § 2000d et seq.
Title VII of the Civil Rights Act of 1964, 42 U.S.C. § 2000e.
U.S. & Ayers v. Fordice, 505 U.S. 717 (1992).
U.S. & Ayers v. Fordice, 879 F. Supp. 1419 (N.D. Miss. 1995).
U.S. & Ayers v. Fordice, 116 S. Ct. 1538 (April 22, 1996).
U.S. & Ayers v. Fordice, 111 F. 3rd 1183 (5th Cir. 1997).
U.S. v. Louisiana, 811 F. Supp. 1151 (E.D. La. 1992).
U.S. v. Louisiana, Settlement Agreement, November 14, 1994.
Weal v. Cavasos, 879 F. 2d 880 (D.C. Cir. 1990).

CHAPTER 13

PODBERESKY AND *HOPWOOD*:
WILL AFFIRMATIVE ACTION SURVIVE
IN HIGHER EDUCATION?

Virginia Davis Nordin

The life of the law has not been logic: it has been experience.
Oliver Wendell Holmes, Jr., *The Common Law.*

This chapter is devoted to a discussion of some of the important policy issues implicit in *Podberesky v Kirwan* (1994) and *Hopwood v. State of Texas* (1996). In *Podberesky*, the Fourth Circuit struck down a raced-based scholarship program at the University of Maryland; in the *Hopwood* decision, the Fifth Circuit invalidated a minority-preference admissions policy at the University of Texas (UT) School of Law. (For a detailed legal discussion of *Podberesky*, see chapter 11, in this volume). These decisions revisit old higher education policy issues: institutional autonomy, academic abstention by the courts, equity, quotas, and diversity. Although none of these issues are new, *Podberesky* and *Hopwood* raise them in a new format and context.

Podberesky and Hopwood:
Their Significance To Higher Education

When the Fourth Circuit released its *Podberesky* decision in 1994, its significance may not have been apparent to all higher education observers A federal appeals court had struck down a modest scholarship program intended to benefit African Americans at a single state university. *Podberesky's* holding, that the program violated the 14th Amendment's Equal Protection Clause, was binding only within the Fourth Circuit's jurisdiction — Maryland, North Carolina, South Carolina, Virginia and West Virginia.

Nevertheless, it quickly became evident that *Podberesky* was but the opening salvo in a protracted legal campaign designed to wipe out affirmative action in all public institutions.   Daniel Podberesky filed the lawsuit with the help of the conservative Washington Legal Foundation. The chief counsel for the Foundation was quite straightforward in stating that the case was intended to set a major precedent, not only in higher education, but throughout the society, and that it was intended to return the United States to a "color-blind" nation.

Indeed, *Podberesky's* rationale was soon adopted by another federal appeals court. In *Hopwood v. State of Texas*, a 1996 case, the Fifth Circuit ruled that the UT School of Law violated the constitutional rights of non-minority applicants by utilizing an admissions policy that gave preference to African American and Mexican American candidates. That decision is binding on the public colleges and universities in three southern states: Louisiana, Mississippi, and Texas.

Together, *Podberesky* and *Hopwood* raise three very important questions for the nation's colleges and universities:

1) Will affirmative action survive as a legal-remedy for racial discrimination in higher education?

2) If affirmative action does not survive, will universities be able to attract and retain minority students in numbers consistent with equal opportunity?

3) Will university autonomy and academic freedom be compromised by the affirmative action fight now going on the federal courts?

It is perhaps ironic that the plaintiff in the first of these cases, Daniel Podberesky, claimed minority status himself. His mother was born in Costa Rico. His father, a lawyer with the U.S.

Department of Transportation, is of Polish Jewish heritage. Mildred Garcia, vice president of the Hispanic Development Project, stated the suit was "not intended to help Latinos, but rather was an effort by the Washington Legal Foundation to dismantle scholarships". The Mexican American Legal Defense and Educational Fund filed an *amicus* brief arguing that minority-targeted scholarships are crucial for the success of all minority students.

Some History of Diversity and Autonomy

To understand the context of *Podberesky* and *Hopwood*, it is important to review recent history. Student diversity first became important to elite national universities early in the twentieth century. O'Neil (1971) cites several sources for the proposition that admissions officers in the 1940s begin to take more and more diversity factors into account, such as musical ability, geography, race, and gender, in making admissions decisions.

The impetus behind these early diversity policies was probably mixed. On the one hand, universities began to understand that a varied student population contributed to the overall educational experience at their institutions. On the other hand, as Dershowitz(1991) has argued, geographical diversity may have been introduced in the 1920s to set off the number of successful Jewish applicants in the Northeast. Indeed, diversity, as the term is currently used, is just another term for race or religious considerations that have been in place at universities for a long time. It does seem fairly certain that there were formal or informal exclusionary quotas for Jews in some institutions in the early twentieth century just as there were for women at that time and just as there are now for Asian Americans in some institutions. In any event, it is clear that multi-faceted diversity considerations are well established historically as legitimate educational concerns. It is only very recently that some have begun to use "diversity" as a synonym for race or racial diversity. Educationally the term has meant, and still means, much more.

When diversity is viewed from a broader historical perspective, it becomes clear that *Podberesky* and *Hopwood* did more than strike down two supposedly defective affirmative action policies. The cases struck a heavy blow to a diversity philosophy that was developed not to benefit particular racial groups, but to improve and enhance the overall quality of the academic experience.

Another historical theme that is important to understanding *Podberesky* and *Hopwood* is the theme of autonomy. Affirmative action policies enforced by the federal government are the first extensive incursions into academic autonomy after the McCarthy era. In fact, many college presidents have expressed concern about these federal intrusions into the domain of higher education. They opposed the application of federal regulation to the university, they said, not because they opposed affirmative action or equal opportunity as concepts, but because the federal government ought not to be interfering with higher education, particularly in the academically sensitive areas of hiring and promoting faculty and admitting students.

Of course, the core reason for maintaining academic autonomy has remained consistent for centuries: free thought is necessary to the expansion of knowledge. When minorities and women first began to ask for fairer treatment on campus, the publicly stated resistance was not to the idea of equal treatment, but to the idea of governmental interference in the business of the university. Over the years, higher education's position on autonomy has remained the same, but its position on affirmative action has changed considerably. Whereas universities once objected to affirmative action on the grounds that forced compliance was an unwarranted interference with university life, they now argue that removing affirmative action is an unwarranted interference with academically sound university goals and values.

The notion of university autonomy may in fact be one of higher education's best policy arguments for retaining affirmative action in the higher education setting. Justice Frankfurter's concurring opinion in *Sweezy v. New Hampshire* (1957), a case that gave academic freedom "constitutional status," listed as one of the four basic freedoms of academia the freedom to choose who will be admitted to study.

Since *Sweezy*, the Supreme Court has supported a university's freedom to choose. In *Regents of the University of California v. Bakke* (1978, p. 320), Justice Powell wrote that a university may legitimately devise an admission program that takes race and ethnic origin into account. (Justice Powell was joined by four other justices regarding this part of his opinion.) Although the decision struck down a public medical school's specific race-conscious admissions policy, the Court affirmed the constitutionality of affirmative action as a legal doctrine.

The Structure and Nature of Higher Education

Another theme that emerges out of *Podberesky* and *Hopwood* is the courts' essential unfamiliarity with the structural and organizational realities of American higher education. For example, in *Podberesky*, the Fourth Circuit rejected the University of Maryland's scholarship program for African Americans partly because it awarded scholarships to African Americans who were not Maryland residents. The university's goal, the Fourth Circuit pointed out, was to achieve a racial composition for the student body that reflected the racial composition of qualified college-eligible high school graduates in Maryland. That being the case, the court ruled that a scholarship program that attracts non-resident African Americans was not narrowly tailored to meet the university's affirmative action goal.

Podberesky ignored the fact that the mission of public higher education is not confined to a single state. Students have always crossed state lines in substantial numbers in pursuit of public higher education, and it has always been the policy of higher education that they do so. Decisions based on state-confined assessments of higher education diversity goals are unrealistic and skewed as a result. The Fourth Circuit's failure to recognize the existence and academic need for geographic diversity in higher education student bodies indicates a disinclination or failure to understand the complexity and sophistication of public higher education systems. A continuation of this myopia will hamper the development of public higher education.

Significantly, the Fifth Circuit's *Hopwood* decision also exhibited a fundamental misunderstanding about higher education's role in the larger society. In that case, the UT Law School had argued that its affirmative action admissions policy was justified by a long history of racial discrimination in the primary and secondary schools of Texas. Given this history of discrimination, some preference for minority law-school applicants was reasonable.

Although the *Hopwood* trial court accepted this argument, it was rejected by the Fifth Circuit. One state actor cannot justify racial preferences based on the actions of other state agencies, the Fifth Circuit wrote. Nor could the discriminatory history of an institution as a whole justify affirmative action plans by one institutional unit.

Both *Podberesky* and *Hopwood* express an inaccurate understanding of the structure of higher education and its relationship with society as a whole. By ruling that a university may not fashion an affirmative action remedy to address discrimination beyond their boundaries, the courts simply misunderstood the nature of public higher education in America, and thereby unnecessarily dealt affirmative action a major setback.

Can A Modified Affirmative Action Model Survive?

A powerful underlying argument against affirmative action to promote equal opportunity is the concern that this policy, if unrestrained, will become embedded in our law and culture. In other words, the argument seems to imply, affirmative action will shift from a narrowly focused equity remedy to a legally-sanctioned and permanent practice of unfair racial preferences.

It is probably a fair criticism to note that some affirmative action programs seem to have become entrenched, full of regulations and subject to misuse, perhaps most notably the minority contractor set aside programs. But because affirmative action is being misapplied in some instances does not mean that the entire legal remedy should be abolished. The question really becomes, is there another way to limit affirmative action or make sure that it is being used properly for racial minorities in higher education?

Time Limits. Two alternative methods immediately suggest themselves: one that is constantly mentioned, particularly in relation to numerical quotas, is a requirement that all affirmative action plans or policies be clearly limited in time. Every affirmative action plan should have an expiration date. At present, most do, but it is a simple matter to require this as a part of all affirmative action plans. Most early proponents of affirmative action programs assumed that such programs would be transitional or temporary.

Substantial Progress. A second method for ensuring that affirmative action does not evolve into racial preferences is one suggested by the district court discussion in the *Hopwood* case, is that progress toward specific affirmative action goals be shown. In *Hopwood*, for example, the district court noted that although minorities had applied in increasing numbers to the UT Law School in recent years, the Law School had not increased the number admitted but retained the affirmative action goal of admitting a proportion of minorities equivalent to the number graduating below majority scores in Texas. The result was that the minority admission score ratings rose; so while they were still below the majority scores, they continued to approach them more closely and had in fact reached the same level as majority scores twenty years ago. These facts show progress, and also the possibility that actual equality might be reached (which would automatically cancel the need for an affirmative plan). The demonstration of such progress toward the kind of equality which cancels the need for affirmative action should be a justification for current programs such as the UT Law School's program.

Desegregation and Affirmative Action

Another interesting policy concern is the relationship between the higher education desegregation cases, currently culminating in the Supreme Court's *Fordice* case (1992), and the anti-affirmative action cases in higher education — *Podberesky* and *Hopwood*. (For review of *Fordice* and the desegregation litigation involving historically black colleges and universities, see Chapters 9 and 10, in this volume). Several southern states are currently under court orders to desegregate their public higher education institutions, and some of these orders require them to institute affirmative action policies to encourage the desegregation process. Do *Hopwood* and *Podberesky* affect these judicially-approved affirmative action plans?

In Maryland where *Podberesky* was decided, and in Texas, where *Hopwood* was decided, the Office of Civil Rights had required state higher education agencies to file affirmative action plans designed to overcome the lingering effects of legally segregated public higher education in those states. In 1992, the Supreme Court handed down an opinion in *Fordice*, the Mississippi higher education case, which sanctioned the use of affirmative action. A central policy issue, then, is why the justifications for affirmative action in the context of higher education desegregation do not apply to affirmative action efforts like the ones struck down in *Podberesky* and *Hopwood*. A major policy concern is that these decisions, occurring as they do in southern states, will undercut the force of the *Fordice* decision in encouraging and enforcing desegregation of southern systems of higher education. The University of Maryland and the UT Law School cited *Fordice* in support of their affirmative action programs, but to no avail. The *Podberesky* court responded by holding that the Banneker scholarship program was outside the narrow confines of Maryland desegregation efforts because it selected and accepted Banneker scholars from outside Maryland. The *Hopwood* court, in a chilling new approach, ruled that only present effects of past discrimination by the law school, without references to the rest of the university, Texas public education, or any other relevant factors, could justify the use of affirmative action for minorities in law school admissions.

Reflections on the Compelling State Interest Standard

Both *Podberesky* and *Hopwood* ruled that racial preference must be subjected to "strict scrutiny" under the Equal Protection Clause and that such practices can only be justified by some compelling state interest. This is, of course, the Supreme Court's established standard for analyzing governmental practices that discriminate by race, and it is a standard that seldom upholds any kind of race discrimination. Indeed, the University of Maryland and the UT Law School vigorously argued that their respective affirmative action programs were justified by a compelling interest, but neither program survived the federal judiciary's "strict scrutiny."

Currently, the only theoretical argument a university can make to justify a racial classification in an affirmative action program is that of compelling state interest. For those waiting with baited breath for a new legal definition of compelling state interest to emerge from the lower federal courts, little has come forth.

A 1996 case involving discrimination against a homosexual, offers a tantalizing suggestion that a legal standard might emerge that is more friendly to affirmative actions plans like those struck down in *Podberesky* and *Hopwood*. In *Nabozny v. Podlesny* (1996), one of the few cases to take a fresh look at classification justifications under the Equal Protection Clause, the Seventh Circuit considered whether an educational institution could justify a discriminatory policy under a rational basis test rather than compelling state interest. In a case regarding the failure of a school district to protect a young male homosexual from physical injury resulting from sexual harassment, the Seventh Circuit wrote, "We are unable to garner any rational basis for permitting one student to assault another based on the victim's sexual orientation ... ."

The facts in *Nabozny* are very different from affirmative action cases in higher education; nevertheless, the willingness of a federal appellate court to rethink classification justification and to find that a rational basis test had not been met is encouraging, since that test has rarely been flunked in the past. Had the University of Maryland and the UT Law School only been required to show a rational basis for their affirmative action plans, they no doubt would have passed constitutional muster. The *Nabozny* case illustrates the possibility that courts will re-examine the Fourteenth Amendment classification categories, but it is far afield from minority scholarship issues.

Affirmative Action as an Insult to Minorities

A final troubling question is whether affirmative action benefits or harms the protected classes. This argument rages the most strongly in relation to African Americans, some of whom argue that affirmative action programs are a continuing insult to the legitimate achievements of African Americans. Ward Connerly, for example, seems to think that African American students might achieve more if they did not have the "crutch" of affirmative action. Brown (1992) develops the argument that any remedy for racial segregation which makes integration the final goal denigrates the minority race because it seems to assume the inherent superiority of the majority race. Brown writes,

> The Court's ideological framework proceeds from an assumption that racial isolation retarded the intellectual and psychological development of only African-Americans. ... As a result, remedies for ... segregation are based upon an assumption of African-American inferiority--the same assumption that pervaded the constitutional violation of de jure segregation.

Likewise, in *Reflections of An Affirmative Action Baby* (1991), Carter writes of his lifelong effort to overcome the stigma of inferiority despite his well-educated, economically secure, and academically accomplished background. High-achieving African Americans bear the burden of white assumptions that their accomplishments are due to affirmative action, not their own excellence. Many such outstanding African Americans think the stigma attached to them because of the existence of affirmative action programs would be lessened if the programs were eliminated.

Other affirmative action critics fear that the permanent reliance of minorities on the crutch of affirmative action will hinder the strength of individual achievement. Steele (1990) writes that young African Americans

> are taught that extra entitlements are their due and that the greatest power of all is the power that comes to them as victims. [Thus,] if they want to get anywhere in American life, they had better wear their victimization on their sleeve and tap into white guilt, making whites want to escape by offering money, status, racial preferences — something, anything — in return (p. 55).

Is this the way for an oppressed race to come into its own, Steele asks. "Is this the way to achieve independence?"

Proponents of this view tend to argue that the special help of affirmative action might be better applied to lower socio-economic groups of all races, and indeed some colleges and universities are using socio-economic status as a substitute for race in their efforts to reach and include more members of racial minorities. It is beyond the scope of this essay to assess the arguments of these anti-affirmative action writers. Nevertheless, the alternate approach to affirmative action that some of these writers suggest may offer a practical strategy for achieving the core goals of affirmative action. The courts may be more friendly to an affirmative action plan that focuses on socio-economic disadvantages than practices that were struck down in *Podberesky* and *Hopwood*.

Conclusion

In conclusion, let us return to three questions that were asked at the beginning of this essay, and consider some tentative answers. First, will affirmative action survive as a legal-remedy for racial discrimination in higher education? Obviously, all depends on whether the Supreme Court ultimately adopts the reasoning of *Podberesky* and *Hopwood*. If it does, then affirmative actions plans now in place in many public universities will be illegal. On the other hand, the Court may approve affirmative action plans like the ones reviewed in those cases, perhaps reaffirming and building on

Bakke. Or it may require some modification that will assure that affirmative action plans are limited in time or scope.

Second, if affirmative action does not survive, will universities be able to attract and retain minority students in numbers consistent with equal opportunity? It seems doubtful. Teddlie and Freeman (1996) have pointed out that colleges are still largely segregated in 12 of the 19 states that set up segregated higher education systems after the Civil War. Flagship institutions, in particular, were overwhelmingly white, while most African Americans attended HBCUs and two-year community colleges.

Moreover, there is solid evidence that the rising cost of higher education, and the trend of financing it through loans, is adversely affecting African American students. This trend partly explains why many African American students forego prestigious institutions in favor of less expensive two-year colleges and HBCUs. Race-conscious admissions and scholarship programs, like the ones litigated in *Podberesky* and *Hopwood* are a good strategy for counteracting racial isolation in higher education. It seems certain, therefore, if these decisions become settled law, that fewer African Americans will attend public flagship institutions.

Third, will university autonomy and academic freedom be compromised by the affirmative action fight now going on in the federal courts? On this question, much depends on the perseverance and ingenuity of the leadership in our public colleges and universities. Many higher education institutions are firmly committed to some form of affirmative action in their admissions and scholarship policies, and these institutions are unlikely to give them up without a clear legal directive. Moreover, even if affirmative action is outlawed, most institutions will continue to strive to develop alternative strategies to assist disadvantaged students to participate in higher education.

All these questions, like affirmative action itself, are difficult, complex and obscure. Facing them should help elevate our society in a sincere, open and civil discussion ensues. In the meantime we must fight the battles that are presented to us.

Miller (1995) believes that American society will find it necessary to work energetically to bring about a convergence of minority-majority educational performance for several generations to come. Consequently, he says: "The nation will need a steady stream of thoughtful strategic integration to chart and reach the most effective course to its destination..." (p. xiv). Educational affirmative efforts are surely part of that progress. Let us hope we can find a way to keep them intact for the good of us all.

References

Brown, K. (1992). Has the supreme court allowed the cure for *de jure* segregation to replicate the disease? *Cornell Law Review (78)*, 1, p. 547-51.

Teddlie, C. & Freeman, J. (1996). With all deliberate speed: An historical overview of the relationship between the *Brown* decision and higher education. In K. Lomotey & C. Teddlie (Eds.), *Readings on Equal Education, Vol 13. Forty years after the Brown decision: Implications of school desegregation for U. S. education* (pp. 7-53). New York: AMS Press.

Carter. S. L. (1991). *Reflections of an Affirmative Action Baby*. New York: Basic Books.

Dershowitz, A. M. (1991). *Chutzpah*. New York: Simon & Schuster.

Edwards, H. & Nordin, V. (1979). *Higher education and the Law*. Boston: IEM (Harvard).

Miller, L.S. (1995). *An American imperative: Accelerating minority educational advancement*. New Haven: Yale University Press,.

O'Neil, R. M. (1971) Preferential admissions; equalizing the access of minority groups to higher education. *Yale Law Journal (80)*, p. 699.

Steele, Shelby. (1990). *The content of our character: A new vision of race in america*. New York: St. Martin's Press.

West, Cornel. (1993). *Race matters*. Boston: Beacon Press.

Table of Legal Cases

Hopwood v. State of Texas, 861 F. Supp. 551 (W.D. Tex, 1994), rev'd and remanded, 78 F.3d 932 (5th Cir. 1996), cert. denied, 116 S.Ct. 2580 (1996).

Nabozny v, Podlesny, 92 F.3rd 446 (7th Cer. 1996).

Podberesky v. Kirwan, 38 F.3d 147 (4th Cir. 1994), cert. denied, 63 U.S.L.W. 3832 (U.S. May 22, 1995).

Regents of the University of California v. Bakke, 438 U.S. 2365 (1978).

Sweezy v. New Hampshire, 354 U.S. 234 (1957).

U.S. v. Fordice, 505 U.S. 717 1992).

SECTION III.

CONCLUSION

CHAPTER 14

FOUR LITERATURES ASSOCIATED WITH THE STUDY OF EQUAL EDUCATION AND DESEGREGATION IN THE UNITED STATES

Charles Teddlie

Introduction

As the Series Editor for the past three volumes of *Readings on Equal Education* (*REE* Volumes 13, 14, 15) I have had the opportunity to read closely some 35 widely diverse, scholarly chapters devoted to the study of desegregation and equal education in the U.S. Additionally, I recently had the opportunity to examine the social psychological literature concerning desegregation while preparing a conference paper (Teddlie, 1997). Reading these diverse sources led me to several conclusions regarding the current study of equal education and desegregation in the U.S.

1. *There are four distinct literatures concerning equal education and desegregation in the U.S.: legal, polemical, geopolitical, and social psychological.* These literatures have seldom been integrated with one another.

2. *Many authors are dissatisfied with the effects that efforts to desegregate institutions of education have had more than forty years after the Brown decision.* This pessimism regarding the

237

effects of desegregation persists despite the obvious gains that have been made, such as the prohibition of all official, public school segregation and "... the overwhelming acceptance by whites of racial integration of schools" (see Rossell, Chapter 5, this volume, p. 64).

3. *Most authors are dissatisfied with the current state of educational attainment of African Americans more than forty years after the Brown decision.* The continued low achievement of African Americans on standardized tests and their disproportionate dropout rates are decried by both liberals and conservatives, yet strategies for addressing these lingering problems, for both the society and the individual, are varied and controversial. [It should be noted, parenthetically, that a recent comprehensive review of school desegregation's impact on elementary/secondary school students indicates that there has been a small, yet measurable, positive impact of desegregation on the reading skills of African Americans (Schofield, 1995; reprinted 1996)].

4. *The federal courts will be less involved in the desegregation of both elementary/secondary and postsecondary educational institutions in the foreseeable future than they were during the 1954-94 period.* Evidence from a variety of recent Supreme Court rulings [e.g., *Missouri v. Jenkins* (1995)] indicate that the court is curtailing the powers of federal judges in desegregation matters. Mawdsley noted that some informed individuals are predicting that the *Jenkins* decision "... will mark the end of court-ordered desegregation within the next decade" (see Chapter 4, this volume, p. 41). If this is indeed the case, then it may be concluded that the more conservative Supreme Court of the mid-1990s, with Judge Clarence Thomas casting the decisive vote (Teddlie and Lomotey, 1996), has determined that de jure segregation has been adequately addressed by the federal court system.

5. *Issues related to de facto segregation appear to be more important at this time than those related to de jure segregation.* De jure segregation comes about either by law or by deliberate acts of education officials, and it has been greatly curtailed over the past forty-plus years as a result of legal activities set into motion by the *Brown* decision. De facto segregation comes from housing patterns and other non-legislative or non-policy factors, and it is not remedial through the federal courts (see Fossey and Kemper, Chapter 2, this volume, p. 6). While some have argued that de jure and de facto segregation are inseparably linked in certain cases [see

Fossey and Kemper discussion of the *Sheff v. O'Neill* (Conn. 1996) case in Chapter 2, this volume, p. 6], federal courts will only desegregate schools where de jure segregation has actually occurred.

For states outside the South, and especially for suburban and rural districts within those states, it is virtually impossible to demonstrate that de jure segregation has ever occurred. Additionally, given the extensive federal legislation and federal court orders aimed at eliminating de jure segregation and its vestiges, it will become increasingly difficult to demonstrate ongoing de jure segregation in the future. Yet, many of our elementary/secondary (see Fossey, Chapter 3, this volume) and higher educational (e.g., Teddlie and Freeman, 1996) systems remain highly segregated. Addressing this de facto segregation is the challenge of the future in the study of desegregation and equal education in the U.S.

6. *Some promising strategies for addressing de facto segregation have emerged in both the elementary/secondary and the postsecondary literatures.* The success of these solutions appears to be context specific; that is, they depend upon characteristics of the specific community in which the strategies are implemented.

7. *It appears that now is the time for scholars, who are interested in the study of equal education and desegregation in the U.S., to rethink the manner in which they examine these phenomena to reflect the changes that have occurred in the society, especially over the past decade.* Indeed, it appears that these scholars need to examine the geopolitical and social psychological literatures more, with less emphasis placed on the legal literature and on polemic discussions.

A major theme of this volume of *REE* has been the decreasing role of the federal judiciary in the desegregation of both elementary/secondary and postsecondary educational institutions in the U.S. In this chapter, each of the four distinct literatures associated with desegregation and equal education will be briefly summarized. In the final section of this chapter, I will argue that legal and polemic writings will play a decreasing role in future dialogue regarding desegregation and equal education, while the geopolitical and social psychological literatures will play an increasing role.

The four types of literatures discussed above have distinct origins and purposes. The following sections briefly discuss each.

The Legal Literature Related to Desegregation
and Equal Education

The legal literature concerning desegregation and equal education dates back at least to the *Pearson v. Murray* (1936) case, which was the first adjudicated lawsuit on behalf of an African American student seeking admission to an all-white professional school. This lawsuit began a legal assault on the separate but equal doctrine of *Plessy v. Ferguson* (1898) that culminated in the *Brown v. The Board of Education of Topeka, Kansas* (1954,1955) decisions. An extensive elementary/secondary desegregation literature has developed surrounding the *Brown* decision and subsequent important decisions concerning elementary/secondary issues such as: "freedom of choice plans" [e.g., the *Green v. School Board of New Kent County* (1964, 1968) case]; busing [e.g., the *Swann v. Charlotte-Mecklenburg Board of Education* (1971) case]; and regional desegregation plans [e.g., the *Milliken v. Bradley* (1974, 1977) and *Sheff v. O'Neill* (Conn. 1996) cases].

A similarly extensive higher education desegregation literature has developed, starting with the case that applied the *Brown* decision to colleges and universities [*Florida, ex rel. Hawkins v. Board of Control* (1956)]. Again, this legal literature concerns issues surrounding the particular measures used to desegregate higher education: lawsuits related to the enforcement of Title VI of the 1964 Civil Rights Act in states where de jure segregation persisted [e.g., a series of cases known collectively as the *Adams* litigation beginning with *Adams v. Richardson* (1973)]; "set aside" placements for minority students (e.g., *Regents of University of California v. Bakke* (1978)]; development of programs designed to attract other race students to HBCUs (historically black colleges and universities) and PWIs (predominantly white institutions) [e.g., *Ayers v. Fordice* (1992) and *United States v. Louisiana* (1994)]; and race-based scholarships (e.g., *Podberesky v. Kirwan* (1994). For instance, the long lasting *Adams* litigation involved methods aimed at the "disestablishment" of dual systems of higher education and the desegregation of student enrollment, faculty, staff and governance (e.g., Teddlie and Freeman, 1996; Trent, 1991; Williams, 1991).

This legal literature weighed the benefits of various judicial remedies to desegregate elementary/secondary or postsecondary education, typically using the paradigm of critical theory. While this legal literature is still important, primarily from a historical point of view, the movement away from further judicial intervention in the areas of desegregation and equal education limits its potential value in the future. This is especially the case with regard to the study of de facto segregation and strategies for attenuating the effect of that type of segregation on equal education opportunities.

Polemic Discussions Regarding Desegregation and Equal Education

According to *Webster's New World Dictionary (Third College Edition)*, "polemic" is an adjective indicating "of or involving dispute; controversial." Thus a polemic discussion is an argument or controversial discussion. Over the past forty-plus years since *Brown*, much of the so-called scholarly writing on equal education and desegregation has involved polemic discussion, rather than empirical (quantitative or qualitative) research concerning the impact of various strategies for desegregation on equal education.

While such discussions are appropriate, and even valuable, in academic writing, they can negatively impact the development of a literature if they are predominant in the intellectual discourse. It is my opinion that such polemic discussions have often overwhelmed research-based approaches in texts devoted to desegregation and equal education, leaving a legacy of argumentation that is counterproductive to scientific inquiry.

Authors who engage in such polemic discussions cover the whole political range from liberal to conservative. Their commonality is their subscription to controversial points of view, which typically do not further constructive dialogue and are not based on empirical evidence, other than "smoke and mirrors." Consider the following two polemic statements:

(1) African Americans are inferior intellectually to whites, especially at the upper end of the IQ scale. Thus, the process of desegregating graduate and professional schools has become a purely political endeavor disguised as "diversity," which necessarily involves the dilution of the quality of the education provided in these schools.

(2) There is a continuing conspiracy among whites to maintain political and economic domination over African Americans by consciously providing inferior educational systems, at both the elementary/secondary and postsecondary levels, for African Americans.

The problem with such declarations, whether or not there is a grain of truth to either, is that a productive dialogue regarding desegregation and equal education is virtually impossible after such statements are made. Indeed, perhaps it is the intent of authors who make such polemic statements to stop productive dialogue regarding these issues.

Both of these arguments, or derivations thereof, have been made by authors writing in the last three volumes of *REE*. Thus, in my role as Series Editor of *REE*, I obviously believe that there is room in the literature for such discussions to occur. Nevertheless, real progress in the mainstream literature on desegregation and equal education will be hindered as long as intellectual energy is misspent asserting and arguing these points.

The Geopolitical Literature Regarding Desegregation and Equal Education

The literature that I refer to as "geopolitical" is characterized by an examination of the impact that both geographical and political factors, separate and in tandem, have had on the success of desegregation efforts and on subsequent equal education opportunities. These factors in elementary/secondary schooling include: historical patterns of segregated housing in urban areas that result in whites and African Americans living in geographically distinct communities, white flight from urban school districts to contiguous suburban and rural districts, white and African American resistance to court-mandated assignment of students to schools outside their own community (especially if accompanied by extensive busing), and community reaction to the lack of parental/student choice in school assignments. These geopolitical factors in higher education include: the geographical location of colleges and universities in predominantly white or African American communities, political support from African Americans for the continued traditional role of HBCUs in their communities, political reaction by the white community to "set asides" and race-based scholarships, and the geographical transfer of educational programs from PWIs to HBCUs (which have a political impact beyond the educational one).

Several chapters from the past three volumes of *REE* contain discussions of these geographical and political factors.

Glenn (1996)

Glenn's (1996) chapter in Volume 13 of *REE* was entitled "'Busing' in Boston: What We Could Have Done Better". In this chapter, he made suggestions about what could have been done to improve the desegregation process in Boston, where the first stage of mandatory desegregation was met with boycotts, antagonism, and chaos. These suggestions included: seeking areas of agreement with school officials, rather than operating in a climate of mistrust; and working with, rather than against, the desire of parents and teachers to make decisions about how children are educated. Glenn concluded that his office spent too much time and energy concerned with legal issues, rather than with political ones:

> Our approach to Boston school authorities was ... too concerned with creating a public record in which we were always "right" and they always "wrong," and not enough with behind-the-scenes problem solving. The fact that our position was ultimately vindicated by the courts does not remove a lingering doubt about whether it has been vindicated by history.... I wish we could have found a way to say to parents and teachers in Boston ... "create the sort of school you want most, provided that parents of both black and white children are persuaded to entrust them to your school." I am now convinced that many ... of those who resisted and sabotaged the desegregation effort would have reacted very differently to a situation in which interracial cooperation had its rewards in improved schooling and more responsive schooling for their children (1996, pp. 147 and 153).

Teddlie and Freeman (1996)

Teddlie and Freeman's (1996) chapter in Volume 13 of *REE* included discussion of the higher education desegregation lawsuits in Mississippi [*Ayers v. Fordice* (1992)], Louisiana [*United States v. Louisiana* (1994)], and Alabama [*Knight v. Alabama* (1991, 1995)]. While these lawsuits had the potential for revolutionary changes, such as the closing of predominantly segregated colleges and universities, the ultimate decisions were much less extreme, due partially to pressures from political constituencies in each state (e.g., those associated with HBCUs). In fact, the hodgepodge of decisions resulting from these cases appear to be determined more by local political realities than by any consistent federal court interpretation of Title VI regulations.

Geographical considerations also played a role in these decisions. For instance, the decision of the federal court in the Louisiana case [*United States v. Louisiana* (1994)] to establish a new junior college in Baton Rouge to be jointly administered by Southern University (an HBCU) and Louisiana State University (a PWI) is a good example of attention paid to the "territorial rights" of the two institutions. This point is highlighted by the decision to locate the junior college in the central part of Baton Rouge, approximately equidistant from Southern University (located in the northern part of the city) and Louisiana State University (located in the southern part of the city).

Garvin (1997)

Garvin's (1997) chapter in Volume 14 of *REE* entitled "There's No Place Like Home" addressed the impact that segregated housing patterns, especially in public projects, have on the education of children. According to Garvin, the social context of where and how people live has a severe impact on where and how they are schooled. The geographical segregation of some 28,000 school age children in New Orleans (99% of whom are African American) makes meaningful desegregation of public schooling in that city, as we now envision it, virtually impossible. While Garvin used as an example public housing in New Orleans, his analysis would have been equally appropriate for other urban inner-city areas, where there is a high concentration of poverty among African Americans (e.g., Baltimore, Boston, Chicago).

St. John and Hossler (this volume)

St. John and Hossler (Chapter 9, this volume) introduced the critical-empirical perspective or framework, which they developed while expert witnesses in the *Knight v. Alabama* case. This framework assesses the impact of alternative policies and strategies on student enrollment choices at the higher education level. Their research indicates that various geopolitical factors can affect the degree of success that these alternative strategies/policies have in influencing student enrollment decisions. These factors include: the percentage of blacks (or whites) living in the geographical areas surrounding HBCUs, support (or resistance) from alumni at HBCUs toward programs designed to attract more whites, the percentage of whites already in the population of HBCUs or African Americans already in the population of PWIs, and whether or not the local political climate will allow the gradual phase in of new programs designed to attract other race students.

The propositions linking strategies/policies to student enrollment decisions, found in Table 1 in Chapter 9, are all dependent on the specific geopolitical context of the institution under study (HBCU, PWI, other). St. John and Hossler convincingly argue that research findings can be used to determine the strategies/policies that are more likely to work given certain geopolitical contexts.

Rossell (this volume)

Rossell (Chapter 5, this volume) presents a convincing argument that what she calls "new freedom of choice" plans are superior to court mandated plans in successfully desegregating elementary/secondary schools. Her analysis is based in part on empirical results from research that examined the impact of certain geopolitical factors, such as "white flight," on the success of desegregation plans.

White flight is a good example of a geopolitical factor that must be taken into consideration when developing a desegregation plan for an elementary/secondary school district. It is "political" because parents leaving a school district due to their dissatisfaction with educational policy are essentially "voting with their feet". It is "geographical" in that it involves the relocation of a group of parents, with certain demographic characteristics, from one geographical locale (typically an urban core area) to another geographical locale (typically a surrounding suburban or rural area). White flight is "geopolitical" in that it affects the political relationships within different geographically defined voting units: typically the urban areas become more African American (and "liberal" in the traditional U.S. political sense; that is more Democratic), while the suburban and rural areas become even more white (and "conservative" in the traditional U.S. political sense; that is, more Republican).

Rossell summarizes the impact of white flight in Chapter 5 as follows:

Of all the forms of white response to school desegregation, white flight is probably the most important because it directly affects interracial exposure, the ultimate goal of any desegregation plan. (pp. 47-48)

The social psychological theory that underlies desegregation efforts is based on the "contact hypothesis" of Allport (1954/1979), which stated that bringing members of different groups into contact with one another would reduce prejudice and result in more positive intergroup attitudes under "certain facilitating conditions" (this hypothesis will be discussed in more detail in the next section of this chapter).

Rossell argues that white flight mitigates the potential positive effects of desegregation by decreasing the chance of contact between whites and African Americans. She further states two empirical relations that have emerged from research studies concerning mandatory assignments of students to schools (see p. 48, this volume):

(1) The greater the reduction in racial imbalance in a district (which is highly correlated with greater white mandatory reassignments), the greater the white loss during the implementation year of the desegregation plan.

(2) Central-city school districts above 30-35% minority, which utilize mandatory desegregation plans, never regain the lost white students.

Rossell used these research results and her longitudinal study of a pair of school districts (Savannah-Chatham County, Georgia and Stockton, California) to argue the superiority of new freedom of choice plans over mandatory court-based desegregation plans.

Mathews and Jarvis (this volume)

Mathews and Jarvis's (see Chapter 6, this volume) article on the history of desegregation efforts in the East Baton Rouge Parish School System describes the impact of several geographical and political factors: continued resistance by the white-dominated political structure to desegregation, de facto segregation in schooling that was partially due to geographically separate housing patterns for whites and African Americans, white flight into adjoining suburban and rural districts, and the loss of community support (both white and African American) for the court-mandated mandatory assignment plans (including busing).

The Social Psychological Literature Related to Desegregation and Equal Education

Three subfields within the social psychological literature are relevant to the desegregation and equal education literature. These are:

(1) *The literature related to the "contact hypothesis."* As noted by Rossell (Chapter 5, this volume) the instrumental value of desegregation relates to the "contact hypothesis," which assumes that increased contact between members of different races will lead to better relationships, given certain facilitative conditions;

(2) *The cooperative learning literature.* The initial writing in this area concerned the creation of classroom settings in which interactions between members of different races could occur in a positive manner;

(3) *The ingroup-outgroup literature.* This area concerns issues related to majority/minority relations, including the assimilation of the outgroup into the ingroup.

The Contact Hypothesis
Allport (1954/1979), in his influential book on the nature of prejudice, presented the contact hypothesis, which stated that bringing members of different groups into contact with one another would reduce prejudice and result in more positive intergroup attitudes under *certain facilitating conditions*. These facilitating conditions included:

(1) equal status between members of the groups,

(2) common goals among members of the group, and

(3) sanction by authority.

This contact hypothesis played a central role in the formulation of the Social Science Statement, which was "a separate non-legal brief that was submitted to *and accepted by* the United States Supreme Court" in its *Brown* decision (Clark, 1979, p. 477, emphasis in original). The Social Science Statement, stated that segregation had detrimental effects in three areas (Miller & Brewer, 1984):

(1) it increased intergroup hostility and prejudice,

(2) it impaired self-esteem among minority children, and

(3) it contributed to poor academic motivation and learning among minority children.

According to the contact hypothesis, increased contact between members of different groups should decrease intergroup hostility and prejudice. Hennigan, Flay, and Cook (1980) concluded that the Social Science Statement employed the contact hypothesis, but gave relatively little attention to the *qualifying conditions*, leading to optimistic social psychological theory about the probable outcomes of school desegregation (e.g., Stephan, 1978; Weyant, 1986). It is clear that the positive qualifying conditions proposed by Allport (e.g., equal status, common goals, sanction by authority) were seldom met in real world desegregation situations.

Subsequently, evidence from field studies in actual school desegregation efforts has yielded contradictory, and often disappointing, results (e.g., Gerard & Miller's 1975 school desegregation study in Riverside, CA; recent reviews by Schofield, 1995, Lomotey & Teddlie, 1996, Orfield & Eaton, 1996; Teddlie & Lomotey, 1997). Schofield (1996) summarized the difficulties in drawing conclusions from studies conducted in such a wide variety of settings as follows:

> ... virtually all of the reviews emphasize the wide variety of situations covered by the existing literature. They often point out that not only do the student bodies in the schools studied vary sharply in their age and social class, but that the proportion of students from different racial and ethnic backgrounds has also varied dramatically. Further, they point out that given the variation in particular circumstances it is reasonable, perhaps inevitable, that different instances of desegregation will have varying effects on intergroup relations. (pp. 95-96)

This contradictory evidence from real world settings led Cook (1979) to write a review entitled "Social Science and School Desegregation: Did We Mislead the Supreme Court?" Cook (1979) concluded that it would be better for social scientists to experimentally study the conditions under which favorable intergroup relations could be met, instead of reactively conducting case studies of whatever desegregation plan local authorities had devised. To that end, several researchers conducted experimental studies in classrooms in which the facilitating conditions prescribed by the contact hypothesis were present. This research area evolved into the field of study known as cooperative learning, and its results have been applied not only to desegregation settings, but also to the more general teacher and school effectiveness areas.

Brief Review of the Research on the Cooperative Learning
Brown and Maras (1995) described the use of cooperative learning procedures in the study of what creates successful desegregated classroom environments as follows:

> One promising avenue to counter these problems is the wider use of cooperative learning groups, particularly when employed in the microcontext of the classroom. In a cooperative learning exercise the class is typically broken down into small ethically mixed groups. Each group is given some task to undertake which requires the collaborative efforts of all its members for successful achievement. Assessment is based partly or wholly on the basis of the collective result. One advantage of this technique is that it satisfies several criteria for optimizing the effects of intergroup contact since participants enjoy equal status and are dependent on each other for the achievement of jointly desired goals. Moreover, learning tasks can sometimes be devised which capitalize on rather than eliminate the ethnic diversity of the group. (p. 326)

Evidence from much of the cooperative learning research indicates that the use of such small multiethnic groups can raise the self-esteem and academic performance of minority group children, while increasing the number of cross-ethnic friendships. A number of cooperative learning techniques were developed for multiethnic classroom situations, including:

- The jigsaw classroom - Aronson, Blaney, Stephan, Sikes, and Snapp (1978).
- Teams-Games-Tournaments (TGT) - DeVries, et al. (1978, 1980).
- Student Teams and Academic Divisions (STAD) - Slavin (1977).
- Learning Together and Alone - Johnson, Johnson, and Maruyama (1984).
- Groups-Investigation - Sharan, et al. (1984).

For instance, Aronson and his colleagues (e.g., Aronson, et al. 1978; Blaney, et al. 1977) began a series of field experiments utilizing the jigsaw technique, which structured desegregated classrooms so that students from different groups would pursue common goals for at least part of the school day. In the experimental condition, each student in a group had one piece of a puzzle, and each student was dependent upon others in the group to complete the total picture. In one study, each student in a six person group was given a part of the entire biography of Joseph Pulitzer. The students had to read their own part and then communicate it to the group. At the end of the experimental time, the students were tested on their knowledge of Pulitzer. In the control condition, each student learned on their own in the traditional manner. The performance dimension of the experiment involved the following:

> ... students are tested on the material and graded individually. Thus the group members are interdependent in studying the material, they gradually learn to help each other and to reward each other instead of competing, but their grade reflects their own individual learning so they aren't penalized if other group members have learned less than they have. (Oskamp, 1984, p. 166)

Results from these studies on cooperative learning indicated that the jigsaw technique increased performance of minority students, liking for group members, self-esteem, cooperativeness, and openness to learning from other students (e.g., Aronson, 1995; Aronson and Osherow, 1980).

While researchers went to great lengths to create the ideal facilitating conditions in the cooperative learning experiments and quasi-experiments, these ideal conditions are seldom met in real world desegregation situations. Oskamp (1984) summarized the differences between the experimental and real world settings:

> There is good research support for each of these principles, but it is striking to note how far the usual desegregated classroom deviates from these specifications. There is too often official resistance to desegregation, and most American classrooms - desegregated or not - fail to meet the other two conditions as well. Their goal structure is usually one of fierce competition rather than cooperation, and there are usually marked status differentials between the "good" students and the "poor" students as well as between the majority group and any ethnic or national minority students in the class. (p. 166)

While the beneficial effects of cooperative learning techniques have been known for some 20 years, it has seldom been used in creating change in real world desegregation efforts. The application of cooperative learning techniques to actual desegregation efforts illustrates a couple of interesting questions regarding the use of experimental results in applied educational settings.

(1) Are the results from laboratory and field experiments on cooperative learning relevant to change processes in real world desegregation experiences, where the *facilitating* conditions for the contact hypothesis are seldom met?

(2) Does the cooperative learning research make any difference if it has no political viability? If policy makers are unaware, or choose to ignore, research that could help desegregation achieve its stated goals, then is experimentation worthwhile in terms of real world applicability?

The Ingroup-Outgroup Literature

An active branch of social psychological research concerns ingroup-outgroup relations. One of the most common ways to categorize people is to divide them into two groups: those in my group (or the ingroup) and those not in that group (the outgroup). There are two major ingroup-outgroup "effects":

(1) we tend to see members of the outgroup as more similar to each other than the members of the ingroup; this may be termed the "they-all-look-alike-to-me" effect (Aronson, 1995);

(2) we tend to see our own group (the ingroup) as better on any number of dimensions and to allocate rewards to our own group more frequently; this may be termed ingroup "favoritism" (Aronson, 1995).

In U.S. society, the ingroup is often white Americans, while the outgroup has often been African Americans. Desegregation may be seen as an attempt to mix members of the outgroup with members of the ingroup. The extensive social psychological literature on ingroup-outgroup relations is, therefore, relevant to the study of the desegregation of public education in the U.S. (e.g., Park and Rothbart, 1982; Tajfel, 1981).

Recent research into the contact hypothesis (Gaertner et al., 1993) indicates that better intergroup relations are fostered in situations in which previous outgroup members can be recategorized as members of the ingroup. This raises the interesting question: do outgroup members want to be assimilated in order to be accepted? If a sizeable portion of the outgroup does not want to be assimilated, then what is the relevance of the experimental research to specific instances of desegregation in which these outgroup members participate? Again, the application of experimental results must be adjusted to the specific social context under study.

What is the relevance of research on the contact hypothesis in situations in which the outgroup in the desegregation context is a member of the majority group in the larger society? For instance, a common practice in desegregation cases now involves white students being bused into special programs in predominantly African American schools and neighborhoods (see Mathews and Jarvis, Chapter 6, this volume; Rossell, 1990). Do the same experimental results noted above regarding recategorization of outgroup members hold in these situations?

Toward a Paradigm Shift in the Study of Equal Education and Desegregation in the United States

It appears that there has been a sea change in the history of the desegregation of elementary/secondary and postsecondary education in the U.S. The Supreme Court, and the rest of the federal judiciary, will no longer be as actively involved in desegregation as it has been in the past. In the future, issues of de facto segregation will be more important to address than issues of de jure segregation. Policy makers, educators, and academics will need to employ a different body of knowledge in addressing de facto segregation than they did when addressing de jure segregation. Legal and polemic arguments will be less important in the future, while evidence from the geopolitical and social psychological literatures will be more important.

A new paradigm for the study of desegregation and equal education will focus on context specific desegregation strategies for individual educational institutions, rather than global, court mandated remedies for all institutions. This new paradigm may evolve from models such as that proposed by St. John and Hossler (see Chapter 9, this volume), which they call the critical-empirical framework. This critical-empirical framework assesses the effects of alternative policies and strategies on student choice at the higher education level. St. John and Hossler posited propositions about the linkages between these alternative policies/strategies and student enrollment choices in higher education (see Chapter 9, Table 1, pp. 130-31, this volume), based on empirical evidence gleaned from previous research.

The current dominant paradigms, or worldviews (Kuhn, 1970), utilized by authors working within either the legal literature or writing polemic arguments are either critical theory or constructivism (Guba and Lincoln, 1994). The critical-empirical framework may employ aspects of these two paradigms, but will rely more heavily on pragmatism (e.g., Cherryholmes, 1992; Howe, 1988; Rorty, 1982; Tashakkori and Teddlie, in press). Pragmatism is a worldview that embraces the utilization of all types of empirical data (quantitative and qualitative) to answer questions that are of interest and value to the investigator. The emphasis in pragmatism is on "what works."

The paradigm of pragmatism applied to the study of desegregation and equal education involves the following steps:

(1) Policy makers, educators, and/or academics must first agree upon goals related to desegregation and equal education. The most basic aspects of this goal formulation involves answering such questions as: "Do we as a group want to have desegregated schools? Do we as a group want to have equal educational opportunities for all our students?" Once these basic goals are agreed upon, then more specific ones will emerge, including operational definitions of desegregation and equal education opportunities. It is important to remember that this definition of desegregation (or equal education) is not imposed by a court, but is derived through dialogue among stakeholders.

(2) The characteristics of the specific school context(s) must then be defined in detail. Research from a variety of sources indicates that specific school context(s) require specific desegregation strategies. For instance, in many cases the effect of the white flight that has already occurred (or is occurring) must be taken into consideration. This white flight should be treated as a social phenomenon that can be understood and addressed, not as an inappropriate political response to be criticized.

(3) A comprehensive literature search, including mainstream sources and the largely "underground" case study literature associated with successful and unsuccessful attempts at desegregation, should be conducted. This search will focus on finding cases similar to the one under study, so that context-specific strategies can be formulated.

(4) The information from this literature search (e.g., desegregation case studies, geopolitical sources, social psychological sources) should then be used to generate predictions regarding the impact of certain strategies on the specific school desegregation situation under study.

(5) The preferred strategies should then be enacted with as much fidelity to the original "intervention" as possible.

(6) Assessment of the success of the strategy should then occur, using multiple outcomes (e.g., degree of desegregation attained, attitudinal indices, cognitive outcomes).

(7) The strategy should be re-assessed and refined based on the evaluation data.

This model for desegregation depends upon the political acumen and will of communities of people working together, not the directives of federal courts. While such a process is necessarily messier than a clear-cut court decision, authorities such as Charles Glenn (1996), writing about the Boston desegregation experience, have concluded that it is the better way to long lasting success.

References

Allport, G.W. (1954/1979 ed.). *The nature of prejudice*. Cam bridge & Reading, MA: Addison-Wesley.

Aronson, E. (1995). *The social animal*. (7th ed.). New York: W.H. Freeman and Company.

Aronson, E., Blaney, N., Stephan, C., Sikes, J., & Snapp, M. (1978). *The jigsaw classroom*. Beverly Hills, CA: Sage.

Aronson, E., & Osherow, N. (1980). Cooperation, prosocial behavior, and academic performance: Experiments in the desegregated classroom. In L. Bickman (Ed.), *Applied social psychology annual* (Vol. 1). Beverly Hills, CA: Sage.

Blaney, N., Stephan, C, Rosenfield, D., Aronson, E., & Sikes, J. (1977). Intedependence in the classroom: A field study. *Journal of Educational Psychology, 69,* 139-146.

Brown, R., & Maras, P. (1995). Integration. In A.S.R. Manstead & M. Hewstone (Eds.) *The Blackwell encyclopedia of social psychology*, pp. 325-326. Oxford: Basil Blackwell Ltd.

Cherryholmes, C. C. (1992). Notes on pragmatism and scientific realism. *Educational Researcher, 21,* 13-17.

Clark, K.B. (1979). The role of social scientists 25 years after Brown. *Personality and Social Psychology Bulletin, 5,* 477-481.

Cook, S.W. (1979). Social science and school desegregation: Did we mislead the Supreme Court? *Personality and Social Psychology Bulletin, 5*, 420-437.

Cook, S.W. (1984). Cooperative interaction in multiethnic contexts. In N. Miller, & M.B. Brewer, *Groups in contact: The psychology of desegregation*, pp. 156-186. New York: Academic Press.

DeVries, D.L., Edwards, K.J., & Slavin, R.E. (1978). Biracial learning teams and race relations in the classroom: Four field experiments on Teams-Games-Tournament. *Journal of Educational Psychology, 70*, 356-362.

DeVries, D.L., Slavin, R.E., Fennessey, G.M., Edwards, K.J., & Lombardo, M.M. (1980). *Teams-Games-Tournament: The team learning approach.* Englewood Cliffs, NJ: Educational Technology Publications.

Gaertner, S., Dovidio, J., Anastasio, P.A., Bachman, B.A., & Rust, M.C. (1993). Recategorization and the reduction of intergroup bias. In W. Stroebe & M. Hewstone (Eds.) *European review of social psychology* (Vol.4), pp.1-26. Chichester: J. Wiley.

Garvin, J. (1997). There's no place like home. In C. Teddlie & K. Lomotey (Eds.) *Forty years after the Brown decision: The current and future sociological implications of school desegregation*, pp. 309-338. New York: AMS Press.

Gerard, H.B., & Miller, N. (1975). *School desegregation: A long-term study.* New York: Plenum.

Glenn, C. (1996). "Busing" in Boston: What we could have done better. In K. Lomotey and C. Teddlie (Eds.) *Forty years after the Brown decision: Implications of school desegregation for U.S. education,* pp. 139-156. New York: AMS Press.

Guba, E. G., & Lincoln, Y. S. (1994). Competing paradigms in qualitative research. In N. K. Denzin & Y. S. Lincoln, (Eds.) *Handbook of qualitative research*, pp. 105-117. Thousand Oaks, CA: Sage Publications, Inc.

Hennigan, K.M., Flay, B.R., & Cook, T.D. (1980). "Give me the facts": Some suggestions for using social science knowledge in national policy making. In R.F. Kidd & J. Saks (Eds.), *Advances in applied social psychology* (Vol. 1). Hillsdale, N.J.: Erlbaum.

Howe, K. R. (1988). Against the quantitative-qualitative incompatibility thesis or dogmas die hard. *Educational Researcher, 17,* 10-16.

Johnson, D.W., Johnson, R., & Maruyama, G.(1984). Goal interdependence and interpersonal attraction in heterogeneous classrooms: A meta-analysis. In N. Miller, & M.B. Brewer, *Groups in contact: The psychology of desegregation*, pp. 187-212. New York: Academic Press.

Kuhn, T. S. (1970). *The structure of scientific revolutions.* (2nd ed.). Chicago: University of Chicago Press.

Lomotey, K., & Teddlie, C. (Eds.) (1996) *Forty years after the Brown decision: Implications of school desegregation for U.S. education.* Volume 13 in the series *Readings on Equal Education.* New York: AMS Press.

Miller, N., & Brewer, M.B. (1984). The social psychology of desegregation: An introduction. In N. Miller, & M.B. Brewer, *Groups in contact: The psychology of desegregation*, pp. 1-8. New York: Academic Press.

Orfield, G., & Eaton, S.E. (1996). *Dismantling desegregation: The quiet reversal of Brown v. Board of Education.* New York: The New Press.

Oskamp, S. (1984). *Applied social psychology.* Englewood Cliffs, NJ: Prentice-Hall, Inc.

Park, B., and Rothbart, M. (1982). Perception of out-group homogeneity and levels of social categorization: Memory for the subordinate attributes of in-group and out-group members. *Journal of Personality and Social Psychology*, 42, 1051-1068.

Rorty, R. (1982). Pragmatism, relativism, and irrationalism. In R. Rorty *Consequences of pragmatism*, pp. 160-175. Minneapolis: University of Minnesota Press.

Rossell, C.H. (1990). *The carrot or the stick for school desegregation policy: Magnet schools or forced busing?* Philadelphia: Temple University Press.

Schofield, J.W. (1996). Review of research on school desegregation's impact on elementary and secondary school students. In K. Lomotey and C. Teddlie (Eds.) *Forty years after the Brown decision: Implications of school desegregation for U.S. education*, pp. 71-116. New York: AMS Press. Reprint of original chapter published in *Handbook of research on multicultural education* by J.A. Banks and C.A.M. Banks (Eds.), 1995, New York: Macmillan.

Sharan, S., Kussel, P., Hertz-Lazarow, R., Bjarno, Y., Raviv, S., & Sharan, Y. (1984). *Cooperative learning in the desegregated school.* Hillsdale, NJ: Earlbaum Associates.

Slavin, R.E. (1977). How student learning teams can integrate the desegregated classroom. *Integrated Education, 15*, 56-58.

Stephan, W.G. (1978). School desegregation: An evaluation of predictions made in *Brown v. Board of Education. Psychological Bulletin, 85*, 217-238.

Tajfel, H. (1981). *Human groups and social categories.* Cambridge: Cambridge University Press.

Tashakkori, A., and Teddlie, C. (in press). *Mixed methods and mixed model studies in the social and behavioral sciences.* Thousand Oaks, CA: Sage Publications, Inc.

Teddlie, C. (1997, July). *What can be learned in education from experiments in social psychology.* Paper presented at the Evidence-Based Policies and Indicator Systems International Conference, Durham, UK.

Teddlie, C. and Freeman, J. (1996) With all deliberate speed: The impact of the Brown decision on institutions of higher education. In K. Lomotey and C. Teddlie (Eds.) *Forty years after the Brown decision: Implications of school desegregation for U.S. education*, pp. 7-52. New York: AMS Press.

Teddlie, C., & Lomotey, K. (1996). Historical perspectives on school desegregation: An introductory view. In K. Lomotey and C. Teddlie (Eds.) *Forty years after the Brown decision: Implications of school desegregation for U.S. education*, pp. 1-6. New York: AMS Press.

Teddlie, C., & Lomotey, K. (Eds.) (1997) *Forty years after the Brown decision: The current and future sociological implications of school desegregation.* Volume 14 in the series *Readings on Equal Education.* New York: AMS Press.

Trent, W. T. (1991). Student affirmative action in higher education: Addressing underrepresentation. In P. Altbach & K. Lomotey (Eds.) *The racial crisis in American higher education*, pp. 107-134. Albany, NY: State University of New York Press.

Weyant, J.M. (1986). *Applied social psychology.* New York: Oxford University Press.

Weigel, R.H., Wiser, P.I., & Cook, S.W. (1975). The impact of cooperative learning experiences on cross-ethnic relations and attitudes. *Journal of Social Issues, 31*, 219-244.

Williams, J. B. (1991). Systemwide Title VI regulation of higher education, 1968-88: Implications for increased minority participation. In C. V. Willie, A. M. Garibaldi, & W. L. Reed (Eds.) *The education of African-Americans, pp.* 110-122. Boston, MA: William Monroe Trotter Institute, University of Massachusetts at Boston.

Table of Legal References

Adams v. Richardson. 356 F. Supp. 92 (D.D.C. 1973).

Ayers v. Fordice. 79 F. Supp. 1419 (1995).

Brown v. The Board of Education of Topeka, Kansas, 347 U.S. 483 (1954).

Brown v. The Board of Education of Topeka, Kansas, 349 U.S. 294 (1955).

Florida ex rel Hawkins v. Board of Control, 47 So.2d 608 (1950), 53 So.2d 116 (1951), *cert. den.*, 342 U.S. 877 (1951), *cert. granted*, 347 U.S. 971 (1954), 350 U.S. 413 (1956).

Green v. School Board of New Kent County, 391 U.S. 430 (1968).

Podberesky v. Kirwan, 38 F.3d 147 (4th Cir. 1994).

Missouri v. Jenkins, 515 U.S. 70 (1995).

Pearson v. Murray, 169 Md. 478, 182 Atl. 590 (1936).

Plessy v. Ferguson, 163 U.S. 537 (1898).

Regents of University of California v. Bakke, 438 U.S. 265 (1978).

Sheff v. O'Neill, 678 A.2d 1267 (Conn. 1996).

Swann v. Charlotte-Mecklenburg Board of Education, 402 U.S. 1 (1971).

United States v. Louisiana, No. 80-3300 (USD/ED, 1994).